2009

THE CHURCH'S BOOK OF
COMFORT

THE CHURCH'S BOOK OF
COMFORT

Edited by
WILLEM VAN 'T SPIJKER

Translated by
Gerrit Bilkes

REFORMATION HERITAGE BOOKS
Grand Rapids, Michigan

Published by
Reformation Heritage Books
2965 Leonard St., NE
Grand Rapids, MI 49525
616-977-0599 / Fax 616-285-3246
e-mail: orders@heritagebooks.org
website: www.heritagebooks.org

Originally published as *Troostboek van de kerk*.
Copyright Den Hertog B. V., Houten, 2005.

Library of Congress Cataloging-in-Publication Data

Troostboek van de kerk. English.
  The church's book of comfort / edited by Willem van 't Spijker ;
translated by Gerrit Bilkes.
    p. cm.
  ISBN 978-1-60178-056-0 (hardcover : alk. paper)
  1. Heidelberger Katechismus. I. Spijker, W. van 't. II. Bilkes,
Gerrit. III. Title.
  BX9428.T7613 2008
  238'.42--dc22
                        2008048477

CONTENTS

PREFACE

Much has been written about the Heidelberg Catechism. The references in this book comprise only a fraction of the bibliography that could be assembled for this classic document, and numerous studies on this catechism will continue to appear in the future. This is a normal development for works in church history that survive the centuries, because they capture a bit of eternity itself. Such is indeed the case with the best-known document of the Reformed tradition. The Heidelberg Catechism owes its "eternal youth" (G. Oorthuys) to the fundamental way it interprets the truth of the gospel, as rediscovered by the Reformation. This new publication brings these features to light.

Although the Catechism can be called a classic document, it is not detached from history. Those who ignore the historical context of this confessional statement will not recognize its special character. For this reason, the first three chapters are devoted to the history of this particular catechism.

Drs. Christa Th. Boerke describes the church and historical events that took place against the background of the Reformation in Germany during the period that preceded the emergence of the Heidelberg Catechism. The German Reformation had a particularly Lutheran character until changes were initiated by Elector Frederick the Wise.

Dr. Wim Verboom addresses the history of the production of the Heidelberg Catechism itself. The history of the Palatinate is traced along political and cultural lines. He describes the antecedents and compilation of this document in a way that makes clear how decisive the choice between Lutheranism and Reformed Protestantism really was.

In the third chapter, Drs. Christa Th. Boerke provides biographical sketches of the people involved in the compilation and publication of the Catechism. Ursinus and Olevianus receive most of the attention, but other participants from Heidelberg University, the consistory, and the government are also included. Thus, we see the varied environment in which the document came to light. This diversity became a hallmark of the Reformed tradition without detracting from its unity.

Dr. Willem van 't Spijker summarizes the theological dimensions of the Catechism. He finds essential agreement in thought and experience with the position that Luther held at the beginning of the Reformation. The classic Reformed formulation of this confession agrees perfectly with the heart of the gospel. The emphasis on communion with Christ is typical. Only in this union with Christ do we partake of salvation, know our misery, experience redemption, and express our gratitude through obedience and prayer.

In the fifth chapter, Dr. Wim Verboom describes the condition of catechetical instruction in the late Middle Ages, revealing the extent to which the Reformation signified a change in religious instruction. Prior to this time, the teaching of the faith was not particularly well established. The catechisms that emerged within the orbit of the Reformation prior to the Heidelberg version reflected a different approach by offering more structured teaching.

Next, Dr. Teunis M. Hofman briefly sketches the history of the Reformation in the Low Countries, describing the background in which the ecclesiastical recognition of the Catechism took place. Official church meetings are ascribed a significant role in this narrative. The evaluation and approval of the Catechism took place over the period from the Convent of Wezel (1568) to the great Synod of Dort (1618–1619). Resistance from the Remonstrants led to a powerful ecclesiastical confirmation of this book of instruction and to its use as a confessional statement of the Reformed Church in the Netherlands.

Preaching and catechetical instruction both functioned as means whereby the content of Reformed doctrine was disseminated. Dr. Willem Jan op 't Hof casts light on the practice of preaching the Catechism in the centuries following the Reformation. He also discusses the significance and circulation of collections of sermons over a period of more than two centuries, from 1576 to 1801. Drs. Marinus Golverdingen focuses on the curriculum and pedagogical principles furnished by the Synod of Dort. He provides an overview of the catechetical instruction material of the seventeenth and eighteenth centuries and describes a few short instruction books popular in those days. Catechism preaching and teaching received only scant attention in the nineteenth and twentieth centuries. To date, very little research has been devoted to this topic.

In the last chapter, a comparison is made with two other confessional statements of the Reformed tradition, namely, the Belgic Confession of Faith and the Canons of Dort. Catechisms of other countries are also compared. The continuing relevance of the Heidelberg Catechism is due principally to the marriage of biblical doctrine and Christian living. An element of great significance in this regard is the ever-present exhortation to focus on the reality of faith. Truth is not only *taught*; it is also *experienced* in terms of the comfort it bestows. Today's generation would greatly benefit from putting into Christian practice the heritage of the Reformation contained in this Catechism.

This book is enriched with many illustrations, most of which derive from old printed sources acknowledged in the captions. Most of these illustrations belong to the photographic archive of the Dutch edition of this volume, Den Hertog, Houten, the Netherlands. In addition, we gratefully acknowledge material obtained from the Bibliotheca Palatina, the Museum of the Electorate of the Palatinate, the Municipal Archives of Heidelberg, and the Theological School of Rotterdam. The illustrations not only make the book more attractive but also help clarify the text. The same is true of the descriptive material placed in boxes, which constitutes source material as well as illustrations. Although the references to source material and literature constitute only a selection, the book reflects the knowledge and insight of the authors based on a broad range of scholarly work pertaining to the Heidelberg Catechism.

This publication saw the light of day not only because of the collaboration of the authors, but also because of the commitment of Dr. J. Versloot and the publisher, Den Hertog of Houten. We thank all those who contributed to the completion of this work.

Apeldoorn, September 12, 2005   Willem van 't Spijker

Preface to the English Translation

The Heidelberg Catechism is part of the international, confessional heritage of Reformed Protestantism. Its formulation and adoption in the Palatinate under the leadership of Elector Frederick the Pious—as he was known—reflected this prince's personal preference for the Reformed confession. It was his desire that this personal conviction would also be commonly held within the political boundaries of his territory and recognized within the broader framework of the European commonwealth. His book of instruction thus acquired a confessional luster that it has never lost. Through its unique approach the Heidelberg Catechism has attained important and lasting significance within Reformed and Presbyterian Christianity worldwide.

From the beginning it was clear that this book of instruction would also become a statement of confession. The church order of the Palatinate originally placed it between the Forms of Baptism and the Lord's Supper. Infant baptism is followed by ecclesiastical instruction in the *doctrine* of the confessing church. This instruction culminates in discipleship: through profession of faith one subjects oneself to ecclesiastical *discipline*. This approach gives structure to the confessing church—marked by the Lord's Supper—in seeking to consist of disciples of the Great Master. The content of the Heidelberg Catechism mirrors this objective. It reveals to some extent the model of the church pursued by Martin Bucer and John Calvin, reflecting an inner strength capable of enduring protracted episodes of particular hardship.

This does not mean, however, that the Heidelberg Catechism seeks preeminence within the Reformed and Presbyterian community. It is the essence of Reformed Protestantism to encompass rich diversity and variation. This has been the case ever since the beginning of the sixteenth century and reflects the ecumenical nature of Reformed Protestantism. Lutherans succeeded in publishing a *Konkordienbuch* (Book of Concord) towards the end of the sixteenth century, capturing the unity of Lutheranism. Similar attempts to achieve the unity of the European Reformed have never gotten beyond the publication of a *Harmonia Confessionum* in Genève in 1581. It presented the content of a large number of Reformed confessions, which demonstrated that despite remarkable diversity there was essential agreement and harmony.

In this way the Heidelberg Catechism has succeeded in playing its role to the fullest extent, as is illustrated by the publication of *Reformed Confessions Harmonized* (edited by Joel R. Beeke and Sinclair B. Ferguson, 1999). Historical antecedents, theological methods, pedagogical objectives, and decisive events can and may contribute to diversity without detracting from underlying unanimity. The fact that in his books of instruction (1537, 1545) Calvin clearly emphasized the need to know and acknowledge God, and thus to glorify Him, does not contradict the need for Christian comfort that the Heidelberg Catechism expounds in its opening question. Neither does the Heidelberg Catechism in any way detract from the glorification of God and the celebration of perfect joy in God, as Westminster Shorter Catechism Q&A 1 stresses. After all, no knowledge of God is possible if it is not imparted to us by the Lord Jesus Christ—through the great Comforter—in whom all wisdom and knowledge are guaranteed. To know Him constitutes eternal life. Practicing communion of faith with Him prefigures the eternal joy of being comforted in knowing God as we have been known by Him.

Thanks to everyone who made an English version of this book possible. We are especially indebted to Lawrence Bilkes (who was so instrumental in making this English translation possible), Gerrit Bilkes (for his fine translation of the book), and Jerry Bilkes (for his suggestions and insights in the translation process). Gratitude is also expressed for the editorial labors of Joel R. Beeke and those helping him at Reformation Heritage Books.

Apeldoorn, January 16, 2009   Willem van 't Spijker

CHAPTER 1
The Reformation in Germany
by Christa Boerke

By the time the Heidelberg Catechism appeared in 1563, Germany had just emerged from a period of turbulence. Beginning in 1517, Europe witnessed the great movement known as the Reformation, which was inextricably connected with Martin Luther (1483–1546), especially in Germany.

Luther initially owed his renown to his famous battle against the Roman Catholic practice of indulgences and other ecclesiastical abuses. In his capacity as a university professor, he became a leading figure in the German Reformation. His forceful involvement in the renewal of the church reflected his personal rediscovery of the gospel and, more specifically, the liberating power of justification by faith—the article, according to Luther, whereby the church stands or falls.

Martin Luther (painting by Lucas Cranach, 1520)

As a young monk, he fought a deep inner battle within the walls of his monastery: Where do I ultimately find the assurance of faith? How can I appropriate God's grace? He found the answer to these questions when he discovered the significance of Romans 1:17, where Paul speaks about justification by faith. This phrase does not signify God's justice in punishing or rewarding mankind, but the righteousness that He will grant to sinners on the basis of Christ's merits. Therefore, the righteous live by faith, focused on the promises of God. It is proof of His immense grace that in His Word God promises us His righteousness and thus seeks to renew and liberate us.

Luther later wrote of this discovery that it was as though, at that moment, the gates of paradise opened to him. His new insight into the Scriptures liberated him. This far-reaching event marked the remainder of his life as well as his theology. Justification by faith—by grace and not by works—remained a frequent theme in his entire life's work. His call for a renewal of the church did not primarily reflect dissatisfaction with abuses but his personal experience with Scripture. From this perspective, he saw the church with different eyes than previously.

The spirit of the time

Luther's rediscovery of the gospel occurred in a time of great social, economic, and political upheaval. Everything was in flux; new tensions were continually emerging. The German nation under the emperor was not homogeneous; it consisted of numerous larger and smaller jurisdictions, each governed by its own monarch. The Palatinate, Hesse, and Saxony represented the crucial regions of the Reformation in Germany. Elector Frederick the Wise (1486–1525) held the scepter over part of Saxony, Luther's cradle. The influence of local princes and a national consciousness increased significantly among the people, provoking a stressful relationship with the emperor. The emergence of cities represented a disturbing element to the countryside, leading to social unrest.

The relationship between the emperor and the pope also created recurrent friction. Depending on the political situation, the pope at times sided with the emperor, and at other times he definitely did not. The rivalry between Emperor Charles V and King Francis I of France also strongly influenced the history of the first half of the sixteenth century. In addition to these tensions, there was a continual threat from the east, where the Turks sought to expand their realm through military action, particularly in Hungary. This threat led to uncertainty within the German realm and to fear among the population. In a sense, this menace actually benefited the Reformation, because it diverted the emperor's attention. In the face of growing national consciousness, Rome sought to centralize its own power and thus to maintain its hold on the German church.

From economic and social perspectives, the ascent of cities was also significant. A flourishing trade had emerged, especially in South Germany. Frequent financial transactions encouraged the growth of the banking industry, which rendered the bourgeoisie increasingly independent. Christian humanism and the recent discovery of the printing press gave rise to an intellectual emancipation. Humanists promoted a return to the Bible and the classic sources of antiquity. They directed heavy criticism at the ruling scholastic theology. Although ethical in scope and optimistic with respect to the abilities of man, humanism nevertheless laid a foundation for the Reformation by strongly emphasizing the study of the Bible and the writings of the church fathers.

Ecclesiastical abuses

There had been abuses in the church for a very long time, but the public's growing self-consciousness pushed them to speak their minds and translate their growing frustration into action. There was increasing criticism of the church among the citizenry, and in the church, there was a growing dissatisfaction on the part of the lower clergy towards the hierarchy who lived in wealth derived from ecclesiastical revenues. And wherever the gospel was rediscovered, people clearly recognized the secularization and moral collapse of the church and the resulting spiritual deficiencies.

Those who expected people to turn away from the church were mistaken. People's interest in the church was quite keen, and not merely in a negative sense. Short Bible commentaries, prayer books, and penance guidelines were in great demand. Printing technology put Bibles, in whole or in part, into the hands of the laity. Religious literature not only enhanced knowledge but also stimulated involvement in contemporary religious activities, which fostered spiritual growth. On the other hand, numerous forms of worship, or superstition, emerged and were sustained. Mary and other saints and relics attracted veneration, and processions and pilgrimages were organized on a frequent basis.

The support that Luther received confirmed the people's hope for improvement. However, he could hardly have anticipated the far-reaching implications of his theology for the sixteenth-century church; both his teaching and his life would have unmistakable consequences for Europe.

The concrete implications of Luther's new insights became immediately apparent in his fight against the sale of indulgences. At the beginning of 1517, the Dominican friar John Tetzel traveled through Germany announcing that his indulgences not only offered remission of punishment but also pardon for sins. The background of these special indulgences was that Rome needed funds for the construction of the new St. Peter's Church. Luther, who was confronted with the fallout of Tetzel's message in the confessional, raised objections in letters and sermons. When these efforts did not help, on October 31, 1517, he posted his ninety-five theses dealing with this subject on the door of the Castle Church at Wittenberg. He sharply condemned the subjective desire to avoid punishment, regardless of the costs. He made a forceful appeal to the pope to end these misconceptions. Furthermore, these theses addressed not merely the concept of indulgences but the ecclesiastical system of penance as a whole. What does the gospel say about repentance? What is the meaning of good works, and what is the real treasure of the gospel as far as faith is concerned?

It took Luther's theses only a few weeks to bring all of Germany into uproar. A sharp war of words ensued in which Tetzel was not too shy to participate. Luther's resistance against the pope was sufficient ground to initiate a heresy process, and the situation was exacerbated by suspicions that his insights aroused. However, Luther did not stand alone in this regard. He had friends and supporters, among whom Philip Melanchthon figured prominently. At the age of twenty-one, Melanchthon had become a professor of Greek at Wittenberg and thus was an immediate colleague of Luther. He became Luther's most important supporter and friend. Even after Luther's death he played a significant role, particularly in the manner in which Calvinism was adopted in Germany in later years.

Luther in Heidelberg

The ninety-five theses of 1517 were not the only ones that Luther wrote in this initial period, although they became the best known. In those days, it was customary at universities to conduct debates on all kinds of topics through the use of theses. Luther had earlier formulated ninety-seven theses against scholastic theology in which he showed little tolerance for Aristotle and William of Ockham. These theses, which were more substantial theologically than the ninety-five of 1517, received no attention from scholars whatsoever, which hurt Luther deeply. Apparently the church became alarmed more quickly when its revenues were at stake. A third collection of theses also attracted little attention, although they definitely invited a reaction. This collection consisted of forty theses associated with the name Heidelberg.

HAIDELBERGA

Neccar   Fluvius.

Heidelberg in 1620 (engraving by Matthias Merian). The Augustinian monastery where Luther presented his debate on April 26, 1518, is marked.

Luther visited Heidelberg in 1518 at the invitation of his confessor and superior, Johann von Staupitz, who asked Luther to lead a debate on April 26 at the chapter meeting of the Augustinian Order, of which Luther was a member. It was a significant gesture on the part of von Staupitz to give Luther the floor on the occasion of the order's anniversary, in the face of the commotion that had emerged. Luther had been district vicar for the preceding three years, and his term of office was expiring.

Luther left for Heidelberg under the protection of the elector, who had informed von Staupitz that Luther was to return immediately after the debate. The work at the University of Wittenberg could not be interrupted for long; neither was he to be transported anywhere else. This precaution was intended to ensure that Luther would not be taken surreptitiously from Heidelberg to Rome.

The forty theses

The fruit of Luther's visit to Heidelberg was a number of splendid theses that offer a concise summary of his early theology. The forty theses comprise twenty-eight theological and twelve philosophical statements, of which the former are the more important. In these theses, Luther's teachings constitute a theology of the cross: on the one hand, the cross deprives man of any option whatsoever to gain salvation on his own, and on the other hand, it causes him to expect everything from the grace of Christ. These theses do not deal with indulgences or penance but address sin, grace, and faith.

The Heidelberg Disputation
Brother Martin Luther, Master of Sacred Theology, will preside, and Brother Leonhard Beyer, Master of Arts and Philosophy, will defend the following theses before the Augustinians of this renowned city of Heidelberg in the customary place, on April 26th 1518.

THEOLOGICAL THESES
Distrusting completely our own wisdom, according to that counsel of the Holy Spirit, "Lean not unto thine own understanding" (Prov. 3:5), we humbly present to the judgment of all those who wish to be here these theological paradoxes, so that it may become clear whether they have been deduced well or poorly from St. Paul, the especially chosen vessel and instrument of Christ, and also from St. Augustine, his most trustworthy interpreter.

1. The law of God, the most salutary doctrine of life, cannot advance man on his way to righteousness, but rather hinders him.
2. Much less can human works, which are done over and over again with the aid of natural precepts, so to speak, lead to that end.
3. Although the works of man always seem attractive and good, they are nevertheless likely to be mortal sins.
4. Although the works of God are always unattractive and appear evil, they are nevertheless really eternal merits.

5. The works of men are thus not mortal sins (we speak of works which are apparently good), as though they were crimes.

6. The works of God (we speak of those which he does through man) are thus not merits, as though they were sinless.

7. The works of the righteous would be mortal sins if they would not be feared as mortal sins by the righteous themselves out of pious fear of God.

8. By so much more are the works of man mortal sins when they are done without fear and in unadulterated, evil self-security.

9. To say that works without Christ are dead, but not mortal, appears to constitute a perilous surrender of the fear of God.

10. Indeed, it is very difficult to see how a work can be dead and at the same time not a harmful and mortal sin.

11. Arrogance cannot be avoided or true hope be present unless the judgment of condemnation is feared in every work.

12. In the sight of God sins are then truly venial when they are feared by men to be mortal.

13. Free will, after the fall, exists in name only, and as long as it does what it is able to do, it commits a mortal sin.

14. Free will, after the fall, has power to do good only in a passive capacity, but it can always do evil in an active capacity.

15. Nor could free will remain in a state of innocence, much less do good, in an active capacity, but only in its passive capacity.

16. The person who believes that he can obtain grace by doing what is in him, adds sin to sin, so that he becomes doubly guilty.

17. Nor does speaking in this manner give cause for despair, but for arousing the desire to humble oneself and seek the grace of Christ.

18. It is certain that man must utterly despair of his own ability before he is prepared to receive the grace of Christ.

19. That person does not deserve to be called a theologian who looks upon the "invisible" things of God as though they were clearly "perceptible in those things which have actually happened" (Rom. 1:20; cf. 1 Cor. 1:21–25).

20. He deserves to be called a theologian, however, who comprehends the visible and manifest things of God seen through suffering and the cross.

21. A theology of glory calls evil good and good evil. A theology of the cross calls the thing what it actually is.
22. That wisdom which sees the invisible things of God in works as perceived by man is completely puffed up, blinded, and hardened.
23. The "law brings the wrath" of God (Rom. 4:15), kills, reviles, accuses, judges, and condemns everything that is not in Christ.
24. Yet that wisdom is not of itself evil, nor is the law to be evaded; but without the theology of the cross man misuses the best in the worst manner.
25. A person is not righteous because he performs many works, but because apart from works he believes greatly in Christ.
26. The law says: 'Do this!' and it never happens. Grace says: 'Be- ʒrything has already been achieved.

   ll the work of Christ an acting work (oper-
   accomplished work (operatum), and thus
   ‹ pleasing to God by the grace of the acting

   not find, but creates, that which is pleasing
   ı comes into being through that which is

These clearly delineated theses reveal the characteristic features of Luther's theology. The first twelve theses deal with the law, which cannot help man to attain righteousness but rather blocks his way. The law points to sin and guilt and brings about death. Human accomplishments are incapable of achieving righteousness; they must even be viewed as deadly sins as long as they are performed apart from grace and faith. In contrast to these human works stand the works of God, which may not appear attractive but which do reflect righteousness. Nowhere else has Luther dismissed man's accomplishments with respect to his own salvation more strongly than here. A person cannot approach God without completely abandoning himself and rejecting his own efforts. This truth is reiterated in statements 13–18, which maintain that since the fall into sin, man's free will is no longer capable of doing good and is totally focused on sin. It is necessary to admit this to God. The law brings about an awareness of sin, which in turn causes humility; humility and doubt make room for grace.

The section that contains theses 19–24 is the best known; here Luther describes his concept of true theology. God lets Himself be known only through the foolishness of the cross, not through intellectual contemplations of His attributes or works. God's actions are hidden in the cross. The theologian of glory—a label for a scholastic theologian—has no inkling of this truth. He reverses the order and focuses on the visible and the external: works, glory, power, and wisdom—which lead only to blindness and hardness of heart. The theologian of the cross, however, considers the cross to be good and works evil. He pursues the foolishness of the cross. This view implies a strong condemnation of scholastic theology, which, according to Luther, does not fathom the hidden manner in which God works in a peculiar manner. The cross alone is our theology.

Next, theses 25–27 address the relationship between faith and works. Justification by faith does not depend on man's own actions but only on faith in Christ. Works proceed from faith and are therefore not really actions of man himself, but rather of God, who performs them through him. The believer can therefore never take any pride in them; Christ accomplishes them in him. The believer's work is in fact the work of Christ, and therefore it pleases God.

The last thesis emphasizes the creative power of God's love, which does not focus on the object but creates the object of His love. It is for this reason that God loves the sinner: not because the latter deserves it, but because God takes the initiative to approach him in love.

Against philosophy

The philosophical material that Luther raises in the next twelve theses stresses his objections against the philosophy of Aristotle, with particular focus on Aristotle's influence on the prevailing theology—a topic that Luther has raised before. The order in which these theses are presented is significant: theology first and philosophy second. Luther's message is clear: theology comes first. Those who wish to philosophize about Aristotle must first become foolish in Christ. True knowledge is impossible apart from Christ. By viewing theology and philosophy from this perspective, Luther denied philosophy an independent role; it became subservient to theology.

It was very important to Luther to be able to demonstrate that scholastic theology sought support from Aristotle in vain. A philosophy without the grace of Christ cannot lead to true knowledge. It is for this reason that he speaks of a theology of the cross opposing a theology of glory: "One is not a true theologian if one focuses on the invisible aspects of God embedded in

His creation, but only if one focuses on what is visible, including the negative side in terms of suffering and the cross."

The sale of indulgences is not mentioned. Here is the heart of the matter: "A person is not righteous because he performs many works, but because apart from works he believes greatly in Christ. The law says: 'Do this!' and it never happens. Grace says: 'Believe in Him!' and everything has already been achieved."

The way in which Luther attacked the prevailing Aristotelian theology in Heidelberg evoked enthusiasm, especially among young students. They considered him to be brilliant and admired his great knowledge of the Bible, as well as the way in which he countered objections. Through this debate, several German theologians were won over to Luther's teachings, including Johannes Brenz and Martin Bucer. Martin Bucer was especially enthusiastic about the Heidelberg debate and began to refer to himself as a "Martinian." Johannes Brenz became a faithful student who understood Luther and his theology well.

Luther defends himself before Cardinal Cajetanus
(woodcut from *Historien der Heyligen Ausserwaehlten Gottes Zeugen*
[Histories of Selected Holy Witnesses of God], by Ludwig Robus, Strasbourg, 1557)

Consequences

That very year, Luther was summoned to appear in Rome within sixty days to account for his obstinate heresies. However, through the intervention of the elector, Luther did not have to appear in Rome, but he was heard in Augsburg from October 12 to 14 by Cardinal Cajetanus. It bore no fruit, however. Luther refused to recant; there was no way he could surrender his beliefs. However, the elector declined to hand Luther over to the pope. Meanwhile, the pope needed the elector's support for his anti-Hapsburg campaign. Thus Luther was safe in the elector's protection and could carry on with his pastoral and academic pursuits.

At a debate in Leipzig from June 27 to July 15, 1519, the conflict between Luther and Rome escalated. Luther and his colleague Karlstadt had been challenged to this debate by Johann Eck. Additional issues were raised, such as the primacy of Rome and the authority of councils. Luther declared that John Huss, who was condemned at the Council of Constance and burned at the stake, had nevertheless taught very Christian and evangelical ideas. Luther thereby openly cast doubt on the decisions of this ecclesiastical council, which made him even more suspect in the eyes of his opponents.

Various events led the faculties of Cologne and Louvain to reject a number of theses contained in Luther's writings. The Sorbonne at Paris sharply condemned his writings and classified Luther as one of the heretics who had come forward throughout the centuries.

Three publications in one year

Luther further elaborated in his writings what he set forth in his theses. Three publications were of particular importance in this initial phase of the Reformation; they contained many religious, theological, pedagogical, and political elements that reappeared in his later works as well as in both of his catechisms.

To the Christian Nobility

Luther's missive to the German nobility was primarily directed at Charles V in the fervent hope that the latter would liberate Christianity from papal tyranny. It appeared impossible to come to an understanding with Rome. He therefore made an urgent appeal to the nobility to abandon their own agendas in favor of supporting the Reformation. When the church abandoned its responsibility, there was a role for the nobility.

Use of the term *nobility* did not imply that Luther addressed the nobility only. He had in mind all those whose position in society carried responsibility for secular matters or government, whether within the empire, within a country, or within a social class. This perspective on the relationship between church and state became characteristic of the Lutheran Reformation.

As a theologian, Luther knew how to mobilize social forces to further his program of change, giving his ideas greater visibility. He was well aware not only of the abuses of Rome, but also of those in the German state and everyday life. Rome had ensconced herself behind three strong "walls" to defend herself and deflect all possible criticism. She maintained that spiritual power surpassed all secular authority, that the pope had final authority to interpret Scripture, and that only the pope could convene a council. Under such circumstances, nothing would ever change! With a reference to Jericho, Luther attacked all three of these walls with cogent arguments. Through baptism, we are all priests and members of the clergy. As Christians, we are all taught directly by God. Members of the local church have the authority to gauge all preaching against Scripture itself. The government, not the pope, has the authority to convene a council.

Next, Luther broadly indicated where reform was required—not only ecclesiastically, but also politically, socially, nationally, and internationally. Even economic abuses of interest and usury did not escape his attention. Academic degrees at universities were to be more transparent. Theology was to be guided by the Holy Spirit, for He alone trains true doctors of knowledge.

If the church declined to convene a council, princes and members of the nobility would be called to deal with ecclesiastical, social, and academic abuses. Luther outlined a complete recovery program consisting of twenty-eight recommendations that reveal the society in which he lived.

Babylonian Captivity of the Church

Luther's second missive followed quickly. He had been asked to write about the sacraments in response to a tract on the Lord's Supper written by a Franciscan monk. On the one hand, Luther's title alluded to a schism that forced the pope to take up residence in Avignon; on the other hand, it invoked Israel's sojourn in faraway Babylon. The papacy represented the Babylonian realm.

If Luther retained any leniency, it is hardly apparent in this publication, in which he vigorously attacked the Roman doctrine of the sacraments. Over against the prevailing practice of the sacraments, he held to the priesthood of all believers on the basis of their baptism. The sacraments of baptism, penance, and the Lord's Supper had been forced into woeful exile by the Roman Catholic *curia*—the pope's cabinet—and the church had been robbed of its freedom. According to Luther, evil in the church went well beyond the matter of indulgences—a fact he could see much more clearly now than before. Instead of seven sacraments, Luther retained only three: baptism, the Lord's Supper, and penance. The key to all of them was the promise of the Word of God and the faith and repentance that would follow. The other four sacraments could be regarded, at most, as customs that lacked any scriptural foundation.

Luther attacked the practice of withholding the cup of wine from the laity. Only priests were permitted to drink wine at the Lord's Supper. And was it not the case that for twelve centuries the church had not heard of the doctrine of transubstantiation? Luther urged his readers to rely on the Word of God. He wrote, "At any rate, I subject my mind in obedience to Christ when I do not understand in what way the bread is the body of Christ. But simply trusting His Word, I certainly believe not only that the body of Christ is in the bread, but also that the bread is the body of Christ. The Holy Spirit has greater authority than Aristotle."

Although philosophy does not understand this mystery, Luther asserted, faith can grasp it. The authority of the Word of God is greater than that of our minds. This sacrament, which does not involve any sacrifice in the sense assumed by Rome, concerns the sign and seal of God's covenant. It signifies His promise, to which we can only respond in faith and not with personal accomplishments. This same emphasis was apparent in what Luther said about baptism. The power of this sacrament lies in its promise and not in the sacrament itself. The Word is more important than the sign; faith is more important than works.

This exposition of the sacraments may be counted among Luther's most important works. A year after its appearance, a refutation was published under the auspices of King Henry VIII of England. The pope was so pleased with it that he granted Henry the honorary title of *defensor fidei* (defender of the faith).

The Freedom of a Christian

When the papal bull denouncing him had been proclaimed and his books were being burned throughout the empire, Luther published his third well-known booklet, *The Freedom of a Christian*. Luther wrote this small book that summarized the entire doctrine of faith at the request of the papal *nuncio*, Karl von Miltitz, who desired to make a final attempt at reconciliation between Luther and the pope because he feared a schism. He asked Luther to describe the essence of his views again, this time avoiding all polemics. The elector would advocate for him so that the matter could be brought to

The diplomatic representative
of the pope, Karl von Miltitz

a good conclusion. It was agreed that Luther would preface the booklet with
a letter to the pope that explained that he did not wish to attack the pope
personally. These considerations contributed to the fairly restrained tenor of
both booklet and letter, although in the letter Luther dismissed the *curia* in
unambiguous terms, ascribing to them the chief responsibility for abuses in
the church.

The core of this work is formed by two theses, based on 1 Corinthians 9:19 and Romans 13:8: a Christian is a free master in every respect and
subordinate to no one; a Christian is the humble servant and subordinate of
everyone. The connection between the theses lies in Christ and His finished
work. In Christ, the believer is justified and free. However, in Christ he is
also subservient; he will behave himself towards his fellowmen as Christ did
for him. This is the so-called principle of reciprocity, which appears throughout the booklet. In communion with Christ, everything that stains me is
removed by Christ, and all of Christ's merits are credited to me — a wonderful exchange, like a wedding. Whatever belonged to the bridegroom now
belongs to the bride, and what belonged to the bride now belongs to the
bridegroom. When the believer realizes what Christ has done for him, he
will in turn dedicate his life to his neighbor. Luther's powerful expression is
that we thus "become Christ to one another."

It is not known whether the pope read this tract on freedom. It became

Luther's best-known and perhaps most widely read work, and it made clear that reconciliation with the church was out of the question.

The Edict of Worms

The papal bull of denouncement appeared on June 15, 1520, demanding that Luther recant within sixty days or face excommunication. His books were burned everywhere: in Cologne, Mainz, Trier, Antwerp, Liège, and Louvain, and also in Utrecht, Amersfoort, and Ghent. In reply, Luther called one more time for a council. He defended himself in a statement entitled *Against the Bull of Antichrist*. There was no way back, and he no longer desired it. He had made his decision. In front of the Elster Gate on Monday, December 10, he burned the bull in which he was condemned, as well as the books of canon law.

In the meantime, Charles V had been crowned sovereign of the Holy Roman Empire in Aachen and had convened the first Imperial Diet of Worms, which was opened on January 28, 1521. The organization of the German state was his highest priority, which included state government and how its responsibilities should be assigned, the Supreme Court, the army, and the threat from France. Charles viewed himself not only as emperor of Germany,

Luther's hearing in Worms (woodcut, Augsburg, 1521)

but also as head of Roman Catholic Christianity. Furthermore, it was of utmost importance to him to win over the pope, a priority that played a role in his attitude towards Luther. He saw himself as the one who carried the sword to combat heretics within the realm.

Having arrived in Worms under safe-conduct, Luther was questioned in the presence of a large audience concerning the content of his books and his willingness to retract them. Luther refused to do so unless he could be convinced on the basis of the Word of God of any errors he might have committed. According to tradition, he ended his defense with the pronouncement: "Here I stand, I cannot do otherwise. God help me, Amen."[1] A meaningful discussion was out of the question. As was customary, the emperor supported the papal ban with a state interdict, so that Luther's statement could be interpreted as *lèse-majesté* (high treason) and punished accordingly. The papal bull of condemnation was sanctioned by state law on May 8 through the Edict of Worms. As far as the church's teaching was concerned, nothing changed.

On his way home, Luther was ambushed, dragged out of his carriage, and spirited away on horseback. This kidnapping was deliberate and had the blessing of the elector. On May 4, Luther was given protection at Wartburg Castle, where he would reside for the next ten months under the alias of Junker (Squire) Jörg. There he began his translation of the New Testament, which was published in Wittenberg in September 1522 and was crucial to the advance of the Reformation.

One cannot say that the Edict of Worms was rigorously enforced. The emperor was too preoccupied with his war with King Francis I of France. The reorganization of the state did not get off the ground, and nothing was done about ecclesiastical corruption. Pope Leo X died near the end of 1521, but his successor seemed equally uninterested in church reformation. The emperor declined to hold a council to review anything because of his antipathy towards Luther.

At Wartburg Castle, Luther did not have peace for long. Chaos threatened in Wittenberg because Karlstadt implemented Luther's teachings too hurriedly. Priests got married, the Lord's Supper was administered in two different ways, monastic vows were broken, and church images were smashed. Despite the interdict, Luther returned to Wittenberg on March 6, 1522, to reestablish order personally. A series of Lenten sermons called *Invocavit* given over the period March 9–16 reestablished peace. Luther followed these sermons with a tract in which all Christians were encouraged to avoid

---

1. "Hier steh' ich, ich kann nicht anders. Gott helfe mir. Amen."

disturbance and chaos: "Everything must be accomplished through the Word of Christ." He urged his readers to acknowledge their sins, pray for deliverance from papal tyranny, and preach and speak according to the will of the Holy Spirit.

Following his return to Wittenberg, Luther devoted himself to the reformation of the mass and the sacraments. His influence increased dramatically at this time, reaching such German cities as Erfurt, Weimar, Augsburg, and Nuremberg. Beyond Germany's borders, strong centers of the Reformation developed in places like Basel, Strasbourg, and Antwerp.

An eventful year

The year 1525 turned out to be eventful in several respects. A conflict with Erasmus arose about free will, the Peasants' War broke out, and a difference of opinion emerged concerning the Reformational view of the Lord's Supper, which ultimately led to a rift between the Germans and the Swiss.

Erasmus was persuaded to attack Luther by his friend John Fisher, Bishop of Rochester, who had written a refutation of Luther. The topic that Erasmus broached with Luther was the capacity of the human will. He published his book *Discourse on Free Will* in Basel in 1524. In it, he rejected Luther's view on grace. In 1525, Luther responded with *The Bondage of the Will*, in which he defended *sola gratia*: man is saved by grace alone; his own will plays no role. Man is incapable of choosing what is good for him, unless it is given to him by grace. His will is like a dumb animal that is either ridden by God or by Satan. Luther could not understand Erasmus's approach to reforming the church: reformation without rupture. It is characteristic of Erasmus that he never left the church and largely kept himself aloof from ecclesiastical strife.

In the same year, the Peasants' War broke out, starting in Austria and South Germany as a social uprising against economic penury. The new evangelical movement gave farmers fresh hope for improvement. In Swabia, peasants and serfs published Twelve Articles, which recast the biblical commands in the form of a social program. In some locations, having gained the support of the lower nobility, the peasant movement had revolutionary overtones that sought the secularization of ecclesiastical properties. In Saxony and Thuringia, Thomas Müntzer was considered to be the instigator. Luther was horrified by this tumultuous interpretation of his message and published a denunciation of the Twelve Articles in which he criticized the feudal lords and rejected the blending of the gospel with socioeconomic politics.

In the midst of the upheaval, Elector Frederick the Wise passed away on May 5, 1525, having just celebrated the Lord's Supper with bread and wine.

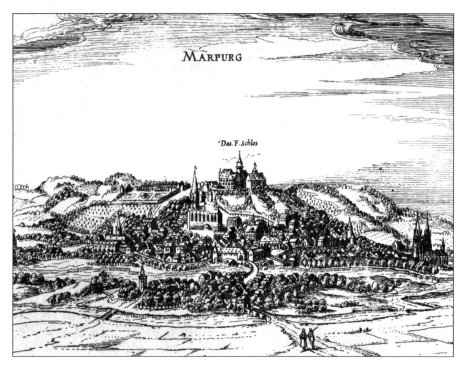

MARPURG

'Das.F.Schlos

View of Marburg in the sixteenth century. The castle where
the discussion took place is at the highest elevation.

The battle increased. Luther produced two more strong protests and thereby
distanced himself openly from the Peasants' War. More than 100,000 peasants lost their lives, and Thomas Müntzer was beheaded.

The third striking event of that year was the dispute between Luther and
Swiss Reformers concerning the Lord's Supper. At the end of 1524, Zwingli
presented his symbolic view of the words of its institution, "This is my body"
(Matt. 26:27) meaning "this is an indication of my body." The Netherlander
Cornelis Hoen had come to this interpretation before Zwingli. Luther interpreted this view as subjectivist fanaticism. He vehemently objected to
everything that smacked of spiritualism. Like Brenz, he maintained that the
body and blood of Christ were truly present in the Lord's Supper, through
the Word.

The debate over the presence of Christ in the Lord's Supper culminated
in a religious debate at Marburg. At the initiative of Philip of Hesse, a discussion took place at his castle in Marburg from October 1 to 4 to try to settle
the differences regarding the doctrine of the Lord's Supper and bring about
a broad-based, united front. On one side were Luther, Melanchthon, Jonas,

and Brenz, and on the other side, Zwingli, Oecolampadius, Bucer, and He-dio. The great question was, in what way was Christ present in the Lord's Supper? Luther connected this presence with the elements of bread and wine. Zwingli maintained his symbolic view. Agreement was reached on fourteen points, including original sin, justification, baptism, and the need to give to the laity not only the bread but also the wine. But on the fifteenth point, the presence of Christ in the Lord's Supper, no agreement could be reached. Lu-ther told the Swiss, "You have a different spirit from us." He could continue to extend Christian love to the Swiss, but not brotherly love. At this point, Luther distanced himself permanently from the Swiss Reformation.

Luther's Small and Large Catechisms (1529)

Luther was well aware of the great need for a book of instruction that would contain a succinct description of the key elements of the new doctrine. On visits to churches, he encountered a great lack of knowledge of the faith and great ignorance on the part of pastors regarding the teaching of the new doc-trine. He was asked to provide a suitable book of instruction. In Wittenberg, Luther commenced a series of sermons on material that he would subse-quently incorporate in his catechisms.

His catechisms, therefore, derived from his homiletic efforts. The Large Catechism, written in 1529, was a detailed book intended primarily to fa-miliarize preachers with the many aspects of Protestant church life. It served as a textbook, a reader, and an aid for meditation for anyone who sought to explore the faith. In the same year, Luther wrote the Small Catechism, which was intended for educating young people within the family, at school, or in church. The same material is discussed in both catechisms—in the Small Catechism in the form of questions and answers, and in the Large Catechism through a broader treatment. For the members of his own household, Luther organized an annual catechism exam that was followed by a festive meal.

These catechisms treat, in succession, the Ten Commandments; the Apostles' Creeds; the Lord's Prayer; and the sacraments of baptism, penance, and the Lord's Supper.

It is not surprising that Luther began with the Ten Commandments, showing that the law teaches people that they cannot possibly keep the com-mandments and that they need God's grace and forgiveness in Christ. His explanation of the Apostles' Creed has a very personal focus, as seen in this passage in the Small Catechism that describes faith in Christ:

I believe in Jesus Christ.... *What does this signify?* I believe that Jesus Christ, truly God—begotten of the Father from eternity—and also true man—born of the Virgin Mary—is my Lord, who has redeemed, purchased, and liberated me—a lost and rejected human being—from all sin, death, and the power of the devil, not with gold or silver, but with His holy, precious blood and through His innocent suffering and death, so that I may belong to Him; live in subjection to Him in His kingdom; and serve Him in eternal righteousness, innocence, and salvation since He is risen from the dead and lives and reigns forever. This is absolutely true.

In the treatment of the sacraments, the strong emphasis on the Word is striking. It is not the water, nor the bread and wine, but the Word of God that is effectual and speaks to us. Luther wished to retain penance as a means of liberating the believer from remorse and fear, but he viewed it in a much broader context: penance need not be administered only by ministers, but rather it constitutes a service that all Christians can render to one another. Although penance is no longer formally practiced within Lutheranism, it continues to play a role in pastoral care.

Through their succinct statements, both books of instruction have left their mark on the Lutheran faith. Those who wish to familiarize themselves with Luther's theology cannot ignore his catechisms, which continue to form part of the confessions of faith of Lutheranism. The model of ecclesiastical instruction provided by Luther was adopted by many other Reformers. For example, churches in England and France eventually adopted catechisms that, like Luther's, often functioned also as confessions of faith—such as the Heidelberg Catechism.

The Diet of Augsburg (1530)

In the meantime, the political difficulties encountered by the followers of Luther had not eased. The First Diet of Speyer, convened in 1526, was intended by the emperor to crush the evangelical movement. The Protestant princes failed to repeal the Edict of Worms. The Second Diet of Speyer, convened in 1529, only aggravated the situation. Ancient rights of Roman Catholic clerics were reconfirmed. Five evangelical princes (among whom were John of Saxony and Philip of Hesse) and fourteen cities presented their *protestatio* (protestation) on April 22, 1529. From then on, adherents of the new movement were referred to as Protestants.

Under these difficult circumstances, the Diet of Augsburg was convened in 1530. Emperor Charles V had the advantage. On his thirtieth birthday, February 24, 1530, he was crowned emperor by the pope in the Cathedral of Bologna, virtually behind the backs of the electors. From this strong position, he intended to uphold the Edict of Worms, but he wanted both parties to spell out their convictions.

The Protestants were successful in ensuring that religious matters were addressed first. A document written chiefly by Melanchthon and signed by four princes who had collaborated on the protestation was read in the presence of the emperor, who did not understand German. This document, consisting of twenty-eight articles, was the *Confessio Augustana* (Augsburg Confession). It was given to the emperor in both German and Latin. Melanchthon himself referred to it as an *apologia*, or a defense and justification. At the same time, however, it was a confession of faith, formulated clearly and succinctly. In it one can recognize all the Reformational themes from a Lutheran point of view.

The opposition could not accept this document. The emperor ordered the preparation of a *confutatio* (confutation) against the Augsburg Confession.

The Diet of Augsburg in 1530 (sixteenth-century copperplate).

The resulting document completely adhered to medieval Roman Catholic theology, and the emperor considered the Augsburg Confession to have been completely refuted.

However, battle lines had been drawn that could no longer be ignored. The princes remained steadfast, and the emperor underestimated Luther's influence. Four cities went their own way, in part because they were not comfortable with the Lutheran doctrine of the Lord's Supper as spelled out in the Augsburg Confession. Strasbourg, Constance, Memmingen, and Lindau wrote their own *Confessio tetrapolitana* (Tetrapolitan Confession), although it was not presented at the Diet of Augsburg. Melanchthon defended his confession against the imperial refutation in an *apologia* that he submitted on September 22, 1530. The emperor, however, refused to consider this more detailed treatise. His aim was now to persuade the pope to collaborate in a general council that should convene that very year. He also decided to renew the enforcement of the Edict of Worms.

The Schmalkaldic League

In Schmalkalden on February 27, 1531, the Schmalkaldic League was formed to fight the implementation of the decisions of the imperial diet and, if necessary, the emperor himself. The league was composed of about ten principalities and a number of evangelical free cities. Bucer and Luther had reconciled. The leadership of the league rested with Saxony and Hesse. The Augsburg Confession, Melanchthon's *apologia*, and the Tetrapolitan Confession constituted the league's foundation. Nevertheless, the Swiss refused to join in; only after the death of Zwingli did the southern regions support greater rapprochement.

As a result of the league's anti-Hapsburg threat coupled with the war with England and France, the emperor agreed to a truce at Nuremburg in 1532 that allowed the Reformation to continue to take root. In their own ecclesiastical districts, the Protestants were left in peace. At the request of Elector Johann Frederick, Luther wrote the Schmalkaldic Articles, intended as a new confession that sought to maintain internal unity. They were adopted by the elector and in other localities, although they were not officially adopted by the league. Luther published them himself in 1538. In 1580, they were incorporated in the *The Book of Concord* and thus became part of the confessional documents of the Lutheran Church.

Growing tensions

In the 1540s, real attempts were made to resolve the religious problems of the empire. Three religious discussions sought to achieve agreement between Protestants and Roman Catholics, first in Haguenau (June 12 to July 16, 1540), subsequently in Worms during the same year, and finally in Regensburg (April 21 to May 31, 1541).

In the meantime, Rome became increasingly conscious of the need for reformation in the church. On September 30, 1544, Pope Paul III convened the Council of Trent, although it did not open until more than a year later on December 13, 1545. During the next imperial diet in Worms, the Protestants rejected this council, desiring instead an impartial, ecclesiastically free consideration of their position. When the emperor learned of this reaction, he declared to the pope that he was prepared to use force against these Protestants. He was indeed to carry out this promise.

Following Luther's death in 1546, the members of the Schmalkaldic League were prepared to fight for their convictions, but they suffered a serious shortage of money. The emperor had the support of the pope and the Roman Catholic princes, not only in manpower but also in funds. The church offered indulgences to those who prayed for the eradication of this heresy.

In 1548 the emperor adopted a new imperial law, the Augsburg Interim, a ruling that yielded very little to the Protestants on the main points of church doctrine, tradition, and the sacraments; at the same time, it left many questions unanswered. Neither Lutherans nor Roman Catholics were pleased with it. It permitted the marriage of clergy, and both bread and wine were permitted in the Lord's Supper. The pope chose to ignore the Augsburg Interim, but Protestants resisted it. Melanchthon sought to resolve the question of Roman Catholic ceremonies that were unacceptable to Protestants. His efforts in this regard were not well received within his own camp, and he lost a good deal of support. In subsequent years the Augsburg Interim's lack of clarity gave rise to many internal disputes within Lutheranism.

It was Maurice, elector of Saxony (1521–1553), who turned the situation around. He was indignant about the humiliating imprisonment of his father-in-law, Philip of Hesse. When the emperor's attention lapsed because the Turks invaded Transylvania, Maurice revolted, supported by other princes. His attack on the emperor at Innsbruck completely surprised the emperor, who barely escaped imprisonment and suffered defeat near Metz. Although Maurice himself was killed in action a year later in 1553, his efforts saved Protestantism in difficult circumstances.

The Peace of Augsburg (1555)
A disillusioned emperor then departed for the Netherlands and left the

Elector Maurice of Saxony

government of Germany in the hands of his brother Ferdinand. The latter convened the Diet of Augsburg, where a religious peace was achieved on September 25, 1555, though not without great difficulty. Subjects were to adopt the religion of their sovereign and adhere to the confession that he supported. The motto devised to capture this principle was *cuius regio, eius religio* (whose region, his religion). Those who did not agree to this principle had to leave. Those who were already Protestant could remain so, but a change of faith could only take place with loss of dignity and property. This provision made the position of a sovereign absolute; he gained complete control not only in secular matters but also in spiritual matters in his territory. The elector was simultaneously the chief bishop, who determined the religion of his domain. Real freedom of religion was not yet granted.

Charles V saw this religious peace as a failure of his imperial policy during these many years. In Brussels on October 22, 1555, he transferred the government to his brother Ferdinand, who succeeded him as emperor upon Charles's death in 1558. Thus the realm entered a somewhat more stable period nine years after Luther's death. The distinction between Rome and the

Reformation, between Roman Catholics and Protestants, was recognized as a reality. In the future, separate religions would coexist. In confessionally split Germany, Protestants rallied around the Augsburg Confession. The pope was furious about the recognition of Protestants, and he refused to recognize the Peace of Augsburg.

The Peace of Augsburg ensured a period of rest and stability that would last about sixty years until the Thirty Years' War.

Calvinism in Germany

However stabilizing the Peace of Augsburg was, it only applied to Lutherans. Calvinists, Zwinglians, and Anabaptists were excluded and could not depend on it. Nevertheless, Calvinism increasingly penetrated predominantly Lutheran Germany during these years. How could this be?

In his theology, Philip Melanchthon, Luther's most trusted friend and supporter, increasingly moved toward Calvinism, especially with respect to his view of the Lord's Supper. In 1540, he rewrote the articles of the Augsburg Confession that dealt with the Lord's Supper. His supporters, who were

Philip Melanchthon

similarly influenced by Calvinism, were referred to as Philippists. They read Calvin's *Institutes* as eagerly as they did Melanchthon's *Loci communes*. Heinrich Bullinger was also highly regarded by these followers. They made no sharp distinction between Lutheranism and Calvinism. Initially, they believed that Calvin's teachings were a consistent application of what Luther had originally intended. However, Lutherans treated Philippists as Calvinists.

Following Melanchthon's death on April 19, 1560, Calvin's influence in Germany increased. His influence was particularly pronounced in higher social circles such as the court, the upper echelons of the civil service, and among Christian humanists. After the Diet of Naumburg in 1561, Calvinism was given some scope because it was recognized as a form of Lutheranism. Accordingly, Calvinists were entitled to a certain degree of protection.

Another factor that furthered Calvinism in Germany was the increasing contact between the University of Wittenberg and the universities of Zurich and Geneva. Scholarly ideas were increasingly exchanged among professors and students. Geneva was known as a center of solid theological education coupled with strong discipline.

A third factor was refugee churches. Calvinist immigrants from the Southern Netherlands established refugee churches, especially in the Rhine region: Frankfurt, Frankenthal, Aachen, Cologne, Wezel, and other places. In the Palatinate, an important church was established in Frankenthal, where Petrus Dathenus worked. Netherlanders who had had to flee because of their faith were readily accepted there. They formed their own church based on their Calvinistic tradition, and they greatly supported their persecuted fellow believers at home by printing Reformational documents, organizing ecclesiastical life, and strongly supporting resistance.

It cannot be denied, however, that the transfer to Calvinism on the part of Elector Frederick III of the Palatinate was of decisive importance for this branch of the Reformation in Germany. That a Reformed catechism should appear in the Palatinate after a lengthy period of predominantly Lutheran church history is largely due to this elector, who, from his own thorough study of Scripture, decided in 1559 to switch to Calvinism.

CHAPTER 2

The Completion of the Heidelberg Catechism
by Wim Verboom

The Palatinate—Heidelberg

The Palatinate

The name of the German region in which the events related to the emergence of the Heidelberg Catechism took place derives from the Latin term *palatium*. It indicates the residence of a prominent person, and from it we derive the word "palace."

The region of the Palatinate in the late Middle Ages and the beginning of the modern era can best be described as a collection of counties or duchies located on both sides of the Rhine, including Neuburg, Zweibrücken, and Simmern. These areas enjoyed a degree of independence, but ultimately they were subject to the emperor. Inter-city conflicts frequently arose. Among those towns, Speyer played a dominant role for a long period of time. Several emperors are buried there.

Centralization of authority emerged when Emperor Frederick I Barbarossa appointed his half-brother Conrad as Pfalzgrafen bei Rhein (Count Palatine of the Rhine) in 1156. One of his successors, Louis I, began to use Heidelberg as a place of residence in 1225. It soon became the center of the Palatinate electorate. Count Palatine Rupert I was the first to be given the title of elector in 1356. The electors mentioned below emerged from this environment.

Heidelberg

Heidelberg was first mentioned in the charters of Count Palatine Henry in 1196. Initially a fishing village located on the Neckar River, it was home to St. Peter's church, which was served by a priest. During the time of Conrad, Heidelberg developed into a city with walls and towers. Two castles were built on the slopes of its hills; one was located where the great castle would later be constructed. Sources refer to a wooden bridge across the Neckar in 1284. The Alte Brücke (Old Bridge), which was built later and has its own history, continues to be a tourist attraction.

Heidelberg (Braun and Hogenberg, *Civitates orbis terrarum*, 1572)

During the thirteenth century, the establishment in Heidelberg of several monastic orders, including the Augustinians, led to new cultural and scholarly developments. The city acquired its influence and prestige partly for this reason. The university was established in 1386, and under the electors Rupert III and Louis III the Church of the Holy Spirit was built, an immense, late-Gothic hall church. At that time, Heidelberg had about 4,000 inhabitants, compared to 125,000 today.

While the electors ruled the Palatinate, the population depended on agriculture, viticulture, and fishing for their livelihood. In addition to trade by way of the Neckar River, the supply of various products to the castle represented a significant source of income.

Political and ecclesiastical developments

The first Palatinate prince on whom we focus is the elector, Philip the Upright. He was one of seven officers in the Holy Roman Empire entitled to vote in the selection of the emperor. He governed his territory from 1476 until 1508, before the Reformation.

We mention this elector first because under his government, a degree of openness emerged for the renewal of education and the arts. He sought to turn Heidelberg into a "seat of the Muses." At his court one could also detect humanistic influences. Although this interest in cultural renewal was not a harbinger of the Reformation, it created favorable conditions for the Reformation, as was the case elsewhere. For example, the famous humanist Rudolf Agricola came to Heidelberg to give a number of lectures, and scholars such as John Oecolampadius and the poet Conrad Celtes taught the elector's children the first principles of literature. Despite significant opposition, Wessel Gansfort gained a certain amount of influence. Luther subsequently referred

Elector Philip the Upright (left) is handed an incunabulum (early printed work).

to him as a kindred spirit. Scholar John Reuchlin served as librarian and professor of Greek and Hebrew.

G. D. J. Schotel wrote that Elector Philip could merely savor the beginning of a "better future." He had succeeded in "creating a breach, which prospered the approaching storm." Unwittingly, Philip had performed incalculable service for the Reformation. If God had granted him a longer life—he passed away in 1508—he would certainly have achieved greater progress in his territories than was the case under his successor, according to Schotel.

Elector Louis V

Philip the Upright's successor was his son, Louis V. The latter reigned as elector palatine from 1508 to 1544. He was known as a thoughtful and conciliatory ruler. During his reign, while the winds of the Reformation began to blow elsewhere in the German empire, there was also noticeable change in the Palatinate. In the midst of the ever-advancing political and ecclesiastical changes, Louis adopted a conciliatory attitude. On the one hand, for example, he required his subjects to attend the Roman Catholic mass, but on the other hand, he maintained a tolerant attitude towards the new Reformational ideas. In Zweibrücken, Count Louis II offered the Reformation some

Elector Louis V

latitude, and he permitted the well-known 1518 debate to be conducted in Heidelberg. During this assembly of Augustinian monks, Luther expounded his Reformational insights. Justification by faith represented an especially important theme. Individuals who subsequently provided leadership to the Reformation, like Martin Bucer and Johannes Brenz, were won over to the cause through this debate.

Louis V himself did not choose between the teachings of the Protestants and those of the Roman Catholics. Following the Protestation of 1529, he sought to mollify the emperor. At this stage there was apparently still some hope for reconciliation. When both parties came together in Nuremberg in 1532, Louis played an important role in establishing the Nuremberg Truce. One of the provisions of this truce was that Protestants would be tolerated at least until a council could be convened. During the religious discussions at Regensburg (1540–1541), Louis was a member of the moderate party. His faction lost ground there in the face of increasingly divergent views, especially concerning the church.

Like his father, Louis took a great deal of interest in the arts and culture,

Elector Frederick II

especially architecture. The construction of the renowned castle of Heidel-berg was completed during his reign, although it had been started earlier.

Elector Frederick II
When Louis V passed away in 1544, his brother Frederick II took over as elector and held this position until 1556. For Frederick, this brought an end to a restless existence. He had traveled a great deal, visiting the Netherlands, Spain, and France, among other countries. In those days, he eagerly sought the favor of the Hapsburg family.

In 1530 Frederick II was present at the Diet of Augsburg. There he gained an appreciation for the position of Luther's followers and acquired the conviction that they should not be punished as heretics. That he sought to accommodate Protestant views in his own territory is obvious from the introduction of a provisional church order whose content was influenced by Melanchthon. The mass was permitted to be celebrated in the German language and the Lord's Supper could be administered with both bread and wine. Furthermore, the marriage of priests would no longer be prohibited. On January 3, 1546, he agreed that the first Protestant church service could be held in Heidelberg. However, we should not conclude that Frederick himself was interested in joining Protestantism; he remained Roman Catholic.

Frederick did not join the Schmalkaldic League formed by evangelicals in 1531. Nevertheless, he did participate in the Schmalkaldic War of 1546–1547 on the side of the Protestants, and thus he found himself among the losers. The provisions of the Augsburg Interim of 1548 had to be implemented. Only the Communion cup for the laity and the marriage of priests were permitted, at least until a council could make some decisions. Apart from these concessions, Roman Catholic doctrines and practices were maintained. Subsequently, Frederick became reconciled with the emperor and collaborated in the Peace of Passau of 1552, prior to the Peace of Augsburg of 1555.

Elector Otto Henry

Otto Henry had an imposing personality. This cousin of Frederick II began to govern in 1556. He ruled for only a short time before he suddenly passed

Elector Otto Henry

away in 1559. His nickname, "the Magnanimous,"[1] suited him perfectly. This generosity did not preclude decisive action, as was proven immediately upon his appointment as elector. He had already shown himself to be an avid follower of Luther, and he was a member of the Schmalkaldic League.

When Otto Henry was invested with the reins of power, he immediately introduced the Reformation by issuing an edict. He prohibited Roman Catholic errors and propagated pure, evangelical doctrine. He was a friend of Melanchthon and was influenced by Melanchthon's ecclesiastical and theological stance. He also immediately issued a church order that took a position intermediate between that of the Palatinate and Nuremburg and that of the Reformer Brenz of Württemberg. This meant, for example, that a church council was established with both secular and spiritual representation. Theologians such as Michael Diller and Johannes Marbach had great influence on the content and the implementation of this church order.

An important event whose consequences Otto Henry could not have foreseen was the appointment of Tilemann Hesshus as general superintendent and councilor with responsibility for canon law. He introduced the

---

1. "der Grossmütige"

The Elector Frederick III pictured with his first and second wives. *From left to right:* Maria Casimir von Brandenburg-Kulmbach (1519–1567) and Amalia Gumberth IV von Neuenahr (1536–1602).

unchanged Augsburg Confession of 1530 as the confession of the Palatinate and required ministers and other officers of the church to obey it. Brenz's Catechism was adopted. Worship services underwent important changes. Latin hymns were replaced by hymns sung in the language of the people. From then on, preaching and the administration of the Lord's Supper had to reflect the views of Luther and Brenz.

Remarkably, Otto Henry took a conciliatory position with respect to Anabaptists. Schotel writes that within a matter of weeks, ecclesiastical life changed completely. Everything was accomplished without quarreling, without division. "The people woke up as from a dream and rubbed their eyes; but this was no dream."

Elector Frederick III

We pay somewhat greater attention to Frederick III, the elector upon whose initiative the Heidelberg Catechism was completed in 1563. The image this elector has left with us is one of a man who served God with his whole heart. He saw his role as a continuation of that of the kings of Israel in the Old Tes-

Frederick III

tament who took up the reformation of their nation and their people. Since Frederick had spent time at various royal courts, including the imperial court of Charles V, David Pareus compares him with Moses, who was brought up at the court of the tyrant in Egypt and became his greatest opponent.

Frederick was born on February 14, 1515, in the Duchy of Simmern as the son of Duke Johann II. In 1537, he married Maria, the daughter of Margrave Casimir of Brandenburg-Kulmbach. Maria was Lutheran, and Frederick joined her religion. At the time of the Augsburg Interim in 1548, we find him on the side of the Protestants. In 1556 he succeeded his father as duke and introduced the Reformation in his territory. At this time, he acted as conciliator of the religious differences that existed among Lutherans, the followers of Melanchthon (Philippists), and the Reformed adherents.

In 1559, Frederic III succeeded Otto Henry as elector. Initially, he remained Lutheran. In this capacity he appointed Lutheran clergy and professors. However, in Heidelberg there emerged a serious conflict between Superintendent Hesshus, who first thought along the lines of Melanchthon but subsequently began to think strictly along Lutheran lines, and Klebitz,

The statue of Frederick III in the Friedrichsbau (Frederick Building) of the castle of Heidelberg.

a deacon who leaned towards the Reformed confession. The conflict concerned the Lord's Supper. Hesshus considered Klebitz to be Zwinglian. He gave orders for Brenz's Catechism to be replaced with Luther's. Frederick disapproved of their fight and threatened exile. Everyone had to adhere to the Augsburg Confession according to the text of the *Variata* (the revised Augsburg Confession of 1540). In these clarifications, Melanchthon took a position on the Lord's Supper that diverged from Luther's and leaned towards Calvin's. However, Hesshus and Klebitz did not terminate their conflict. Frederick therefore removed both of them from their offices. He subsequently requested Melanchthon to describe clearly his position on the Lord's Supper again. Melanchthon did so in a so-called *Gutachten* (expert opinion). In it, he rejected the Lutheran view that Christ is physically present in the Lord's Supper *in*, *with*, and *under* the symbols of bread and wine and, by implication, is physically omnipresent.

Frederick now sought to arrive at a position of his own. He steadily leaned more and more towards the Reformed view. His son-in-law, Johann Frederick of Saxony, vehemently objected to this change. He visited his father-in-law and debated with him for five days. It became known as the Heidelberg Debate of 1560. It was through this dispute that Frederick completely switched to the Reformed position. His son-in-law and many others opposed his views; Frederick stood virtually alone. Yet, he wished to remain loyal to the Augsburg Confession, and he met with German princes in Naumburg to sign it. Although his son-in-law left the meeting prematurely and did not sign the confession, the others did sign. Frederick hoped that the more moderate Lutherans would thereby share in the Peace of Augsburg of 1555. At the same time, the unity of the empire would be assured. The Reformed theologian Theodore Beza of Geneva stayed at Heidelberg in 1559, and Frederick was greatly influenced by his teaching. The elector was also attracted to the thinking of Bullinger. The Reformed theologians Zacharias Ursinus and Caspar Olevianus were the next to visit Heidelberg.

Following the meeting in Naumburg, Frederick pursued the Reformation along Reformed lines. He had images, baptismal stones, altars, crucifixes, and similar items removed from churches, and he forbade the playing of organ music. The publication of a document by Thomas Erastus concerning the Lord's Supper, entitled *Gründlicher Bericht, wie die Worte Christi: das ist mein Leib, zu verstehen* (Comprehensive Report on How the Words of Christ, "This is My Body" Should Be Understood), gave the final push to his switch to Calvinism. When the Heidelberg Catechism appeared in 1563, it was incorporated into the Palatine church order. This church order was entirely

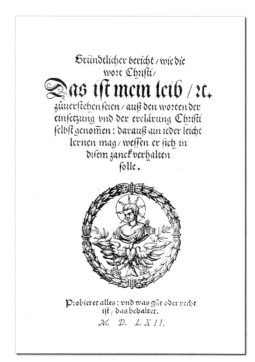

Title page of *Gründlicher Bericht*
(Comprehensive Report,
Heidelberg, 1562)

Reformed, and it was put together in the spirit of the church order of Calvin for Geneva and that of Łaski and Micron for the Netherlands refugee church at London. Frederick III retained the role of superintendent.

In the account of the completion and introduction of the Heidelberg Catechism below, Frederick III became completely isolated. The attacks on the elector and his catechism became quite fierce. At the same time, during his reign, Heidelberg became a sanctuary for Reformed refugees, including Huguenots.

In a letter to his son-in-law, Johann Frederick, dated June 10, 1562, Frederick included a confession of his faith that clearly demonstrated how he experienced his faith: "I thank my dear God, who has taught me to pray, namely, the Lord's Prayer. When I say, 'Father of ours' or 'Our Father who art in heaven,' then I believe and know for sure that I am His child. Since I am His child, I am also a brother of God's Son, our Lord and Savior Jesus Christ, and the fellow heir of all those spiritual benefits that He has acquired for all His believers through His incarnation, suffering, death, resurrection, and ascension into His spiritual Kingdom. No devil, hell, world, or any human being can take these away from me; I am as certain of this through faith as though I held them in my hands. Let this be to me a true foundation, established on the cornerstone Jesus Christ, of whom Paul says in 1 Corinthians 3:11, 'For other foundation can no man lay than that is laid, which is Jesus Christ.'"

Following his publication and defense of the Heidelberg Catechism, Frederick continued to fight. In Heidelberg, a violent dispute arose about the way in which discipline was to be practiced. Since this event is beyond the scope of our discussion, we do not address it. Frederick III passed away on October 26, 1576. A historian of the Palatinate writes that when Frederick died, the territory lost its noblest and greatest prince.

Developments in education and scholarship

Since the educational and academic context played an important role in the reformation of the Palatine church, we now focus on this aspect of its history.

The university

Heidelberg had a university since 1386. As was true elsewhere, the academic climate of this university was long influenced by scholasticism, and the philosophy of Aristotle reigned supreme. There were also realists who thought along the lines of Thomas Aquinas; according to them, reason and revelation

Hohe Schule zu Heydelberg (*University at Heidelberg*, woodcut from Sebastian Münster, *Cosmographia*, Basel, 1614)

formed a unity. There were nominalists who saw a dichotomy between faith and knowledge and who emphasized that faith depended solely on the authority of the church. When Louis V became elector and tendencies towards reformation emerged, the university resisted these tendencies. Although a number of formal improvements were made to the academic program, such as the establishment of chairs in Greek and Hebrew, the scholastic climate as such continued to dominate the university.

No substantial changes were made until Frederick II became elector. In 1546, the Lutheran Heinrich Stoll was appointed rector. Under his leadership, the dichotomy between realism and nominalism was overcome. Nevertheless, further substantial renewal stalled as a result of wars and the Augsburg Interim of 1548. Matters improved when new professors were appointed and the university's budget was increased through a transfer of assets from the Augustinian monastery of Heidelberg. Otto Henry sought Melanchthon's advice for the reorganization of education. The result was that in 1558 the university was permanently liberated from the scholastic philosophy of education. The university now had three faculties: theology, law, and philosophy. Furthermore, it obtained a splendid library, namely, the Bibliotheca Palatina, first established under Louis III at the beginning of the fifteenth century.

As could be expected, under Frederick III the university experienced a shift in the Reformed direction. In addition to Olevianus and Ursinius, professors such as Hieronymus Zanchius and Immanuel Tremellius were appointed. At this time the university enjoyed a period of vigorous growth.

The Pedagogical Academy
In 1546, Elector Frederick II opened the Paedagogium (Pedagogical Academy), an institute to prepare students for university study. From the start, despite opposition from the old core of the university, education here was no longer scholastic, but Ramistic, named after the French humanist Pierre de la Ramée (1515–1572). An important characteristic of Ramée's philosophical views was the connection between theory and practice—quite different from scholasticism, which occupied itself with interminable, abstract distinctions. The Paedagogium offered a three-year program based on the model provided by the humanist Johann Sturm of Strasbourg, and it undoubtedly had a positive influence on the university. However, the program deteriorated under Otto Henry, who favored a restoration of the old Neckarschule (Neckar School), which was the Latin school. To this end, he had a new school order developed. Under Frederick III, the Pedagogical Academy re-

The Neckarschule, where at one
time the Collegium Sapientiae
was housed.

covered, and in 1565 it was merged with the Neckar School, forming a new
institute for classical training.

The College of Wisdom
In 1555 Frederick II opened the *Collegium Sapientiae* (College of Wisdom), an
institute for poor students. Having become Protestant under Otto Henry, it
acquired a Reformed character through the reforms implemented by Frederick III and became a seminary for prospective ministers. In 1560 Olevianus
was appointed as its head; he was succeeded by Ursinius in 1561.

It is obvious that Heidelberg was a center of scholarship and education
under Elector Frederick III. It was well placed to produce a booklet of instruction such as the Heidelberg Catechism, especially under the inspiring
leadership of the elector.

Religious instruction in Heidelberg
To explain how and why the Heidelberg Catechism came into being, we first
focus on how the principles of the new doctrine were disseminated among
the population, especially children, after the reformation of the Palatine

church. As was the custom, religious instruction took place within the triangle of family, school, and church. Concentrating on Heidelberg, we focus on each of these spheres and draw a number of conclusions.

The family
Outside the Roman Catholic Church, the role of parents is an important factor in the religious instruction of children. The covenant of grace, to which the children belong and of which they bear the sign and seal through baptism, calls for their response to the promise of God's salvation. Parents who offer their children for baptism promise to instruct their children in the doctrine of godliness, led by the Holy Spirit. Luther explained this task to parents in his Small Catechism because he encountered an astounding degree of ignorance. It was no different among those of the Reformed tradition. Thus, in the Palatine church order of 1563, the minister conducting a baptism was to state, "In particular, however, you as parents and baptismal witnesses must make every effort to instruct this child in the right knowledge and fear of God and the Lord Christ, according to the articles of the Christian faith and the doctrine of God revealed from heaven and contained in the Old and New Testaments."[2]
   A variety of instructional booklets appeared, as well as various ecclesiastical stipulations that required parents to send their children to catechism classes, both at church and school.

The school
Heidelberg's various institutions of learning brought their own perspectives to the religious instruction of children and young people. Not isolated entities, these schools had varying connections with the church and the government, as is evident from the school orders, programs of instruction, and inspections.
   School instruction had three aspects. First was instruction in the faith, followed by cultural development, and, finally, social involvement. It is not surprising that catechetical instruction had a prominent place in the overall program. A 1556 school order established for the Latin school specified that all students would receive catechetical instruction twice a week, on Wednesdays and Saturdays. As was true elsewhere, the teaching of catechetical material

---

2. "Insonderheit aber jr vater und gevattern allen fleisz anwenden, dasz disz kind in rechter erkanntnusz und forcht Gottes, laut der artickel des christlichen glaubens und der lehre, welche von Gott ausz dem Himel offenbaret, und in alten und neuen Testament begriffen ist, dem Herrn Christi aufferzogen werde."

The Schoolmaster (woodcut
by Albrecht Dürer, 1510)

was embedded in the teaching of literature. The catechetical material was recited in church after it had been studied at school.

In more advanced education, the study of Holy Scripture was connected with the study of languages. Furthermore, children had to memorize Bible verses at home and recite them in school. Music education included the learning of spiritual songs. Psalms were memorized. Lutheran and Reformed instructional booklets were used interchangeably at school and at home.

The church

The main emphasis in religious education in Heidelberg was placed on instruction within the church. In the church order of 1563, a curriculum was developed for this instruction. First, it prescribed the reading of the Heidelberg Catechism in Sunday morning services. It further stipulated that in cities where two services were held in the afternoon, a summary of the Heidelberg Catechism was to be read in the first service. In places where only a catechism service was held on Sunday afternoons, the reading of this summary was to take place prior to the service. Much attention was paid to this catechism service, which was conducted not only for the children of the congregation but also for the adults.

As prescribed in the church order of 1563, a service proceeded as follows:

1. Song
2. Prayer
3. Reading of the Ten Commandments or its summary
4. Instructional talk by the minister with the children
5. Catechism sermon for the entire congregation
6. Recital of the week's section of the Catechism by children who had memorized it, in the presence of the congregation
7. Discussion of the next set of Catechism questions and answers
8. Prayer

We see that the catechetical method in this service consisted of a combination of monologue and dialogue. Monologue occurred in readings and preaching; dialogue took place in the instructional talk with the children, the recital of memory work, and the discussion of the upcoming Catechism questions and answers.

Profession of faith by young people and others who were to participate for the first time in the celebration of the Lord's Supper took place on the Saturdays preceding such celebrations. The requisite knowledge was taught to them by their parents or by others on their parents' behalf. This responsibility of the parents was part of a continuous sequence from baptism, through instruction and profession of faith, to conscious membership in the church. For those planning to make profession of their faith, it was not merely a matter of attending a special class. Profession of faith itself took place in the midst of the congregation and consisted of an examination in the chief doctrines of faith. Little is known about the age of the prospective candidates.

Not until the turn of the sixteenth to the seventeenth century does the available information refer to a specific age for making a profession of faith, namely, fourteen years. The instructional content of ecclesiastical catechism teaching was intended to be an interpretation of Holy Scripture. It consisted of the following classical components: faith, commandments, prayer, sacraments, combined with Bible verses and songs. Although there were several instruction booklets available for children, ministers used a guide prepared by Ursinus entitled *Explicationes catecheticae* (Exposition of the Catechism).[3]

---

3. A later Dutch translation of this work, *Het Schat-boeck der Christelycke Leere ofte Uytlegginghe over den Catechismus* (The Treasure Book of Christian Doctrine or Exposition of the Catechism), was known in the Netherlands as *Schat-boeck* (Treasure Book).

Conclusions

From the characteristics of religious education in Heidelberg, we can draw the following conclusions:

1. Religious instruction in Heidelberg reflected a covenantal perspective.
2. Religious instruction was intended to be wholly biblical.
3. Religious instruction envisaged a personal profession of faith.
4. A special feature of religious instruction was the inclusion of an element of comfort in the teaching material. This undoubtedly reflected the religious persecution of the time.

Religious instruction booklets prior to the Heidelberg Catechism

We now consider what instructional booklets or catechisms were available in the Palatinate before the Heidelberg Catechism appeared in 1563. In the Palatinate, as elsewhere, the Reformation led to lively creativity in the creation of catechetical literature. The aim was to prepare instructional booklets that described the key elements of the faith in simple terms, based on the Bible and adapted to the local situation. These booklets also identified and fought errors that were encountered in those days.

In this context we must take into account the widespread ignorance of the general population. Most people could neither read nor write. The publication of the instructional booklets therefore reflected the implementation of education programs for the general population. Children had to go to school to learn to read so that they could absorb the contents of the Bible, which had been published in their mother tongue, as well as principal catechetical concepts contained in the instruction booklets. The impact of these develop-

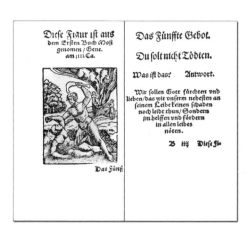

Page from Luther's Small Catechism: the fifth commandment

Title page of Luther's
Small Catechism

ments can also be recognized in the Palatinate. From the beginning of the Reformation the following booklets were used there:

Luther's Small Catechism (1529)
Luther's Large Catechism (1529)
Brenz's Catechism (1535)
Eine Kurze Ordenliche Summa (A Brief Orderly Summary, 1558)
Ursinus's Shorter Catechism (1562)
Ursinus's Larger Catechism (1562)

We consider each of these in turn, briefly looking at their content and providing an evaluation. It is immediately obvious that these booklets clearly reflected the ecclesiastical and religious developments in the Palatinate.

Luther's Small Catechism (1529)
When Luther published his Small Catechism in 1529, he could not have anticipated the enormous influence it would have in Lutheran countries and churches, including the Palatinate. The 1557 church order of the Duchy of Zweibrücken prescribed the use of this very booklet. Luther wrote it primarily for families, with parents being charged to use it for teaching their

children. It was also used in schools and other places of instruction. Like many catechisms, the booklet follows the question-and-answer format, which probably derived from practices associated with penance. Such a format provided the confessor with a means of testing the knowledge of the candidate. The Small Catechism is a typical example of Luther's style. Simple and practical, with a pastoral orientation, the booklet is directed at children and their level of experience.

As far as the content of the Small Catechism is concerned, the Lutheran sequence of law and gospel form the framework: (1) the Ten Commandments, (2) the Apostles' Creed, (3) the Lord's Prayer, (4) baptism, (5) penance, and (6) the Lord's Supper. These divisions are followed by morning, afternoon, and evening prayers. This catechism also contains household rules with Bible verses. It is noteworthy that the booklet also offers instruction on penance, something that is not true of subsequent catechism teaching among Reformed churches. Luther insisted that penance should have a pastoral emphasis. The booklet encourages confessors to speak words of comfort to people who were troubled by their sins. Naturally, in this booklet we encounter Luther's views on the sacraments. Baptism to him was the sacrament of water and the Word: it offers forgiveness to those who believe in the Word. In the Lord's Supper, the body and blood of Christ are physically present in the elements of bread and wine. The Lord's Supper constitutes the visible Word, and one receives its benefits through faith.

Luther's Large Catechism (1529)

In the same year the Small Catechism appeared, Luther published his Large Catechism, also referred to as the German Catechism. The Small Catechism was intended for students and the Large Catechism for teachers. A few of the church orders in the Palatinate explicitly prescribed the use of this catechism. It was intended primarily for ministers and offered them material for preaching and catechetical teaching. At the same time, this booklet of instruction offered more substantial material to church members who sought to advance beyond the Small Catechism. The Large Catechism follows a concentric approach: the material is covered several times, each time in greater depth.

The Large Catechism does not follow the question-and-answer format but presents doctrinal explanations of principal concepts of the Christian faith. It is rather detailed, but quite accessible and pastorally oriented.

The booklet begins with a preface in which Luther explains the importance of instruction. He himself continued to study on a daily basis. He said, "I still behave as a child who is taught the catechism; I read and recite it word

Johannes Brenz

by word every morning, and when I have time, the Lord's Prayer, the Ten Commandments, the Creed, the Psalms, and so forth. Although I read and study every day, I still have not arrived where I would like to be; I must remain a child and a student of the catechism and am happy to be so."

After the preface, the following topics are discussed: (1) the Ten Commandments, (2) the Apostles' Creed, (3) the Lord's Prayer, (4) baptism, (5) the Lord's Supper, and (6) penance.

A number of features stand out. The Apostles' Creed is not discussed as twelve articles, but as three following a trinitarian subdivision. In this way Luther wished to emphasize that faith in the Triune God is the foundation of the Christian faith. Furthermore, the explanations of baptism and the Lord's Supper are entirely in line with those of the Small Catechism. The Large Catechism strongly emphasizes that the sacrament represents the visible Word and, as such, the Word in action. This does not mean, however, that through participation in the sacrament one automatically shares in salvation. In the discussion of the Lord's Supper, for example, we read that "those who hear it said and *believe* it to be true share in it. Those who *do not believe*, have nothing" (italics added). The catechism presents penance as an institution that people are at liberty to use. It consists of two parts: confession of sins and acceptance of acquittal by God. These two elements correspond to the basic structure of the Lutheran faith: law and gospel.

Brenz's Catechism (1535)
Johannes Brenz, the Reformer who led the Reformation in Württemberg, among other places, wrote several catechism booklets. One of these appeared in 1535 and was usually known simply as Brenz's Catechism. This booklet, intended for young people, was also called *Fragstück des Christlichen Glaubens für die Jugend* (The Question of the Christian Faith for Young People). When the moderate Lutheran elector Otto Henry introduced a new church order in the Palatinate in 1556, he prescribed Brenz's Catechism as an educational tool for instruction in the Christian faith, instead of the Small Catechism of Luther that might have been expected.

Brenz's Catechism also follows the question-and-answer format. He offers brief and simple information, taking into account the age and level of children's comprehension. The framework of the information is the identity of the learning child. The catechism therefore begins with a question about baptism as a sign of being a Christian. The child confesses that he is a Christian for he has been baptized. Subsequently, (1) the meaning of baptism is further explained; followed by (2) a discussion of the Apostles' Creed, which leads to instruction in the doctrine of justification by faith and the receiving of the Holy Spirit. We need the Holy Spirit to live prayerfully according to God's commands. Next the catechism discusses (3) the Lord's Prayer, (4) the Ten Commandments, and (5) the Lord's Supper. The booklet ends with (6) an explanation of the keys of the kingdom as they apply to preaching (Matt. 16:19).[4]

This booklet departs from the typical Lutheran approach of starting with the law. The law topic is not treated until after a discussion of the Lord's Supper, which may be a reflection of Melanchthon's influence. At any rate, the performance of good works is treated separately here, as distinct from the average Lutheran catechism. Consider the following question and answer:

---

4. "The reference in Mt. 16:19 to the giving of the keys of the kingdom of heaven to Peter has given rise to considerable debate about what the power of the keys is. On the one side Roman Catholicism insists, on the strength of this saying, that the Roman communion to which Peter came as the first bishop has inherited his prerogative; it is the church in which forgiveness is validly proclaimed, entrance to the kingdom insured, and binding ecclesiastical rules established. On the other side, the churches of the Reformation contend that Peter represents the apostles and that the keys refer to the total apostolic mission, being used to convey the message of remission of believers' sins and to order rightly the Church's life and ministry" (*International Standard Bible Encyclopedia*, rev. ed., ed. Geoffrey W. Bromiley [Grand Rapids: Eerdmans, 1986], s.v. "keys, power of the.")

Title page: *Eine Kurze Orden-liche Summa* (A Brief Orderly Summary, 1558)

Q. Why should we perform good works?

A. So that we shall give evidence of our faith through good works and be grateful to our Lord God for His goodness shown towards us.

Here a life of gratitude is spelled out in a nutshell. In the explanation of the Lord's Supper, it is taught that Christ is present, but not in the typical Lutheran fashion—that Christ is present *with, in,* and *under* the bread and wine (consubstantiation). It is not surprising that Hesshus, once he had adopted strict Lutheranism, did not care for this interpretation of the Lord's Supper and wanted to get rid of Brenz's booklet of instruction. Another striking aspect is that in the discussion of the keys of the kingdom, no reference is made to penance—as was usually the case in Lutheran booklets of instruction—but instead to the preaching of the law and the gospel. All in all, we conclude that this booklet reflects a different spirit from the catechisms of Luther himself and the instruction booklets strongly influenced by him. Here we detect influences of Melanchthon's theology. Subsequently Frederick III was able to use it as a foundation for the Heidelberg Catechism.

Eine Kurze Ordenliche Summa (A Brief Orderly Summary, 1558)
In 1558, another catechism was introduced in Heidelberg. It was a reprint of

a catechism written by Nicolaus Gallus for the city of Regensburg in 1554 (or possibly 1547). This booklet was primarily aimed at instructing families in the faith, as is immediately obvious from its structure. Its content proper is preceded by an explanation of Christian rules for the family.

The booklet does not follow the question-and-answer format but contains explanations that serve as commentary on illustrations. This approach was frequently followed in instruction booklets prior to the Reformation. For example, we see on a left-hand page an illustration of a church service, full of symbolism, and on the corresponding right-hand page an explanation of faith that comes about through the operation of the Word and the Spirit as a consequence of preaching. The nature of the text is quite simple and yet very informative.

The booklet consists of three sections. It first discusses the law and its role in teaching us that we are sinful people. The second part deals with the gospel and faith, through which believers partake of Jesus Christ and share in the benefits of the gospel. This section also discusses the significance of baptism, the keys of the kingdom associated with penance, and the Lord's Supper. The booklet concludes with a third section dealing with good works as the fruits and signs of faith. It interprets the new life as being in line with the Ten Commandments — that is, a life of gratitude. It also addresses cross-bearing from the perspective of future glory. This catechism ends with *Ein kurze Christenliche Bekenntnisz für junge kinder und einfeltigen menschen* (A Brief Christian Confession for Young Children and the Mentally Handicapped). Here a child confesses three things: (1) I am a poor sinner, (2) I am saved by Christ, and (3) I confess that I am called to gratitude.

What strikes us immediately in this moderately Lutheran booklet is the division into three sections that treat three aspects of faith: knowledge of misery, knowledge of deliverance, and knowledge of gratitude. This division into three parts forms the structure of both the booklet and the concluding personalized confession of faith. We will return to this structure in the discussion of the Heidelberg Catechism. It is further noteworthy that the Lord's Supper is interpreted in the spirit of Melanchthon. Christ's presence in the Lord's Supper is not confessed in accord with the strict Lutheran view, but in the spirit of Melanchthon's *Variata* (the revised Augsburg Confession of 1540). The role of faith in partaking of salvation in the Lord's Supper is stressed. Furthermore, the classical doctrines of faith, commandments, and prayer are not presented analytically (point by point), but synthetically (in summary form).

Viewing this booklet as a whole, we can say that though it is Lutheran in approach, it leans towards the Reformed view of faith on issues like the doctrine of the Lord's Supper and the use of the term *gratitude* to indicate living according to God's commandments. The law here serves not only to reveal man's sinfulness but also constitutes a rule for the new life of faith.

Ursinus's Shorter Catechism *(1562)*
In 1562 Ursinus wrote his first catechism for children, the *Kleine Catechismus* or *Catechismus minor* (Shorter Catechism). This booklet was published in Heidelberg and therefore was the first Reformed instruction booklet in the Palatinate. This catechism is a direct precursor of the Heidelberg Catechism, which was to appear the following year. Containing 108 questions and answers, the booklet adopts a very simple, personal, and pastoral style. It is remarkable that this accessible document came from the pen of the learned Ursinus. The booklet begins with two questions about a Christian's comfort:

Q. 1. What comfort does your heart depend on in both life and death?
A.   That God will certainly forgive me all of my sins for Christ's sake, and has granted me eternal life, for which I glorify and praise Him.

Q. 2. How do you know this?
A.   The Holy Spirit testifies this in my heart through God's Word, the sacraments, and growing obedience to God.

The booklet continues with the familiar three-part structure organized around misery, deliverance, and gratitude. The role of the law is stated to be the source of knowledge of sin. An explanation of the Apostles' Creed follows. Special emphasis is placed on justification by faith. A discussion of the sacraments is followed by the Ten Commandments and the Lord's Prayer.

The three-part organization of this instruction booklet, which appeared shortly after the publication of *Eine Kurze Ordenliche Summa* in Heidelberg, justifies the supposition that Ursinus knew the latter booklet and probably adopted its structure. We may conclude that the organizing concepts of misery, deliverance, and gratitude were not exclusively Reformed but instead reflect the unique theological and spiritual climate of the Palatinate, where there probably were more instances of agreement between Lutherans and Reformed believers than elsewhere. In this context, the interpretation of predestination stands out. Instead of a detailed explanation of two-sided predestination, we find a carefully formulated, pastoral question:

Q. But are you not tempted to doubt your salvation when you learn that only those predestined by God will be saved?

A. Not in the least; on the contrary, in all my temptations I now have well-founded assurance; for if I desire to believe and obey God with a serious resolve of my heart, then this constitutes strong proof that I am counted among those who have been predestined to eternal life and therefore can never be lost, however weak my faith may be.

Ursinus's Larger Catechism *(1562)*

Ursinus completed another book of instruction in 1562, the *Catechismus major* (Larger Catechism),[5] which appeared in Latin. This document was a textbook for the lessons in dogmatics that Ursinus taught to the students of the Collegium Sapientiae — the first Reformed textbook of dogmatics in Heidelberg. It must have been intended to replace the *Loci communes* (1521) and the *Examen ordinandorum* (1553), written by Melanchthon.

This detailed catechism consists of 323 questions and answers. In view of its purpose, it is not primarily pastoral and personal in emphasis, but rather dogmatic and impersonal in nature. It was entirely suited for the schooling of prospective preachers. This catechism also starts off with a question dealing with comfort, and the covenant plays an important role in the explanation followed by the central themes of the Christian faith: the law (in summary form); the gospel (Apostles' Creed); conversion and gratitude (living according to the Ten Commandments); prayer (the Lord's Prayer); and the institution of the ministry of the church, in which preaching and the sacraments are discussed in detail. The textbook ends with a chapter on discipline.

The threefold pattern of misery, deliverance, and gratitude is only implicitly present in the Larger Catechism, and so from a theological point of view it did not play as major a role in the development of the Heidelberg Catechism as did the Shorter Catechism. It also makes plain that Ursinus was a covenantal theologian. In line with his teacher, Melanchthon, he distinguished between the covenant of nature (or the covenant of creation) and the covenant of grace. He also frequently discussed predestination. It is noteworthy that the expressions "believers," "those who have been born again," and "those who have been predestined" are used interchangeably. As in the Shorter Catechism, the Decalogue is presented according to the Reformed

---

5. Another name for Ursinus's *Larger Catechism* was *Summa theologiae* (Summary of Theology).

format; in Lutheran catechisms, the first two commandments were combined and the tenth commandment was split up into two parts.

The completion of the Heidelberg Catechism
Motivation

We now come to the question of how, in 1563, the Heidelberg Catechism came to replace the instruction booklets discussed above. It is not surprising that the initiative for this change came directly from Elector Frederick III. After the Peace of Augsburg, the principle of *cuius regio, eius religio* (whose region, his religion) allowed a prince to determine the religion of his region. However, that this initiative led to the completion of a catechism that not only replaced the preceding booklets but continues to have great influence on the Reformed church and theology today was more than Frederick could ever have anticipated.

Frederick III was Reformed. We have already seen that he considered it to be his calling to educate his people in the Reformed religion. A new catechism was one means to this end. In his preface to the Catechism, Frederick III gave several reasons for introducing a new catechism. A uniform approach to religious instruction was lacking. There was also a great deal of

Title page of the first edition of the Heidelberg Catechism of 1563

Lutheran Tilemann Hesshus (1527–1588) was professor at Heidelberg

ignorance and, by implication, a great deal of false teaching. A simple instruction booklet that could be studied by anyone and in which the principles of the Reformed confession were clearly set out would address these problems.

Completion

Precisely how the Heidelberg Catechism was completed has not yet been fully determined. There is no record of its genesis in the library of the Vatican, where the precious Bibliotheca Palatina was transferred following the return of the Palatinate to Roman Catholicism. It is possible that the archival documents are somewhere in Heidelberg or its surrounding vicinity, but they are not located in the official archives of the church and the city.

Researchers have developed a number of theories for the completion of the Catechism. For a long time it was thought that Frederick III assigned the task of compiling a new textbook to the two theologians Zacharias Ursinus and Caspar Olevianus. H. Alting and, later, J. C. Koecher and J. I. Doedes were proponents of this theory. However, others now believe that Ursinus was the primary author of the Heidelberg Catechism. M. A. Gooszen, J. M. Reu, and W. Hollweg think along these lines, and I concur with them.

In view of the preface by Frederick III, it is perhaps best to imagine the course of events as follows. In 1562 the elector gave Ursinus the task of writing a new catechism. By then, Ursinus had already authored two catechisms, and he drew on those for this new assignment. For example, in the new Catechism the question about the church is virtually identical to the one in his Shorter Catechism. Ursinus proposed a document that was discussed by a committee composed of members of the theological faculty and the consistory of Heidelberg. That was followed in January of 1563 by a discussion among the superintendents and the most important ministers of the Palatinate church. Frederick III himself was also directly involved in this work. In the final phase of the discussions, Olevianus played an important role as superintendent.

Finally, the committee approved the manuscript unanimously on January 18, 1563. The Catechism was then printed by publisher Johann Mayer, a Heidelberg publisher. Its publication may be viewed as the apex of the Reformational work of the elector. He did not refer to it as "his" Catechism without justification.

A broad consensus?

There is more to be said about the completion of the Heidelberg Catechism. It is important to keep in mind, as we saw earlier, that in the Palatinate there were various ecclesiastical movements: consummate Lutherans, Lutheran followers of Melanchthon (Philippists), and Reformed believers. It is possible that by working with a committee composed of these various factions, Frederick sought to achieve as broad a consensus as possible. He hoped that the Catechism would gain the support of the non-Reformed groups, which was very important. With the publication of this Catechism, however, didn't Frederick risk the possibility of disturbing the Peace of Augsburg? Achieving as broad a consensus as possible, including Melanchthon's movement, would minimize this risk. Sadly, Frederick was not successful in this regard.

The publication of the Catechism was met with a storm of protest from Lutherans. Although attempts had been made to avoid opposition from Lutherans wherever possible, they treated the Catechism with the greatest animosity, publishing various polemical reactions against it. The Lutheran professor Tilemann Hesshus of Heidelberg wrote *Treue Warnung vor dem Heidelberger calvinischer Katechismus, sammt Widerlegung ettlicher Irrthümer derselber* (Legitimate Warning against the Calvinistic Heidelberg Catechism, together with a Refutation of Several Errors Contained in It). Matthias Flacius Illyricus also reacted negatively and wrote *Wiederlegung eines kleinen, deutschen, calvinischen Katechismus, so in diesem MDLXXII Jahr ausgegangen* (Refutation of a Short German Calvinistic Catechism Published in This Year 1572). The Catechism also received sharp response from Roman Catholics. For example, Engelbertus Kenniphovius wrote *Refutatio catechismi heidelberg*. Publications that defended the Catechism appeared as well. Ursinus himself wrote *Antwort auff etlicher Theologen Censur über die am Rand des Heidelb. Catechismi aus Heiliger Schrifft angezogene Zeugnusz, nebst Antwort und Gegenfrag auf sechs Fragen von des Herren Nachtmahl, 1564* (Reply to Various Critical Theologians concerning Scripture References in the Margin of the Heidelberg Catechism, together with Replies and Counter Questions regarding Six Questions about the Lord's Supper).

In 1564, a religious discussion of the Catechism at the monastery of Maulbronn in Württemberg ended in a heated exchange. In 1566, Frederick had to defend his book of instruction at the Diet of Augsburg. The emperor and most of the princes of the empire opposed him. However, contrary to everyone's expectation, he made a deep impression through his appearance. He defended his Catechism with the following words:

"As far as my catechism is concerned, I acknowledge and confess it. In its margins it is supported with arguments and proofs from Holy Scripture to such an extent that it has thwarted all attempts by theologians to refute it and with God's help will continue to thwart them…. Furthermore I comfort myself with the sure confidence that my Lord and Savior, Jesus Christ, has given me and all believers the sure promise that everything that I shall lose for His Name's sake, will be restored a hundredfold in the age to come."

At the end of the diet, August of Saxony said, "Fred, you are a better man than any of us." The Margrave of Baden added, "Why do you attack this man? He is godlier than any of us."

Frederick III Makes His Defense

Having defended a number of measures to introduce the Reformation in his territory before Emperor Maximilian II at the Imperial Diet of Augsburg (1566), the elector's discourse became quite personal:

"As far as religion is concerned, in the name of Your Majesty I have been earnestly charged and enjoined to abandon and change my religion, because it is believed to be in conflict with the Augsburg Confession and contaminated with Calvinism. In this regard I have already personally informed Your Imperial Majesty that in matters of conscience and religion I do not recognize more than One Lord, who is Lord of all lords and King of all kings. I continue to be of this view and opinion. Religion is not merely a matter of the flesh, as they say. On the contrary, it pertains to the soul and its salvation. In this regard I serve under the command of my Lord and Savior Christ, and He expects me to keep religion safe for Him in reverence. Therefore I cannot concede to Your Imperial Majesty that you would have authority over it. Only God who has created [religion] can command it.

"It is my desire to seek from Your Imperial Majesty nothing less than that you will not proceed to the execution of judicial prosecution. And since I have never read the books of Calvin, as I can testify before God and my Christian conscience, I cannot in the least be aware what is meant by Calvinism. On the contrary, I have signed and sealed a decree in Frankfurt and subsequently in Naumburg, thereby signing and sealing the Augsburg Confession, together with the most prominent secular electors and princes who adhere to the said confession. Of those a considerable number are present here today. I hope to be able to persevere in this, all the more because I know that it is founded on the Word of God, i.e., in the Holy Scriptures of the Old and New Testaments. No one has any basis of truth for accusing me of having acted contrary to the Bible, which I would be loath to do at any rate.

"As far as my catechism is concerned, I confess it. In its margins it is also so solidly grounded in Holy Scripture that it has proven to be irrefutable. Indeed, thus far you yourself have not succeeded in doing so and I hope that with God's help it will continue to be irrefutable for a much longer period to come.

"And it is the case, as I have specifically declared to Your Imperial Majesty and also to the Council of Electors in plenary session, as well as to numerous friends here present: If it turns out that someone, whether young or old, learned or uneducated, friend or foe, indeed, the very lowest kitchen or stable servant, can more successfully teach or inform me on the basis of God's Word about the biblical Scriptures of the Old and New Testaments, outside of which there is no salvation, then I shall be grateful to him, beside God, and shall thereby offer the required obedience to God and His Holy Word. If in this assembly there would be any gentlemen or friends of mine here present who would like to deny this, then I would gladly hear this from them; we can soon enough come up with a Bible here.

"However, if Your Imperial Majesty yourself should be prepared to take the trouble to take this upon yourself, then for the sake of Your Imperial Majesty I shall do my utmost to defend myself, which I consider to be my bounden duty. Given this, what I believe to be, Christian offer I very humbly hope that you will continue to be most gracious and will not initiate judicial proceedings, just as the late Emperor Ferdinand (of laudable memory), your deceased father, left me alone and did not burden my conscience—although His Majesty would have loved to have seen me participate in the abominable papal mass at the occasion of your royal coronation in Frankfurt.

"If, however, my most humble confidence should turn out to have been idle and despite this Christian and honest offer of mine one were to take action against me in earnest, or plan to do so, then I shall comfort myself with the sure promise given to me, and all believers, by my Lord and Savior Christ Jesus, that everything that I shall lose for the sake of His honor and Name, will be restored to me a hundredfold in the other world. With this I desire to commend myself to the grace of Your Imperial Majesty."

Introduction and further elaboration

As we have already noted, a new church order also appeared in Heidelberg in 1563. It included the Heidelberg Catechism between regulations pertaining to baptism and the Lord's Supper. Thus it formed a link—a path of instruction, as it were—between both sacraments. The child who has been baptized receives instruction in order to respond to baptism and subsequently to be admitted to the Lord's Supper. In this church order we also find regulations concerning the way in which instruction in the Catechism should proceed.

The first edition of the Catechism included 128—not yet 129—questions and answers, but they were not numbered. The margins indicated chapters of the Bible as references, but they did not include specific verses. In 1563, second and third editions appeared. The second edition changed the question concerning Christ's conception by the Holy Spirit and birth of the Virgin Mary and incorporated the question about the mass. The third edition added a condemnation of the mass as a response to the "anathema" of the Council of Trent regarding the Reformational doctrine of the Lord's Supper (Q. 80). In the church order of 1563, the Catechism was divided into fifty-two Lord's Days and nine lections. The tenth lection contained Bible verses for everyday life. It was the intention that every Sunday, a lection would be read in the church service. The text of this third edition was called the *textus receptus* (standard text). A Latin translation of this third edition was produced by Josua Lagus Pomeranus and Lambert Ludolf Pitheopoeus.

In the 1573 edition, the number of Bible references was expanded and the 129 questions and answers were numbered. In 1576, an abridged version of the Heidelberg Catechism appeared under the title *Kleine Heidelberger Katechismus* (Shorter Heidleberg Catechism) because the unabridged Heidelberg Catechism turned out to be too difficult for children.

The Heidelberg Catechism was translated into the Dutch language a number of times. The best-known Dutch translation is by Petrus Dathenus;

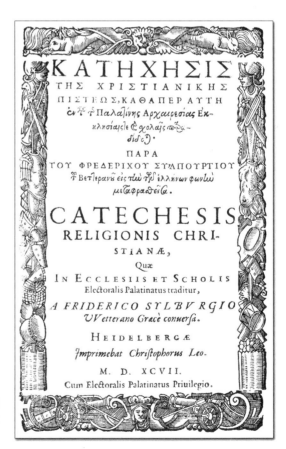

A Greek-Latin edition
of the Catechism

it appeared in 1566 together with his Psalter. This is the translation that is found in various versions of Dutch church service books today.

Summary

From an early date, the Palatinate was open to new ideas. Philip the Upright took great interest in the renewal of the arts and culture. Various institutes of education in Heidelberg provided the infrastructure for a complete renewal of the church and theology.

This breakthrough occurred when Elector Otto Henry assumed power in 1556. He was a follower of Luther and introduced the Lutheran religion, only one year after the Peace of Augsburg. The influence of Melanchthon ensured a moderate, peaceful climate. Otto Henry's successor, Frederick III, gradually adopted the Reformed persuasion. He personally implicated himself in religious issues of his time and ultimately arrived at a religious point of view that was close to Calvin's, and probably even closer to Bullinger's. On the one hand, the University of Heidelberg influenced these events, and on the other, developments within its walls reflected the events in the church and in society at large. From Frederick III's point of view, the Collegium Sapientiae also represented a powerful instrument for the dissemination of the Reformed faith. Here theologians such as Olevianus and Ursinus trained future preachers for the Palatinate.

In the period preceding Frederick III, various booklets were used for instruction in the faith. They were all influenced by Luther's catechism, although they offered their own nuances. *Eine Kurze Ordenliche Summa* of 1558, a Lutheran catechism, contained the threefold pattern of misery, deliverance, and gratitude that became the typical structure of Ursinus's Shorter Catechism (1562) and the Heidelberg Catechism (1563). Although the precise course of events leading to the appearance of the Heidelberg Catechism remains obscure, historical research of the last few years has led to the conclusion that Ursinus was its chief author. A draft prepared by him was approved by a team of collaborators from various factions, among whom Olevianus carried the most weight.

The Heidelberg Catechism is altogether Reformed, but at the same time it sought a consensus with the views of the followers of Philipp Melanchthon. Strict Lutherans, including Hesshus, vehemently opposed this Catechism. It also had strong defenders, including the Elector Frederick III himself. At the Diet of Augsburg of 1566, he succeeded in extinguishing the fire of hatred against the Catechism. He immediately introduced the Catechism in the Palatinate, and it gained a prominent place in the church order of 1563. The

Catechism was of such exceptional quality that within a short time it became known everywhere and was introduced in many Reformed churches in Germany and beyond. In the Netherlands, Petrus Dathenus played a prominent role. His 1566 translation of the Catechism was combined with the publication of his Psalter. The Heidelberg Catechism continues to have great influence in many churches in the Netherlands and elsewhere in the world.

CHAPTER 3

The People Behind the
Heidelberg Catechism
by Christa Boerke

Tradition held that Zacharias Ursinus and Caspar Olevianus were the authors of the Heidelberg Catechism, commissioned by Elector Frederick III of the Palatinate. This was the prevailing view among historians as late as the nineteenth century. The actual theological work would have been performed by Ursinus, while Olevianus would have been responsible for the final editing of the text. But how true is this supposition? Were only these two men involved, or was there a broader circle of contribution? There is no consensus today on the authorship of the Catechism, and it appears unlikely that there will ever be a conclusive answer. So far, no documents have been unearthed that reveal who did what in the development of the Heidelberg Catechism.

Yet there are several clues. The elector wrote a preface to the first edition of the Catechism, dated January 19, 1563, in which he recounts that the theological faculty, the church superintendents, and the principal members of the consistory made their contributions to the Catechism. The elector mentions

Frederick III

no names, not even those of Ursinus and Olevianus. This omission can be considered to be a wise and sympathetic gesture; a broad foundation would be much more readily accepted by the general population, and at the same time it would prevent Lutherans from possibly holding a few identifiable persons responsible for the introduction of this Reformed doctrine of faith. At the same time, the Elector indicates that more than one or two authors participated in the production of the Catechism.

Preface to the printed edition of the Heidelberg Catechism of January 1563

We, Frederick, by the grace of God, Count Palatine on the Rhine, Arch Reeve and Elector of the Holy Roman Empire, Duke of Bavaria, et cetera, offer all our superintendents, ministers, preachers, church and school office bearers of our Electorate, the county of the Palatinate on the Rhine, our favor, and we greet you. We communicate to you the following:

Keeping in mind the Word of God as well as our natural obligation and bounden duty, we have felt called and have finally decided to exercise the office entrusted to us by God and to accept our responsibility of governance. Not only in order to let our subjects live in rest and peace, to live modestly, uprightly, and virtuously, but also and particularly to point out to them ever more the true fear of the Almighty and to guide them to the right knowledge of His saving Word as the only foundation of all virtues and all obedience, we wish to encourage them from the bottom of our heart not to lack in zeal when it comes to their eternal and transitory well-being—and on our part we undertake to continue to assist them thereto.

From the very beginning, however, when we agreed to take on the government of this region, we have noticed the following: although our dear relatives, ancestors, counts palatine, electors, etc.—held in glorious and blessed memory—have taken various useful measures, and have made efforts to promote God's honor, to maintain discipline among our citizens, and to establish and exercise civil rule, yet they have not pursued this everywhere as much as necessary. Even to a far lesser extent have their efforts borne visible fruit. To us this provides justification not only for renewing all of these efforts, but also—as necessity demands—for making improvements, providing clarification, and offering support.

In this regard we have discovered no small shortcomings: everywhere—at the schools and in the churches of our electorate—our youth, in the bloom of their younger years, are very inadequately admonished and instructed in the Christian doctrine and to some extent not at all; to some degree it is taught very inconsistently, and not guided by any solid, reliable, and generally acceptable catechism. Everyone works according to his own plan and pleasure. Apart from other, various gross errors, this is the reason why our youth frequently grow up without the fear of the Lord and without knowledge of His Word, without receiving coherent instruction, or are burdened with cumbersome and unnecessary questions, sometimes even with a doctrine that is at variance with the Word.

Since both Christian and secular offices, government, and the economy cannot be otherwise maintained on an ongoing basis; similarly, in order that discipline and all other virtues on the part of our subjects might improve and flourish, and our young people from early on and before anything else might be pointed out the pure and unambiguous doctrine of the holy gospel and the true knowledge of God and would continually practice these, we have considered it to be absolutely necessary, as one of the priorities of our administration, to gain significant insight in these matters, to eliminate evil and inconsistency, and to implement the necessary improvements.

For this reason, on the advice of our entire theological faculty here, also in cooperation with all superintendents and the chief ministers of the church, we have had prepared and compiled in both German and Latin a concise booklet of instruction or catechism of our Christian religion extracted from the Word of God. This was done so that in the future not only will our young people be instructed in the Christian doctrine in a godly manner and admonished in unanimity, but also so that pastors and schoolteachers themselves will have a reliable model and a solid standard as to how to approach the instruction of our young people, and so that they will not change one thing or another on a daily basis or introduce a contrary doctrine.

We hereby admonish and command each and every one that—for the sake of God's honor, to the benefit of our subjects, and for your own benefit—you will gladly and earnestly accept this catechism or instruction hereby offered to you, and that you will impress this cat-echism, correctly interpreted, on our young people at school and in church, and further also from the pulpit on our people with diligence; that you will use it for instruction, will act and live in accordance with it—and that in the indubitable hope and in the indubitable confidence that, if our young people are thus instructed earnestly with respect to the Word of God and thus educated, the Almighty will grant and cause to experience improvement of life, i.e., both transitory and eternal well-being. As we have indicated above, in closing we wish to express the hope that the same will be true with respect to you.

Date: Heidelberg, Tuesday, the nineteenth day of the month of January, following the birth of Christ, our dear Lord and Savior, in the year one thousand, five hundred and sixty-three.

Frederick III instructed his theologians to compile a compendium that would support the unity of the church yet constitute a guide for instruction. Ursinus thereupon presented two documents, which he must have produced shortly after his arrival at Heidelberg: a Larger Catechism, which was a summary of theology for adults, and a Shorter Catechism, which was an instruction booklet for children. It is noteworthy that these two documents contained elements that subsequently turned up in precisely the same form in the final version of the Heidelberg Catechism; the three divisions of misery, deliverance, and gratitude are one example. The elector, however, desired a single document that would be suitable for both audiences and would be a doctrine of faith and a book of instruction.

It is likely that the Catechism was compiled from the two documents prepared by Ursinus and that the circle of Heidelberg theologians reviewed it and provided improvements and additions towards the end of 1562. From January 13 to 18, 1563, the entire committee of theologians, superintendents, and members of the consistory met to decide on the final text. The editing process was therefore not solely the responsibility of Olevianus.

That the Heidelberg Catechism was based on two documents by Ursinus leads to the conclusion that he was the original and principal author, although he is nowhere referred to as such. The more recent view that the Heidelberg Catechism was primarily the work of this particular court theologian of Frederick III is consistent with this conclusion. One could even question significant collaboration on the part of Olevianus, although he must have been involved, since he was both superintendent and member of the Heidelberg Consistory.

The text demonstrates that Ursinus made use of existing catechetical material produced by Luther, Melanchthon, Calvin, Bullinger, Jud, and Micron. Also in this sense the Catechism has more than one author. It should not be overlooked that the elector himself influenced the text. For example, question 80, which concerns the difference between the Lord's Supper and the papal mass, reflects one of Frederick's own preoccupations, and some of the Scripture references in the margin come from his pen.

Ursinus was thus surrounded by a circle of collaborators who supported him, perhaps more critically than creatively. Who were these professors, superintendents, and church ministers? As far as the theological faculty is concerned, there were three professors when the Catechism appeared: Zacharias Ursinus, Petrus Boquinus, and Immanuel Tremellius. Of the college of superintendents, we know of Johannes Anastasius Veluanus, Johannes Willing, Johannes Sylvanus, Johannes Eisenmenger, and Caspar Olevianus. The office of superintendent was introduced in 1556 by the previous elector, Otto Henry. Since that time there were nine superintendents whose respon-

Zacharias Ursinus

sibility it was to visit the congregations in their districts twice each year, to ordain ministers to their office, and, whenever necessary, to conduct church services.

The Heidelberg church council or consistory comprised both laymen and theologians charged with the oversight of general ecclesiastical life. Around 1563 this council consisted of the laymen Wenceslaus Zuleger (chairman), Stephan Zirler (secretary), and Thomas Erastus, and the theologians Michael Diller, Petrus Boquinus, and Caspar Olevianus. The council met on a regular basis and followed the completion of the Catechism with interest.

These men witnessed the circumstances under which the Catechism was formulated and provided their views on the document. Although their role can no longer be traced with precision, it is worth the effort to get to know them better and thus to gain a better understanding of the circle within which the Catechism emerged. Zacharias Ursinus is considered first, followed by Caspar Olevianus. In this sense we follow the line of tradition after all. Subsequently, we focus on the broader circle of those who were involved, as described by the elector.

Two Crown Witnesses
Zacharias Ursinus

Ursinus[1] resided in Heidelberg as of 1561. He was born at Breslau (modern-day Wrocław) in 1534 as the son of a deacon. On April 30, 1550, he began his studies at the University of Wittenberg, where Philip Melanchthon was his sponsor. Melanchthon made arrangements for the young Ursinus's study program and living expenses to be paid by one of his friends, Crato von Crafftheim, a physician and prominent patrician. The income of Ursinus's father was insufficient to pay for his son's education. Melanchthon also monitored the progress of Ursinus's studies and in 1577 took him along to a religious debate in Worms. From there, Ursinus made a longer study tour through Heidelberg, Strasbourg, and Basel to Geneva. On this journey he personally met, among others, Theodore Beza, Heinrich Bullinger, Peter Martyr Vermigli, and John Calvin, and he was influenced by the Reformed heritage. From Geneva he went on to Paris, where he studied Hebrew for a year.

Having returned to Wittenberg, he received a request in 1558 to become an instructor in Breslau at the Elisabeth School, which he had attended as a child. Once there, he initially kept quiet about his Reformed convictions. A year later, however, he came forward with a number of theses concerning

---

1. The Latin word *ursus* means "bear."

the Lord's Supper that demonstrated his change from a moderate Lutheran to a clear follower of Calvin. In his view of the Lord's Supper he supported Melanchthon, who had strongly moved in the direction of Calvin—a position not looked upon favorably by everyone. Since Ursinus wished to avoid conflict in Breslau, he offered the city council his resignation. The offer was accepted, albeit reluctantly. At his farewell event on April 24, 1560, he received from the council a very positive evaluation and a request to remain available to the city, in case the council should ever need to consult with him. With the financial support of Crato von Crafftheim, Ursinus traveled to Zurich, where he wished to consult with theologian Peter Martyr Vermigli on the doctrine of the Lord's Supper. Secretly he hoped for a new position somewhere in Switzerland.

In the meantime, tensions had emerged in the Palatinate because Elector Frederick III sought to introduce the Reformed doctrine. Friction was also beginning to arise between Lutheran and Reformed theologians. At this time, Frederick III established a program of studies for ministers (*Collegium Sapientiae*) in Heidelberg and invited Vermigli to head it up. Vermigli, however, was unable to leave Zurich and referred the elector to Zacharias Ursinus. The latter accepted the offer and arrived in Heidelberg in 1561. Shortly after his arrival he succeeded Caspar Olevianus at the local university; Olevianus had occupied a chair in dogmatics for only a few months, but at his request he had been appointed minister of the local St. Peter's Church. On August 28, 1562, Ursinus was promoted to doctor of theology, thus being in a position to take up a professorship three days later. In the same manner the other chairs of theology at the University of Heidelberg were filled with theologians of the

The city of Breslau (Hartmann Schedel, *Liber Chronicarum*, 1493)

Calvinist persuasion. These included Ursinus's colleagues Petrus Boquinus and Immanuel Tremellius.

Following the death of Frederick in 1576, his son, Louis VI, attained the electoral throne. He sought to restore the Lutheran religion to its full glory, and therefore Ursinus and the other Reformed professors were removed from their positions. In 1578, Ursinus agreed to the request of Count Palatine Johann Casimir to join his recently established theological school, the Collegium Casimirianum in Neustadt (modern-day Neustadt an der Weinstrasse). On May 26 of that year, he was installed and gave a lecture on the interpretation of Isaiah. Ursinus spent the last few years of his life in Neustadt. He died on March 6, 1584, and was interred in the local church two days later. On his memorial plaque his colleagues described him as "an upright theologian, a sharp opponent, in speech and in writing, of heresies concerning the Person and Supper of Christ, a bright philosopher, a sagacious human being and a strict educator of young people."

Ursinus's forty works were republished shortly after his death. There appeared a Neustadt edition[2] in two volumes, in 1584 and 1589, and a Heidelberg edition under the direction of his successor at the university, Quirinus Reuter. In his lectures on dogmatics, Ursinus covered topics such as the Scriptures, God, creation, providence, sin, free will, and the law. According to Ursinus, dogmatics represented an introduction to Holy Scripture. It was the summary of truth and must enable the student to defend his faith. His *Summa theologiae* (also called Larger Catechism) includes chapters on the Ten Commandments, the Apostles' Creed, the Lord's Prayer, ecclesiastical office, the sacraments, and ecclesiastical discipline. In his analysis we encounter elements of Bullinger's theology of the covenant, Calvin's doctrine of the sacraments, and Zwingli's doctrine of predestination. Ursinus's *magnum opus* is without doubt his *Exposition of the Catechism*, which was published in 1598 by David Pareus and which became known in the Netherlands as *Schat-boeck* (Treasure Book).[3]

Caspar Olevianus
Born the son of a master baker and member of city council in Trier on August 10, 1536, Caspar Olevianus (Olewig) was sent to Paris at the age of

---

2. Neustädter Ausgabe

3. *Het Schat-boeck der Christelycke Leere ofte Uytlegginghe over den Catechismus* (The Treasure Book of Christian Doctrine or Exposition of the Catechism). It is published in English as *The Commentary of Dr. Zacharias Ursinus on the Heidelberg Catechism*, trans. George W. Willard (Columbus: Scott & Bascom, 1852).

thirteen to further his education. Subsequently, he studied law in Orléans and Bourges, acquiring his doctorate in 1557. A year earlier, in a situation of great distress, he had made a vow to devote himself to the study of theology and the dissemination of the gospel if he stayed alive. What had happened? During a walk by the Loire River, in the company of his friend Hermann Ludwig, eldest son of the future Elector Frederick III, they met a group of students belonging to the German nobility. In a somewhat reckless mood and tipsy condition, this group went up the river in a boat, taking the young prince with them. From the shore, Olevianus noticed that the boat had capsized as a consequence of excessive swaying. He jumped into the water to make a rescue effort, but he ran into problems himself as he struggled to avoid sinking in the muddy bottom. An attendant, who thought he was rescuing the prince, brought him back to safety. All of the passengers of the little boat drowned. From that day on, Olevianus dedicated himself to the study of Holy Scripture.

Shortly after his promotion to doctor of law, he traveled to Geneva via Strasbourg in March 1558 to study theology with Calvin. Presumably he had already come into contact with Huguenots during his studies in Bourges. He also studied with Heinrich Bullinger in Zurich to learn to preach; there he met Peter Martyr. In Lausanne, he met Theodore Beza, and then traveled back to Geneva.

Partly at the insistence of William Farel, he did not enter the ministry at Metz but returned to Trier, where, in 1559, he offered his services to the city council, first as instructor of Latin and philosophy, and subsequently as a preacher. Through his powerful action and stirring speech, the small Protestant church grew by leaps and bounds, attracting a third of the population of Trier. In the eyes of the city council and the guilds, this went too far. The archbishop and the electors were galvanized into action and forbade him to preach anymore in the city. Trier was not considered to be an imperial or free city, and in their view, therefore, it was not subject to the Peace of Augsburg. A number of Protestants were imprisoned and would not be freed unless they promised to return to the Roman Catholic faith or else leave the city. Olevianus spent about ten weeks in jail. Ultimately, the Reformation in Trier failed.

In 1560, Elector Frederick III invited Olevianus to come to Heidelberg to direct the *Collegium Sapientiae*. In the summer of 1561, he became professor of dogmatics at the university, for but a short time. Within a year he became a preacher and worked as theologian within the Heidelberg consistory. His involvement in the Heidelberg Catechism is beyond question, but the precise nature of his role today is less clear than was formerly supposed.

Caspar Olevianus

For example, there is some evidence that he was not entirely satisfied with the text of the Catechism. In a cover letter to Calvin on April 3, 1563, he referred to numerous Germanisms in the text. He also would have preferred that Calvin review the text prior to publication. At the first synod in the fall of 1570, he expressed the view that the Catechism was incorrect as far as Christ's conception was concerned (question 36), and therefore ministers could not accept the Catechism without qualification as being in accord with the Scriptures. One would not expect such statements to come from an editor-in-chief. It is more likely that Olevianus provided input as a member of the editorial committee.

Olevianus was not only deeply involved in the transition to the Reformed confession in the Palatinate, he was also interested in church order. He participated in the drafting of the Reformed church order of the Palatinate, which was published in November 1563. To many, its presbyterial-synodical elements were totally new: the state-wide *consistorium* (consistory) of the prince was replaced by a synod, and locally a *presbyterium* (presbytery) maintained discipline instead of the government.

Olevianus accompanied the elector as his advisor at religious discussions in Maulbronn (1564), Oppenheim, (1565), and Amberg (1566). After the death of Frederick III and the installation of his son Louis VI (1576–1583), Olevianus was forced to leave Heidelberg. In 1577, Count Louis of Sayn-Wittgenstein in Berleburg appointed him at his court as chaplain and teacher. Olevianus promptly introduced the Catechism. During the years 1578–1580, he wrote commentaries on the epistles to the Galatians, Romans, Philippians, and Colossians, in each case with a preface by Beza. He also influenced the progress of the Reformation in the entire county.

In 1584, Johann VI of Nassau-Dillenburg brought Olevianus to his territory to establish an academy in Herborn, which opened its doors that same year. Olevianus became its first headmaster. The academy consisted of a complete Institute of Higher Education and a Gymnasium, or preparatory school. As a dogmatician Olevianus stressed the doctrine of the covenant, as it had developed starting with Zwingli. In his *magnum opus*, *De substantia foederis gratuiti inter Deum et electos* (The Substance of the Covenant of Grace between God and the Elect, 1585), he placed the entire history of God's involvement with humanity within the framework of the covenant. God established a covenant of nature with Adam, which was broken by man through sin. Thereupon God established a new covenant with him, a covenant of grace, which He

Olevianus was a preacher at the Church of the Holy Spirit
in Heidelberg (pen drawing from the eighteenth century)

The city church at Herborn where Olevianus is buried

sealed with the death of His Son. The core of this covenant of grace is man's election, which is an important ground for certainty of salvation.

A last high point in Olevianus's life was the General Synod of Herborn (1586), at which the Reformed churches of Nassau-Dillenburg, Wittgenstein, Solms-Braunfels, and Wied-Runkel were represented. Olevianus had made every preparation to provide these churches with a church order of their own. In coming to an agreement, the twenty-six theologians present overcame for the first time the territorial nature of the Reformed church in Germany. At the conclusion of lengthy discussions, they accepted a church order that sought a balance between a presbyterial and a consistorial system. All aspects of church organization were discussed, in addition to the way in which baptism was administered and the Lord's Supper was celebrated. Those who read the regulations will notice the great similarity with those that were adopted at the Synod of Middelburg in 1581. Olevianus had thoroughly studied this synod's proceedings ahead of time.

Olevianus passed away on March 15, 1587, due to complications resulting from an accident in December 1586. He had fallen several times on a slippery road, contracting internal injuries. He was not quite fifty-one years old. His last will and testament was a true testimony to his faith; he especially called on churches to support each other, to continue the work of schools and printing books, and to conduct regular synods and church visitations. He was interred in the church at Herborn.

The damaged epitaph
of Olevianus

In addition to his book on the covenant, his guide to the Catechism was especially popular: *Fester Grund, das ist, Die Artikel des alten, wahren, ungezweifelten christl. Glaubens (A Firm Foundation: An Aid to Interpreting the Heidelberg Catechism)*,[4] published in Heidelberg in 1567. In addition, he left various writings about the Lord's Supper, mostly in the form of sermons, and an explanation of the Apostles' Creed.

The Theological Faculty
Petrus Boquinus

Petrus Boquinus (or Pierre Bouquin) came to Heidelberg several years ahead of Olevianus and Ursinus, at the request of the former Elector Otto Henry. In 1558, a year after his arrival, he became professor of theology. He steadily developed into a Calvinist, and he regularly called on Calvin for advice. In 1560, he was already such an important representative of the Reformed heri-

4. Trans. Lyle D. Bierma (Grand Rapids, Baker, 1995).

tage that Frederick III appointed him dean of the theological faculty and member of the Heidelberg consistory.

Boquinus was born in western France some time between 1510 and 1515. He studied theology at Bourges, where several instructors sympathized with the Reformation, and he obtained a doctorate in 1539. Shortly thereafter he entered the Carmelite Monastery of Bourges, where he was elected prior. Because of his Protestant persuasion, acquired during his studies and stimulated by personal study of the Scriptures, he had to leave the monastery and his native land in 1541. He traveled through Basel and Leipzig and eventually arrived in Wittenberg.

When Martin Bucer asked Melanchthon if he knew of a theologian who could carry on the exegetical work of Calvin in Strasbourg, Melanchthon referred him to Boquinus, who in September 1542 commenced lecturing on the Epistle to the Galatians. However, at the end of 1542, Boquinus returned to Bourges for unknown reasons; there, he taught Hebrew and gave lectures on the Old Testament. By dedicating his writings to Queen Marguerite of Navarre and her daughter, Jeanne d'Albret, he gained favor at the court,

Petrus Boquinus

which led to his appointment as a preacher at the cathedral. Since his theological position had not yet crystallized, Boquinus met with some distrust on the part of Reformers at this time. He probably had not yet made up his mind on all points of the Reformed faith. As a result of his evangelical style of preaching, he lost his office and was summoned to Paris to defend himself before the archbishop. In 1555 he fled to Strasbourg, where he became minister of a church established by French refugees. However, because of his past and because he was suspected of Lutheranism, the congregation protested so vehemently that he was soon replaced.

Once in Heidelberg, he participated in theological debates, including some on the Lord's Supper. He also published a number of writings on the Supper. In 1561 he set out with court chaplain Michael Diller to participate in the Colloquy of Poissy. However, they did not arrive there until after the discussions had ended.

Like the other professors, Boquinus lost his office after the death of Frederick III in 1576. After working in Heidelberg for twenty years, he was forced to leave. Two years later he became a professor and minister in Lausanne, where he carried out his duties until his sudden death in 1582.

In several writings, Boquinus crossed swords with Lutherans concerning the Lord's Supper. He also wrote polemical pamphlets against Roman Catholicism, and he translated Calvin's catechism into Greek.

Immanuel Tremellius

Beside Ursinus and Boquinus, Immanuel Tremellius was the third member of the theological faculty at Heidelberg. He was of Jewish descent, born in Ferrara, Italy, in 1510. At an early age he was already quite familiar with the Hebrew language. Having come into contact with Christians as early as 1530, he was baptized ten years later in the home of Cardinal Reginald Pole, who felt an affinity with the new evangelical movement.

In the summer of 1541, Tremellius became an instructor at a new monastic school in Lucca, where he taught Hebrew. In 1542, when the Inquisition was established by Pope Paul III, he fled Italy and became an instructor at the academy in Strasbourg, where Peter Martyr Vermigli also worked and Johann Sturm was in charge. There he married a widow from Metz.

Following the defeat of the Protestants in the Schmalkaldic War, he left Strasbourg and tried to establish himself in Switzerland. Despite personal recommendations from Calvin and Farel, this proved not to be a simple matter; for a long time he and his family led a nomadic life. Archbishop Cranmer invited him to England, where he participated in the completion of the *Book*

Title page of a New Testament published by Tremellius

of Common Prayer. He became a professor of Hebrew at the University of Cambridge in 1549, but when Bloody Mary came to power in 1553, he fled once again to Strasbourg with his family. He was not able to find work there, Bern, or in Lausanne. When he stayed with Calvin in Geneva, Duke Wolfgang of the Palatinate-Zweibrücken invited him to serve as a teacher for his three children, ages four to eight. This work did not particularly suit him, and his relationship with the duke was not without friction. Several times, the duke seemed to stand in the way of new opportunities for Tremellius. Tremellius failed to obtain a professorship in Old Testament studies because the duke was not prepared to release him. The duke's increasingly Lutheran orientation ultimately led to the departure of his court teacher on March 7, 1561. For a brief time, Tremellius resided among the Protestants of Metz, where he took an interest in their freedom of religion and in greater unity between French and German believers.

This time Tremellius did not have to wait long for a new position. Elector Frederick III appointed him to the University of Heidelberg as professor of Old Testament studies. He was offered the position on March 4, 1561; he started working on July 9, 1561, and in the meantime he was promoted to doctor of theology. In Heidelberg, his literary output increased markedly. He directed the publication of lectures given by Bucer in England, and he published a commentary on Hosea as well as a Chaldean and Syrian grammar. Subsequently, he devoted himself to his most important work, the translation of the Old Testament into Latin in collaboration with his future son-in-law, Franciscus Junius. This work was published in five volumes over the period 1575–1579. In addition to his work as professor and author, he also conducted diplomatic missions for the elector.

Tremellius was dismissed as professor after the death of Frederick III. At sixty-seven years of age, he again had to find a new home country. Once again he became a professor, this time in the Hebrew language at the newly opened academy in Sedan. There he worked until his death on October 9, 1580.

Tremellius was one of the greatest experts of his time in Near Eastern languages and was particularly renowned as a translator. He even translated Reformational writings into Hebrew, including Calvin's catechism.

Superintendents

Johannes Anastasius Veluanus

A Netherlander known as Johannes Anastasius Veluanus (born Jan Gerritsz. Versteghe) was added to the circle involved in the Heidelberg Catechism. He was born in Stroe, in the municipality of Garderen, in 1520, where he worked as a Roman Catholic priest from 1544 to 1550. He prepared his sermons along thoroughly Reformational lines. In his writings, he took the side of Luther and expressed dissatisfaction about the deplorable circumstances in which Protestants found themselves following the Schmalkaldic War. Because forbidden books and notes for an antipapal document were found in his presbytery, he was imprisoned by the Inquisition on January 1, 1550, and taken to Arnhem. During the interrogation, he was placed under so much pressure that he recanted his position three weeks later. He suffered deep remorse over this event for the remainder of his life. He was imprisoned in Hattem in a ramshackle castle without windows, being fed only bread and water and treated as a penitent. After two years, he was provided with writing material, a Bible, and the writings of a number of church fathers so that he might prepare a defense of the pope that was as long as the work in which he had formerly criticized the pope. This he refused to do.

Through the intervention of Governess Maria, Versteghe was set free in 1553, on the condition that he would present himself at Louvain within a fortnight to study Roman Catholic theology as a form of punishment. On his way to Louvain, Veluanus opened the letters that the inquisitor had sent with him. Their content made him decide to flee to Strasbourg, where he wrote the book *Der leken wechwyser* (The Laymen's Guide), which appeared in April 1554 and for which he became famous. It covered the main points of the Christian faith and criticized Roman Catholic doctrine in important areas: the mass, penance, veneration of images, purgatory, good works, and so on. He also ridiculed the great ignorance of priests. Out of remorse for his earlier recantation, Versteghe called himself Anastasius Veluanus, which means "the resurrected Veluwenaar."[5] Since there are similarities between The Laymen's Guide and the Heidelberg Catechism, Veluanus's participation in the compilation of the Catechism is highly probable. In 1554, Veluanus also became minister in Steeg near Bacharach on the Rhine.

Veluanus's *Vom Nachtmal Christi* (On Christ's Supper) was published in Zurich in 1557 by Froschauer under the pseudonym of Adamus Christianus because in it Veluanus combated the Lutheran doctrine of the Lord's Supper. The elector at that time, Otto Henry, was Lutheran, and Veluanus was in danger of being dismissed and banned. In 1561, he published *Bekantenisz von dem waren Leib Christi* (Confession of the True Body of Christ) in his own name because by then the Reformed Frederick III had become elector and Veluanus was able openly to refute sacrifice in the mass.

Veluanus was originally attracted to Erasmus, but he sided later with Luther and subsequently with Zwingli and Calvin, which clearly came through in his view of the Lord's Supper. In line with Zwingli, he expected a great deal from collaboration between the government and the people in reforming the church. It is noteworthy that he referred to the doctrine of predestination as highly pernicious and placed much emphasis on rebirth and new life. He ascribed to man a modest free will that could foster salvation to some extent. His advice to ministers was to study the Scriptures a great deal and to read Melanchthon's *Loci communes* and Calvin's *Institutes*. Except for Roman Catholics, Veluanus was quite considerate toward his opponents. He held that heretics should not be killed but only fined or excommunicated.

In 1561, Veluanus became a member of the college of superintendents in the Palatinate. He died in Bacharach in 1570.

Johannes Willing
It is not known how Johannes Willing ended up in the Palatinate. Perhaps Bullinger had a hand in this choice and assisted Willing when he was in distress.

Willing was born in Ravensburg in 1525, and his parents decided that he

---

5. A Veluwenaar is an inhabitant of the Veluwe region in the Netherlands.

should enter the priesthood. He was consecrated in 1545, but one year later he wanted to become a Reformed minister. On October 10, 1546, the town clerk of Ravensburg recommended him to Bullinger in Zurich, who took him into his home and arranged for the city council to grant him a student bursary. In 1548 he continued his education in Wittenberg before returning to Ravensburg, where he turned down an appointment as minister because he did not want to submit to the Augsburg Interim. He worked as a minister in Pfaffenhofen from 1549 to 1552, and then he was called again to Ravensburg. He did not have an easy time there; he was suspected of Zwinglianism, although he continued to insist that he subscribed to the Augsburg Confession.

In October 1554, he was dismissed because of his Zwinglian doctrine of the Lord's Supper. He visited his friend Bullinger and sent a letter to Calvin from Zurich. An aristocrat from Ulm invited him to the village of Reutti on the Danube. Ulm, which controlled this village, had already implemented the Reformation there. Willing started out in Reutti by producing a new prayer book. At the beginning of 1558, his position was threatened because the superintendent of Ulm, Ludwig Rabus, announced that he would eliminate all non-Lutheran elements. Willing was investigated by the Ulm town council concerning his views on the Lord's Supper. He had to submit to an examination, which he did with positive results. On the basis of this test, the council of Ulm officially called him as minister on May 19, 1559. This fact was remarkable since nearly all other theologians with Reformed sympathies in the same district lost their positions.

Shortly after his installation, however, Willing was attacked by Lutheran theologians. Although he reendorsed the Wittenberg Concord, new objections were raised about him around Christmas 1560 because of two sermons on the Lord's Supper that were thought to be Zwinglian. From that time on, material against him was amassed for purposes of raising the matter at the July 8, 1561, meeting of ministers. Willing was asked to reject Zwingli openly, which he refused to do. The following August 4, he was dismissed by the council of Ulm.

Soon thereafter Willing entered the service of the elector. Near the end of November 1561, he was taken on probation as court chaplain in Heidelberg. He received his official appointment as early as December 10. In his sermons, he defended the Reformed view of the Lord's Supper. In 1565, he was involved, along with Olevianus, in the introduction of the Reformation in Oppenheim. A year later he accompanied the elector to the Diet of Augsburg and formed part of the elector's circle of secretaries and clerks. In

Augsburg he preached several sermons that he also published and for which both he and the elector were heavily attacked.

Towards the end of 1566, the elector went to Amberg to introduce his Reformed view, taking Willing along as his adviser and minister, in addition to Olevianus. The population objected. Upon their return to Heidelberg, the elector rewarded Willing for his good services and appointed him to the consistory.

When an attempt was made in 1569 to introduce discipline similar to that practiced in Geneva and Willing joined the opposition, Frederick III lost confidence in this court chaplain. Willing relinquished his position and became a minister in Bretten. There, too, he lost his position after objecting to the introduction of the Genevan church order and implicating himself in developments concerning the theologians Sylvanus and Neuser, who were accused of Arianism. In 1571, he was again appointed court chaplain, this time at the court of Johann Casimir in Kaiserslautern. Since a conflict loomed with the consistory concerning ecclesiastical discipline, Johann Casimir made efforts to transfer Willing as preacher to Speyer. He succeeded in doing so in April 1572, although the council of Speyer actually preferred a Lutheran. Little more is known about Willing during this period, except that he reformed the liturgy according to Reformational lines. Willing died on July 10, 1572, leaving a widow and young children.

From a theological point of view, Willing displayed a close kinship with Bullinger, whom he regularly asked for advice. As far as ecclesiastical discipline was concerned, he sympathized with the ideas of Thomas Erastus, who closely followed Zwingli. Willing's publications consisted exclusively of sermons.

Johannes Sylvanus

Johannes Sylvanus is proof that someone involved in the completion of the Heidelberg Catechism could end up in a far different situation. He was a Reformed minister in the Palatinate but was eventually beheaded for not supporting the Reformational views concerning the Trinity. It is a sad story of someone who was counted among those known as the antitrinitarians.

Sylvanus probably came from South Tyrol, but we know nothing about his youth. In 1555, he was a preacher in the service of the bishop at the Cathedral of Würzburg. By then he had read sermons by Luther and the works of Melanchthon, which convinced him of the correctness of Reformational teachings. He remained in his post for a long time and did not flee until 1559, when the situation became hopeless. In Tübingen he switched to Lutheranism; in 1560, he became a minister in Calw. Closer study of Reformational writings drove him to the Zwinglian doctrine of the Lord's Supper.

Sylvanus appears to have had early contact with Elector Frederick III, whose service he entered in 1563. He became a minister and superintendent in Kaiserslautern. He got himself into difficulties there in 1565–1566, and the town council complained to the elector. As his father's representative, Prince Johann Casimir took this theologian into his protection against these complaints.

In November 1566, Sylvanus went to Heidelberg to join Olevianus and others in journeying to the Netherlands. Upon his return he requested a new position; in January 1567, the consistory appointed him as minister and superintendent in Ladenburg. He participated in the Heidelberg Bible translation and traveled to Zurich. Like his colleague Willing, Sylvanus objected to the introduction of the Genevan model of ecclesiastical discipline in the Palatinate. At this time he must have already begun to doubt the doctrine of the Trinity. He kept in touch with other antitrinitarians in the Palatinate, including Adam Neuser, minister at the St. Peter's Church in Heidelberg. Both men gave the impression of not having a strong character. Sylvanus leaned strongly

Beheading of Superintendent
Johannes Sylvanus on
December 23, 1572, in the
market square of Heidelberg

on Neuser, who wrote an antitrinitarian confession of faith in 1570. They supposed that the doctrine of the Trinity was only invented by the church fathers and that it could not be found directly in Scripture; they sought to return to the "ancient faith in the only God and the Messiah Jesus."

Neuser and Sylvanus were also in touch with antitrinitarians in Transylvania, a group led by Giorgio Blandrata, an Italian. In a letter to Blandrata and the Turkish Sultan, Sylvanus wrote that he hoped soon to be able to come to Transylvania to be delivered from idolatry. This letter fell into the hands of Olevianus and was subsequently passed from the emperor to the elector, who accused the two men of Arianism and had them imprisoned. Neuser managed to escape, and suspicion was focused entirely on Sylvanus. When Neuser's confession of faith was found in his possession, he sought to avoid the impending disaster through recantation. Olevianus and Ursinus insisted on the death penalty for Sylvanus; the government advised leniency. The elector initially hesitated, but when Wittenberg and Geneva turned out to support the elector, Sylvanus was beheaded in the marketplace of Heidelberg on December 23, 1572. The elector looked after his widow and twelve-year-old son. Neuser fled through Transylvania to Turkey, where he converted to Islam.

Johannes Eisenmenger

Little is known about the fourth superintendent. Johannes Eisenmenger, originally called Isenmann, was born in 1495 in Schwäbisch Hall. In 1513, he registered at the University of Heidelberg as Johannes Ysenmenger, befriended Johannes Brenz, and like him became a minister in Hall in 1523. From then on he was the friend and closest collaborator of his future son-in-law Brenz. Both of them, having been chased from Hall as a result of the Augsburg Interim, found a new place of work in Württemburg.

Eisenmenger subsequently became superintendent in Urach and, in 1572, in Tübingen. He eventually became a prelate in the monastery of Anhaufen. He passed away in 1574, four years after the far better known Reformer Brenz.

The Consistory

Boquinus and Olevianus were both members of the Heidelberg consistory. Besides them there were two other theologians: Zirler and Diller. About the latter two relatively little is known. Of the two lay members of the consistory known to us, Erastus and Zuleger, the former became the better known, especially since an ecclesiastical system was named after him: Erastianism.

Stephan Zirler

Of Zirler we know only that he served as private secretary to the previous elector, Otto Henry, and retained this role under Frederick III. Married to a cousin of Melanchthon, he was also a follower of that Reformer. In 1556, he was referred to as a Zwinglian, and in 1563, as a Calvinist. The secretary of the consistory was reportedly a peace-loving man who enjoyed corresponding with Bullinger.

Michael Diller

Of the initial period of Michael Diller's life we do not know much. He was probably born in the vicinity of Speyer. Beginning in the summer of 1523, he studied in Wittenberg. It is not known when he became a monk and the prior of the Augustinian monastery in Speyer. Diller preached in the monastery and the city in an evangelical manner and openly supported Luther's doctrine of justification. At the end of 1538, he was appointed by the city council as its first evangelical minister and was also protected from the bishop. He enjoyed great confidence on the part of the citizenry. Like his colleague, Anton Eberhard, he had so many citizens in his audience that the church turned out to be too small and the town council had to take action. Simultaneous services were then held at two different places. The bishop passively permitted this practice because the council protected both ministers.

Emperor Charles came to Speyer on two occasions, in 1541 and in 1544 during the imperial diet from January to June. Both times, Diller left the city, to return as soon as the emperor departed again. The emperor was disturbed about the new doctrine that Diller advanced in his sermons and instructed the

The city of Speyer (Sebastian Münster, *Cosmographiae Universalis*, 1550)

city council to put a stop to this teaching. Diller defended himself in a document that was sent by the council to the emperor. Following the departure of the emperor, he could carry on with his work without interference. He also gradually introduced changes in the celebration of the Lord's Supper.

The success of the emperor in the Schmalkaldic War and the announcement of the Interim of Augsburg in 1548, however, made it impossible for Diller to continue his work. He left Speyer just before the arrival of the emperor, who commanded the council never to admit Diller into the city again. For the time being, this meant the end of evangelical preaching in Speyer. In 1555, when the Peace of Augsburg was established, the council decided in favor of the Lutheran faith. By 1553, however, Diller was court chaplain in the service of Count Palatine Otto Henry in Neuburg on the Danube. At Henry's command, he undertook, along with Johannes Brenz, a church visitation in the principality of Neuburg, and participated in 1544 in the production of a new church order for the Palatinate-Neuburg.

Following the death of Frederick II, the Palatine electoral dignity was transferred to Otto Henry; Diller joined the new elector in going to Heidelberg. At the elector's behest he collaborated that year with Johannes Marbach and the Heidelberg professor Heinrich Stoll on a church order for the Palatinate. He accompanied the elector in church visitations and established himself as an influential member of the consistory. Frederick III, who succeeded Otto Henry in 1559, confided in Diller and involved him in the reorganization of education in Heidelberg.

Together with Boquinus, Diller was sent by the elector as a delegate to the Colloquy of Poissy in 1561, where they arrived too late to attend. However, in Maulbronn he fully participated in the discussions. From then on he had little more public involvement.

Diller was originally a Lutheran who took a soft and conciliatory attitude in theological controversies; he tended to interpret the Augsburg Confession fairly broadly. Partly for this reason, Philip of Hesse once remarked that he found the elector rather fierce in his actions, but that his court chaplain was quite reasonable. Gradually Calvinism gained the upper hand in Diller's convictions. He devoted much of his effort to transforming the Palatine church into a Reformed church. Diller passed away in Heidelberg in 1570.

Wenceslaus Zuleger

The chairman of the Heidelberg consistory was born in Joachimsthal in 1530 and belonged to a simple, Lutheran, middle-class family. Following the early death of his father, he made his living as a clerk, first for the city of Worms and, as of 1552, in the service of the army of Charles V. In this latter function he laid the foundation for his subsequent, considerable wealth. Zuleger completed his formal education by going to France as a tutor of young German noblemen and subsequently studying law and theology at French universities and in Geneva. Having completed his studies in law, he entered the service of Count Palatine Wolfgang von Zweibrücken in Neuburg as adviser, and he subsequently served Elector Frederick III in 1559.

Despite being not quite thirty years of age, Zuleger was named chairman of the Heidelberg consistory. Within this body he worked closely with Olevianus, his former fellow student, to remold the churches in the Palatinate along Calvinist lines. During September 12–18, 1562, he served as chairman of a conference in Fulda, where emissaries of the evangelical princes assembled. They sought to counteract the decrees of the Council of Trent. In the spring of 1563, he was given the honor of presenting a copy of the Heidelberg Catechism to the Roman Catholic King Maximilian at the Diet of Augsburg.

In the struggle surrounding the introduction of ecclesiastical discipline in the Palatinate, we find Zuleger among its strong supporters. From this time forward his talents in the areas of church politics and diplomacy shone prominently. In various ways he sought a rapprochement with William of Orange and the Netherlands. He also envisioned a leading role for the Palatinate from a political point of view.

The wish by the Lutheran Prince Louis to dismiss Zuleger was rejected on the grounds that Zuleger played too significant a role in the Palatinate's diplomacy with France. Johann Casimir appointed him to the cathedral of Neustadt, where he looked after the Reformed believers who had been driven from the Palatinate, and he played a role in the establishment of the Casimirianum. During the Dutch campaign of 1578, he represented his lord at the court of William of Orange, but he fell out of favor when he failed to achieve Casimir's demands. This brought an end to his official career. He bought an estate near Heidenheim and went to live there. In subsequent years he made new efforts to establish relations with Orange, but he was not successful. Aged and ailing, he moved to Heidelberg, and following the death of his wife, he relocated to Frankenthal, where he passed away in February 1596.

Wenceslaus Zuleger was an upright and passionate fighter for the Reformed faith, to which he also brought his political activities.

Thomas Erastus
Thomas Erastus was a lay member of the Heidelberg consistory. The term

"layman" should not be misinterpreted, for Erastus had studied theology extensively without entering the ministry. His actual profession was that of a physician.

Erastus, or Lieber, was born in Baden, Switzerland, on September 7, 1524, the son of a poor farmer. Strongly influenced by Oswald Myconius, Erastus studied theology in Basel from 1542 to 1544. Escaping the plague, he left for Bologna to study philosophy and medicine there. After living in Italy for nine years, he became the personal physician of the count of Henneberg and in 1558 of Otto Henry of the Palatinate. The elector simultaneously appointed him professor of medicine at Heidelberg. He soon became known as one of the best German physicians of his time. He became headmaster of the university and strongly influenced its reorganization.

Throughout his life, he continued to occupy himself with theological and ecclesiastical issues. He defended trials for witchcraft, and he vehemently opposed astrology and the medicine of Paracelsus. As a theologian he remained faithful to the Basel tradition. Under Frederick III he applied himself to give the state church a Reformed character. His steadfastness gained him the elector's confidence, so that in 1564, as a secular member of the consistory, he was sent as a delegate to the religious discussions at Maulbronn. As far as the Lord's Supper was concerned, he supported the Zwinglian view of interpreting the words of its institution symbolically, as he wrote in his anonymously published work on the Lord's Supper.

Around 1568, attention turned to the church order and ecclesiastical discipline in the Swiss church as well as in the church of the Palatinate, and disagreement arose over the required degree of strictness. As a Zwinglian, Erastus sharply attacked the more Calvinist view of Olevianus and others. Olevianus pleaded in favor of a presbyterial order, a college of presbyters with their own power and authority. Erastus rejected this model and considered ecclesiastical excommunication or exile and prohibition to participate in the Lord's Supper to be an arbitrary, unbiblical, and unjustifiable practice. In his view, all Christian community was based on faith and love, and so was the use of the sacraments; therefore, according to him, no one had the right to exclude others, even if they were blameworthy. Something that could bring about reconciliation with God and offer access to salvation should not be denied to anyone. Erastus also feared that the desired presbytery would lead to a new form of ecclesiastical hierarchy, especially if it were also to have the authority to practice discipline. He was more in favor of the Zurich model, where power was largely concentrated in the state. His view naturally encountered a great deal of resistance, as did that of Beza, with whom Erastus

Thomas Erastus

corresponded. Eventually both the presbytery and ecclesiastical discipline were implemented in the Palatinate in 1570, albeit in a relatively mild form.

Once Elector Louis VI had come to power in 1576 and the Palatinate reverted to Lutheranism, Erastus lost his position in 1580. He left Heidelberg that year. His last years of work were spent in Basel, where he continued teaching medicine and theology and offered his services for debates. He passed away in Basel on January 1, 1583, where he was honored with a statue. His five medical works were republished simultaneously.

In England, Erastus was soon viewed as the representative of those who rejected all ecclesiastical hierarchy and discipline and sought to subject the church to the authority of the state. In England and Scotland of the seventeenth century, this position was given the name Erastianism.

Conclusion: Epitome of Reformed doctrine

The Heidelberg Catechism emerged in a variegated environment, among people with divergent feelings and personalities. What held them together was the Reformed religion and theology, through which they all felt united, even though not all of them persevered. The same is true today. The Heidelberg Catechism is recognized by many as an epitome of Reformed doctrine, but there is also great diversity in the interpretation of its content and the conclusions that are drawn from it. Yet the Heidelberg Catechism continues to serve as a standard that has yielded invaluable benefits. The church and theology would be shortsighted not to accept and pass along this heritage.

CHAPTER 4

The Theology of the Heidelberg Catechism

by Willem van 't Spijker

The positive reception of the Heidelberg Catechism just after its completion implies that it superbly captured the message of the Reformation. The Catechism has stood the test of centuries in this regard, and for this same reason in our own time it continues to attract a great deal of attention. As a summary of the proclamation of Holy Scripture, this catechism continues to provide crucial support to the church and theology today.

Theological sources

The theological content of the Heidelberg Catechism reflects a multiplicity of factors. Its compilers allowed themselves to be led, in their time and in their view, by what had become a growing consensus among many Christians. The gulf between the Reformation and Rome had become obvious and was unlikely to be bridged any time soon. The Reformation itself encompassed such a diversity of movements that the need for a clear choice was imperative. Friction between Lutherans and Calvinists concerned not only the Lord's Supper and the confession of God's gracious election; it also reflected issues over the structure of ecclesiastical offices. Differences of view emerged between Geneva and Zurich that could no longer be ignored. In short, the times called for making choices; there had to be a clear indication of the direction to be taken.

Within this environment, a booklet of instruction was produced that was simultaneously intended to be a confession. It contained a road map for the implementation of the Reformation in the Palatinate. The nature of this catechism clearly reflected the desire for it to be easily understood by unsophisticated users. At the same time, it addressed a number of complicated theological issues without resorting to polemics. The positive tone of the Catechism contributed significantly to the readiness with which it was accepted.

In addition, it can safely be assumed that the entire domain of the Reformation offered potential material for this catechism. The booklet's wide circulation reflected the broad scope of its origins. An analysis of its components demonstrates that nearly all major Reformers were represented not only in their diversity but also in their essential unity. This is already obvious from the circle of its compilers. If we must first mention Zacharias Ursinus and Caspar Olevianus, it is clear that in these two young theologians we can immediately recognize the influence of Luther, Zwingli, and Calvin. As a student of Melanchthon, Ursinus was familiar with Luther's thought, as transmitted by Melanchthon—albeit in modified form. Zwingli and his followers must not be ignored, and with Calvin we should also mention Beza.

It cannot be denied that other catechisms resonated in some way in the questions and answers of the Heidelberg Catechism. The instruction booklets used in London and Emden come to mind. The material is varied and broad in scope. It is precisely for this reason that the impact of the Catechism of Frederick the Pious, as incorporated in his church order, was so remarkable. The focus of this chapter is to reveal the sources and literature that figured in the compilation of the Catechism and molded its character, and in so doing to describe the theological nature of this work.

The Catechism's influence was particularly great because it fit in a unique way into a centuries-old tradition of catechetical instruction. It continued to pass down the faith, commandments, and prayer by means of the Apostles' Creed, the Ten Commandments, and the Lord's Prayer. What was different about this new catechism was the renewed significance that the Reformation brought to faith, commandments, and prayer. The unique character of this catechism lies in its positive presentation of the essence of the entire Reformation as a unified movement.

A third Reformation?

In this connection, we encounter an issue raised by Dr. M. A. Gooszen, professor at Leiden University near the end of the nineteenth century. He associated the Heidelberg Catechism with a third Reformation. In addition to the Reformations of Luther and Calvin, he distinguished a uniquely German Reformed movement that originated with Bullinger. According to Gooszen, the Catechism's dogmatic character reflected the genesis of this Reformed Protestantism. The first phase involved the laying of a Protestant foundation. Then came the acquisition of a Reformed character. Finally, the new catechism was thought to have captured the movement's ultimate soteriological and biblical direction. Proponents of this view ascribe crucial significance to this third phase. The Protestant nature of the Catechism was clear, and its Reformed emphasis was also beyond question. But within this Reformed

Heinrich Bullinger

Protestantism, there were thought to be demarcations that played a role in the formation of this new catechism of the Palatinate.

Gooszen saw a far-reaching distinction between the nature of the Reformation in Geneva and that which took root in Zurich. To him, the views of Bullinger and Calvin differed substantially, especially on belief in predestination but also on the structure of the church. The Reformation in Zurich did not involve an independently operating consistory with the authority to implement ecclesiastical discipline, as was the case in Geneva—at least according to Calvin's principles. This difference in ecclesiastical structure was thought to reflect a deeper distinction that was rooted in the idea of predestination. Calvin incorporated this concept into his theology as a powerful principle, while Bullinger—in line with Melanchthon—did not recognize predestination as a guiding doctrine. In Gooszen's view, these differences in theological approach explained why, in Heidelberg, it was not Calvin but Bullinger who became the dominant influence. This line of thought saw the Catechism as a confessional document in which the value of the covenant and the significance of the church played relatively large roles in God's acts of salvation. The Catechism, according to this view, was the result of a third type of Reformation.

This idea of a *tertium genus* ("third kind") attracted the attention of scholars for a period of time, but today it is viewed as an interesting theory that is not supported by the facts. Aside from the point that the concept of a third Reformation has been adapted to include Anabaptist movements in the recounting of Reformation history, there are additional objections to invoking a *tertium genus*. The compilers of the Catechism were not only guided by Bullinger but were also influenced by Calvin and Beza. Besides, the facts demonstrate that its compilers were accomplished theologians with views of their own, and they took an independent approach. They modestly called attention to predestination by God within the context of the church of Christ. They also interpreted God's covenant as an indispensable factor in the doctrine of the sacrament of baptism. But in these very matters, they followed only the approach taken in the catechisms of their time.

The Catechism is not a theological reference book. It presents doctrine based on Scripture in an accessible way; for details, one must look elsewhere. Because of its broad focus on the entire Reformation, it is incorrect to ascribe it to a third type of Reformation. There is no problem, per se, in alluding to German Reformed Protestantism to emphasize its Reformed character. The essence of the Reformed confession is indeed its diversity. Reformed Protestantism in Germany could adopt its own signature, as was the case in France, Hungary, Scotland, and the Netherlands. Though the Heidelberg Catechism does not represent a third type of Reformation, it may be considered to be unparalleled, because it reflects the entirety of the Reformation in a unique manner that has stood the test of time.

Book of instruction and confession
The special character of the Heidelberg Catechism is due, in part, to its being a self-contained confession. As a catechism of instruction, it played an important role in educating the church. The church order that incorporated this catechism said that "in our Christian religion, the Catechism represents a short and simple oral statement concerning the most important elements of Christian doctrine, whereby ordinary young people are given the opportunity to feed back what they have learned. For from the very beginning of the history of the Christian church the godly have done their utmost to teach their children at home, at school, and in the church, the fear of the Lord." The primary objective was to prevent the collapse of church and society as a consequence of people's sinful nature. Furthermore, God explicitly commanded

to instruct the young. Finally, children who had been baptized as a sign of the covenant needed to be instructed in the Christian faith and conversion "so that, before being admitted to the Lord's Supper, they could make profession of their faith before the entire Christian congregation." Under the papacy, people were brought up without a catechism. This shortcoming had to be corrected through instruction in doctrine, and the church order prescribed the way in which this teaching was to be carried out. The Catechism was an instruction book par excellence, and its purpose was to encourage people to participate consciously in the life of the church.

At the same time, the Heidelberg Catechism served as a confession of the church. Through the Catechism, the position of the churches of the Palatinate were clearly identified within the German realm. The special history of those churches gave this book of instruction its confessional character. The battle that Elector Frederick the Pious had to fight to gain recognition for his position as a Reformed prince, placing himself under the protection of the regulations of the Imperial Diet of Augsburg (1555), was characteristic of the confessional nature of this book of instruction. The Peace of Augsburg recognized those who subscribed to the Augsburg Confession (1530). The opposition encountered by the elector came not only from princes who recognized the papacy but also from a number of Lutheran princes. When Frederick III so ably defended the Catechism at the Imperial Diet of 1566, this book of instruction was implicitly interpreted as a confession of faith. The significance of this event can hardly be overestimated. The position of the Reformed church within the German empire was thereby secured, even though all difficulties did not vanish overnight.

The Heidelberg Catechism had gained ecclesiastical significance. It also placed the Augsburg Confession in a different light. The age of confessionalization had arrived. Lutheranism gradually gained a higher profile, as evidenced by the Book of Concord (1580). Thanks to the theological stance of the Heidelberg Catechism, friction with Lutherans—at least from the Reformed side—was not carried to an extreme. However, confessionalization did mean that theologies began to raise their relative profiles, sometimes in opposition to each other.

Certain developments in the history of theology had transpired. Luther's resistance to Aristotle's influence, which Luther said implied a rationalization of faith, was compromised by the position taken by Melanchthon. The scholastic method thereby acquired legitimacy in Lutheran theology. Something similar was true of Reformed theology. In his own work, Calvin continually managed to maintain a certain distance from scholasticism as practised in

The *Konkordienbuch* (Book of Concord) was the book of doctrinal confessions for Lutherans

Roman Catholic universities. Beza, however, was an active proponent of this theological method which, in formal thinking, gave precedence to Aristotle.

The Heidelberg Catechism largely escaped the scholasticization of theology. Within the circle of its originators we recognize theologians of the school of Aristotle, but there were also those who preferred the method of Petrus Ramus. Thus, the Catechism, which constituted a basis for confessional theology, escaped a dilemma that could have led to frustration. It elevated itself beyond its own time because it sought its foundation by appealing directly to Scripture. The elector insisted on letting Scripture speak for itself. This approach is responsible for what a later observer termed "the eternal youth of Heidelberg."

The Catechism also anticipated subsequent developments, inasmuch as it contained elements that influenced what later would be labeled as Pietism. It played a prominent role in Pietism as well as in the Dutch Further Reformation because of the vitality of its ideas, which were derived directly from Scripture; focused on the act of faith; and placed in a framework of godliness that linked spirituality, sincerity, utility, and ethics.

The place of the Catechism in the church order

The place that the Catechism occupies in the church order that was released on November 15, 1563, is noteworthy. As is true of every Reformed church order, this order consists of regulations that support doctrine. Its title speaks for itself: "Church order, maintained with respect to Christian doctrine, the holy sacraments, and the ceremonies of the electorate on the Rhine."

In the preface to this document, Elector Frederick III refers to the Catechism that had been completed that very year. According to his preface, the regulation of ecclesiastical life has no other purpose than to promote the consistency of education and to achieve consistency in the conduct of the sacraments and religious ceremonies.

The concepts of doctrine and order are closely related. Doctrine has to do with preaching, the proclamation of the gospel. The regulation of the entire ecclesiastical structure is directed towards this proclamation. Through this combination of doctrine and order, the Heidelberg Catechism reached back to the relationship established between *doctrina* and *disciplina* in the early church. The church teaches and proclaims the gospel in the church in order to have it put into practice through witness and service to the outside world.

The *Kirchenordnung*
(Church Order) of 1563

Doctrina indicates instructive preaching; *disciplina* puts learning into practice. It may be said that the Reformation reconnected these two concepts. The regulation of church life establishes and sustains conditions that recognize that the Word of God cannot be bound. In the earliest Reformed church orders, one almost invariably encounters a brief explanation of doctrine.

Such is the case with the church order that incorporates the Heidelberg Catechism. It begins with a paragraph about doctrine and preaching. The central thought is a need for knowledge of God, including eternal life; we obtain this knowledge from the Word of God. In this opening paragraph, the reference to three distinct elements—misery, deliverance, and gratitude—is noteworthy: "The Word of God aims to direct doctrine primarily so that first it brings people to awareness of their sin and misery; subsequently it instructs them in how they can be delivered from all sin and misery; and in the third place it shows how grateful they must be to God for this deliverance. In the texts they expound, preachers must therefore diligently pay attention to these three elements and continually seek to apply the remedy correctly according to the need of the wounded conscience. They must also organize their sermons in recognition of the limited understanding of ordinary people, so that the articles of the Catechism pertaining to the doctrine that they seek to impart are consciously incorporated and taught to the people in an understandable manner." Here it becomes clear that the Catechism, in its explanation of biblical teaching, indicates the framework within which preaching is to take place. The Heidelberg Catechism therefore serves as a standard for scriptural preaching.

Of further significance is the role that the church order assigns to the Catechism. Every Sunday before the sermon, one tenth of the Catechism was to be read aloud, because people had grown up without the Catechism and were prone to forget elements of the Christian religion. In addition, in the afternoon service a Catechism sermon had to be preached with children especially in mind. The children were then asked questions that gave them an opportunity to recite parts of the Catechism. In this way, the importance of solid instruction in Christian doctrine was stressed.

This instruction was backed by the Reformed view of the nature of the church. It was a church in which baptism was administered on the basis of God's promises and in which communion with Christ was actively practiced at the table of the covenant. These two sacraments were linked through instruction in the Catechism, whose purpose was to provide admittance to the Lord's Supper to those who had made profession of faith.

This model of the church corresponded to that of Geneva. It was the goal that Oecolampadius and Bucer, and subsequently Calvin and Beza, had set themselves: a living church that upheld the significance of the covenant as the foundation for baptism and, at the same time, a church that sought to maintain the holiness of the Lord's Supper; only those who had professed their faith as taught in the Catechism were admitted. This view is reinforced by the regulations that the church order incorporates concerning the preparation for the Lord's Supper. It contains a short summary of the Catechism and speaks of faith that seeks and finds strengthening at the Lord's Table. The forms for the administration of baptism and the Lord's Supper that are incorporated in this church order closely resemble the classical forms of the Dutch Reformed tradition. They express the "doctrine as taught here in these churches as the doctrine of complete salvation."

The Catechism of the Palatinate represents a significant component of the church order, a set of regulations that governed doctrine and preaching in the church. This church order could not have been implemented without the Catechism. Conversely, the Catechism would not have been done justice without its being assigned a role in canon law. The theology embedded in this catechism was part and parcel of the living church in which it was meant to function. The elector gave an inkling of this reality when he reported that the entire faculty of theology of Heidelberg was involved in this work, along with the superintendents and the most prominent ecclesiastical office bearers. The church and academia joined hands in the conviction that the theology of the Heidelberg Catechism was not merely an academic matter: it emerged within the church, served the church, and could only function properly within preaching, baptism, and the Lord's Supper, through which the church of Christ reveals herself in this world.

Method and structure

The Heidelberg Catechism owes its vitality and lasting relevance not least to the plan and method of its treatment of the catechetical material. The chief purpose of this book of instruction—its perspective of comfort—marks the whole. The opening question does not merely serve as an introduction, which could well have been achieved in a different manner. Instead question 1 indicates the content of what is to follow and describes Christian comfort as an all-encompassing reality. The secret of Christian comfort is not held in our own hands, but in the faithfulness of the Savior, who has made payment and thus has redeemed us and now takes us into His protection. This interpretation is completely *Christological* in nature and focuses on man's salvation without lapsing into anthropology.

Calvin's chief theme, namely, the conjunction of the knowledge of God and of ourselves, resurfaces here. Luther's view of one's certainty of salvation is also clearly recognizable. It is not a theoretical or contemplative knowledge but one that is existential and experiential in nature. It concerns the knowledge of God, who is to justify us, and the knowledge of man as sinner having to be justified before God. Deliverance from sin through atonement represents the essence of salvation.

The approach of the Catechism is at the same time *trinitarian*. The confession of the Triune God and His work in atonement, redemption, and preservation is interwoven with the confession of comfort. This perspective reappears throughout the Catechism. Salvation derives from the Triune God. But we only know this trinitarian perspective on the basis of the richness found in Christ. It is through Him that the Father preserves us. It is also through Him that the Holy Spirit does His work. What the Holy Spirit does in sanctification and the assurance of eternal life, He does as instructed by Christ. It is Christ, therefore, who assures us and sanctifies us through His Spirit. This strong emphasis on the work of Christ is maintained throughout this book of instruction: in the explanation of the creed, in the description of the life of conversion, and in the pronouncements concerning prayer.

This sequence of treatment differs from that of Luther's catechisms. Luther starts with a presentation of the law followed by a discussion of faith, an order that reflects Luther's view concerning the law and the gospel. The Heidelberg Catechism begins with a discussion of faith; the law is covered in connection with the perspective of gratitude, in which the "third use" of the law is given the major focus—namely, as instruction unto life after justification and the renewal of life. The focus on faith instead of the law has become characteristic of Reformed theology.

Of special significance is the threefold pattern presented at the outset that permeates the entire work: misery, deliverance, and gratitude. These three factors explain one's sole comfort and are inextricably intertwined with it. A three-part scheme is a biblical approach that can be found in the Psalms and in the writings of the apostles. Luther was familiar with it, and Melanchthon also employed it. Since it was present in other books of instruction used in the Palatinate, it is not a unique approach. But it is striking how this three-part structure characterizes all of the aspects of faith, law, and prayer. It therefore does not constitute a formal principle or methodology. Awareness or knowledge of these three aspects is not a matter of intellectual insight. The key is the knowledge of faith, which continually leans on the testimony of Scripture. It would not be correct to state that knowledge of misery is gained from an encounter with the law, which then leads to faith, and subsequently results in acts of gratitude. The threefold division does not imply stages in the experience of faith, in which one moves from one phase to the next. At each stage there is knowledge of sin and guilt.The Catechism does not say, "How great my sin and guilt *were*." On the contrary, the Catechism points to a lasting state of lostness that exists apart from communion with Christ. But this knowledge unites us all the more with our faithful Savior Jesus Christ. When we live in Him, He gives us true humility and gratitude.

These three elements are interwoven with the entire content of the Catechism. They do not primarily constitute an organizational scheme, but they should be viewed as interdependent aspects of the comfort of the Christian life that together describe its richness. All of them are indispensable to living and dying "happily." They do not indicate stages that we shall ever leave behind in this life. They are continually present, as we have already seen, in the right proclamation of the gospel. They also return continually in the instruction that the church receives in the administration of baptism and the celebration of the Lord's Supper. The liturgical forms that were used in the Church Order of 1563 and are found today at the back of the Psalter contain the same three elements of the knowledge of misery, deliverance, and gratitude. We are continually informed that no Christian comfort is attainable if these essential elements are lacking. The Catechism presents these three elements in everything that is said about faith, commandment, and prayer. They reemerge in the sacraments and ecclesiastical ceremonies and play a role in justification by faith. They directly touch on the heart of the Reformational message as revealed to us in the gospel.

No comfort from philosophy

At the very beginning of the development of theology as an academic discipline in the Middle Ages, we meet Anicius Boethius (480–524). He has been referred to as the last Roman and the first scholastic theologian. Through his work the writings of Aristotle, Plato, and many others entered into the theology of the West. He developed a theological method that was adopted and elaborated on by subsequent generations. Boethius gained special renown through a tract about the comfort of philosophy, *De consolatio philosophiae*. Great theologians such as Thomas Aquinas drew from this work. Their influence had a greater reach than the Reformation and even affected Reformational theology to some extent. It is for this reason that we are curious about how Ursinus viewed the significance of philosophy for the practice of theology. No less important is the question of whether a philosopher can come up with arguments that can lead to real comfort.

Ursinus refused to derive church doctrine from the contemplations of philosophers. Teachings of the church originate in God; His divine testimony satisfies our conscience. The law is kept pure within the church; outside the church it is only present in a mutilated form. As far as the gospel is concerned, no sects, pagans, philosophers, Jews, or Muslims have any inkling of it. As far as the heart of Christian doctrine is concerned, only the church can provide the truth.

Yet there is a great deal of philosophy that can be accepted as truth. At the moment of creation, God's truth entered into the spirit of mankind as a ray of His wisdom. The light of nature could penetrate this spirit. Although this power might not be recognized by philosophers themselves, it is a fact. And therefore a Christian is permitted to practice philosophy, which can be quite helpful. Nevertheless, there remains a difference between philosophy and church doctrine.

Boethius

This difference emerges in various ways. First, principles of philosophy are physical in nature, whereas the most important aspect of church doctrine—namely, the gospel—is revealed to us by the Son of God who is in the bosom of the Father. Second, there is an important difference in terms of content. The church possesses the pure and flawless doctrine of the law and the gospel; philosophy can only present external obligations, and those only imperfectly and obscurely. Third, philosophy cannot penetrate the source of all evil—namely, sin. Only church doctrine can do so. According to Ursinus, it can offer our conscience a living and true comfort, by pointing out the way in which we can escape misery, sin, and death and receive certainty of eternal life. Philosophy does not know the cause of our disasters; it cannot fathom what comfort is and therefore is unable to offer comfort to us.

Only the church possesses true comfort in the face of sin and death, in the forgiveness of sins and eternal life. True philosophy is imperfect, although it is not in conflict with the Christian faith. This distinction must be kept in mind for the sake of the glory of God and our own salvation. Our faith and comfort are more secure to the extent that our doctrine is more eminent than that of everyone else. The certainty of the existence of the church in this life is similarly more secure and richer than that of everything that is found apart from it. For this reason the message of the gospel is so much richer than anything the world could offer.

In a separate elucidation, Ursinus further elaborated on the difference between the comfort that the world can offer in its wisdom and the comfort that is derived from the Word of God. Our heart demands something that does not vanish with death. Only the church offers us something that never perishes: "Even though philosophers and all sects seek and promise something that will be a sure comfort for mankind in both life and death, they do not possess it and cannot deliver it without the conscience immediately doubting again and our emotions demanding something else. Only church doctrine offers such a benefit and brings us true comfort that puts our conscience at rest." Christian doctrine shows us the origin of all misery: sin. It also provides us with the means to escape this misery through Christ. "Therefore Christian comfort is the only certain comfort in life and death: reliance on the forgiveness of sin by grace and reconciliation with God through Christ for His sake, the certain expectation of eternal life, as this is inscribed in our hearts by the Holy Spirit and through the gospel, so that we shall not doubt whether we belong to Christ and are loved by the Father for His sake, yes, and will also be preserved to eternal life, according to the Word: 'Who shall separate us from the love of Christ?' (Romans 8:35)."

To Ursinus, truth is truth, whether we know it from nature or from natural knowledge that sends out its beams to us in creation. But this truth remains inadequate when it comes to true knowledge of God and ourselves. And whatever kinds of truth might be known by philosophers, they can never contain the riches revealed to us in the gospel concerning Christ. Human thinking does not direct us to the way of comfort that is adequate for both life and death. Only the gopel of atonement and forgiveness through God's mercy in Christ can grant full riches of comfort that are adequate for life and will not put us to shame in death.

Treasury of Scripture proofs

Strictly speaking, the Heidelberg Catechism does not include a separate chapter on Holy Scripture such as can be found in later dogmatic works, usually by way of introduction. The Catechism was meant to be nothing more and nothing less than an interpretation of Scripture. Its original edition was already provided with Scripture proofs. The elector ensured that biblical references were added to both questions and answers, and he personally supplied a large number of these. Subsequent editions of the church order incorporate a brief summary of the Catechism, together with a list of the most important Bible verses explained in it.

The church order does include a short article on the significance of Holy Scripture. Scripture is first of all a place where God reveals Himself, and therefore it offers the foundation for preaching—which, as we saw earlier, is to follow the scheme of misery, deliverance, and gratitude. Preaching also must cover the content of the Catechism. Scripture resonates in preaching according to established doctrine.

That the compilers of the Catechism expected a great deal from scripturally faithful preaching is also apparent from what the Catechism testifies about Scripture. A strong emphasis is placed on the fact that Scripture is God's revelation. In Scripture, God makes Himself known as the Triune God: "because God has so revealed Himself in His Word" (Q. 25). In Scripture, God's revelation has both an evangelical and a redemptive-historical character. It begins in Paradise, where God first makes Himself known. It follows the paths of the patriarchs and prophets, who proclaim the gospel. It is foreshadowed in sacrifices and other ceremonies, and it culminates in the sending of God's only begotten Son (Q. 19). Scripture is the testimony par excellence of God's revelation.

The Catechism recognizes the distinction between the law and the gospel. The law plays a prominent role in the initial part by disclosing our misery to us. The gospel is summarized in the creed and contains everything that God has revealed to us in His Word. Faith holds the gospel as truth. The confidence of faith is worked in our hearts by the Holy Spirit through the gospel (Q. 21), or, as it is expressed in connection with the doctrine of the sacraments, the Holy Spirit works faith in our hearts through the preaching of the gospel (Q. 65). The Spirit and the Word work together in the preaching of the Word of God and in the administration of the sacraments. The Word of God, as presented in the Catechism, recognizes the distinction between the law and the gospel. But the emphasis falls on the gospel. The preaching of the gospel is the means whereby people are brought to faith and their faith is increased.

The Catechism does not include any theory about Holy Scripture. The Word is the means whereby Christ and His Spirit gather the church (Q. 54). Within this church, the Holy Spirit engenders confidence in people's hearts, as encouraged by the gospel. There the Word comes to us in the form of proclamation. This is how God reveals Himself. God's revelation is fulfilled in Christ. And thus we share in the benefits of Christ through the Word and the Spirit. Assurance and comfort become our portion through the work of Christ, applied through His Spirit.

The law as schoolmaster pointing us to Christ

In the second question, knowledge of man's misery is mentioned as the first of three elements that constitute a Christian's life within the comfort proclaimed by the gospel. It is an essential element. Knowledge of our guilt reminds us of the great distress and death from which we have been delivered.

It is apparent from the response to the second question that misery is not a stage that must be passed or that God's children leave behind them following their conversion. The response does not speak in the past tense about the great, one-time extent of my sin and misery. The answer is given in the present tense. This reply should not be separated from the aim of the Catechism. The testimony of the unique comfort in life and death resonates even in the section dealing with our misery. Indeed, our comfort rests always and entirely beyond ourselves in the Lord Jesus Christ. And the knowledge of our misery does not constitute a prelude, a phase that precedes salvation. It is an essential aspect of salvation. It is not a different type of knowledge from that of the second or third sections. Also, we only learn to know and confess our sin and guilt because it is communicated to us. It is a matter of confirming God's judgment over our lives.

Practically all representatives of the Reformation associated self-knowledge with knowledge of God. The approach of Calvin's *Institutes* is particularly well known: "The quintessence of our wisdom, to the extent that it can be considered to be true and perfect wisdom, consists of two elements: knowledge of God and knowledge of ourselves. But since these two are interrelated in many respects, it cannot easily be established which of these two precedes and generates the other." Calvin correctly gives priority to the knowledge of God. One can only know himself in God's presence. Outside the light of the Word of God, it is possible to imagine something good on the part of man, but biblical anthropology does not picture man any differently from how God sees and judges him. Calvin interprets this to mean that there is no single doctrine in the entire understanding of faith that is not affected by this knowledge. He appeals to his turning this principle into the methodological starting point of his entire theology. This manner of speaking gives his work the inner glow of the experience of faith. Salvation takes place in the encounter between God and man. Man is driven to Christ outside of himself and placed on the road of redemption and renewal.

That Calvin's insight was common across the entire Reformation is apparent from the writings of Luther, Zwingli, Bucer, and other Reformers. The way in which Luther discussed these concepts in his 1532 commentary on Psalm 51 is well known. To him, the key was theological knowledge of man and theological knowledge of God. It is neither a matter of reflection nor a philosophical, juridical, or medical observation. It has to do with man as a sinner. Luther strongly emphasized that the knowledge that is meant here is a purely experiential knowledge. "This knowledge of sin is not merely a thought or a reflection produced by the mind, but a real experience and an extreme distress of the soul." To Luther it was a matter of true theology: "The real object of theology is man guilty of sin and the God and Savior who justifies the sinner. Everything in theology that is sought or treated apart from this object constitutes error and poison."

We need to see the question about the origin of the knowledge of misery in this light. "Whence do you know your misery? Out of the law of God" (Lord's Day 2, Q. 3). "Out of the law" means by the will of God as it is summarized in His law; not by the law apart from God, but by the law as it comes to us directly from the mouth of God Himself. Christ teaches us what the law says.

Ursinus's explanation of this question points in the same direction. Experiential knowledge of our misery, which is knowledge based on experience, is an aspect of comfort in a Christian's life. According to Ursinus, this knowledge is a prerequisite for comfort, not because it constitutes comfort itself in whole or in part, but because it brings about a longing for deliverance and encourages gratitude to God for deliverance. Ignorance about the enormity of evil does not foster gratitude. It diminishes our ability to appreciate the greatness of our deliverance. We are then less likely to gain a proper understanding of the gospel, and therefore we are less likely to obtain the assurance of faith.

Knowledge of misery can be viewed as a preparation for the reception of grace as long as we keep in mind that such preparation is not a prerequisite that we can meet on our own. Knowledge of sin is a gift of grace that is freely granted to us and is therefore a merit of Christ and the work of His Spirit. At the cross of Christ we certainly come to know the depth of our misery, for sin is so great that God, rather than leaving it unpunished, punished it in His own Son through the bitter and shameful death of the cross. Knowledge of sin forms part of the theology of the Reformers and that of the Catechism.

Scholasticism in the doctrine of atonement?

The question of whether, in insisting on the necessity of atonement, the Catechism allowed itself to be guided by remnants of medieval scholastic theology becomes particularly relevant at the beginning of the questions that deal with the second division of deliverance. According to many, questions 12 through 19 appear to be inconsistent with the methodology of the Catechism. The question "Is there no way by which we may escape that punishment and be again received into favor?" is not immediately answered as in the gospel: "Believe on the Lord Jesus Christ, and thou shalt be saved." It is as though the Catechism takes a breath by first asking a number of other questions. Some consider this part of the Catechism to be its weakest. Ursinus appears to have been guided by Anselm's thinking (1033–1109) and the methodology that the latter used in his well-known tract, *Cur Deus homo* (Why God Became Man, 1099). Anselm sought to demonstrate, on reasonable grounds, that the coming of Christ for the redemption of people was necessary. He addressed himself to unbelievers and wished to show that even though one might be ignorant of Christ or the gospel, atonement and the satisfaction for sin could be proved in a reasonable manner. However, his tract presupposed faith, which is itself subject to clarification. His view was not that understanding led to faith, but rather that faith led to insight.

It seems far-fetched to associate this method of reasoning with the Catechism. In the first place, no one can convincingly demonstrate that Ursinus was aware of Anselm's thinking. But if this were the case, Anselm's method of conducting theology would have been adopted by all subsequent great

Anselm of Canterbury

theologians. Anselm was indeed convinced of the deadly gravity of sin. Through reasoning, he sought to prove that Christ had to become human in order to deliver men from sin. He attempted to prove his point "by setting Christ aside" (*remote Christi*). But can Christ really be removed from Christian thinking?

At any rate, the Catechism takes an entirely different approach. It employs a methodology that is quite different from Anselm's. The method of proof employed in questions 12 through 19 is not based on reasoning, but on text derived from the arsenal of Scripture, which is God's revelation. This methodology does not bypass Holy Scripture. Furthermore, the manner of proof is entirely catechetical. The student asks questions and the instructor replies by obtaining arguments from the Bible.

The starting point of the Catechism is also entirely different from Anselm's. It is not a matter of apologetic reasoning with unbelievers. To oblige them, Anselm could indeed pretend that he was ignorant with respect to Christ; he nevertheless spoke a language learned from Christ. The Catechism does not address unbelievers, but those who seek their comfort in Christ, as they have already confessed.

In the discussion of Lord's Day 1, Ursinus has already indicated that here we have the content of the entire Catechism in embryo. Questions 12 through 19 thus do not fall outside the framework of the unique comfort that is found in the knowledge that we belong to the Lord Jesus Christ. Not one of these questions therefore falls outside the justice or mercy of God as He has revealed them in Christ. Redemption, satisfaction, justice, and mercy are to be found in Christ and in Him only. This is what the Catechism seeks to demonstrate. One can therefore simply say that this book of instruction is based, in principle, on the confession of our Lord Jesus Christ in questions 18 and 19, in which the confession of question 1 with respect to comfort is reproduced: It is our Lord Jesus Christ who has been given to us by God for wisdom, righteousness, sanctification, and complete redemption. The next answer points to the source of this knowledge: the revelation of God, which comes to us in the history of redemption and is fulfilled in Christ.

The Catechism does not lay out the way to salvation apart from Scripture and apart from knowledge of Christ. It argues on the basis of the unique comfort of salvation in Christ that this way of redemption is completely in line with God's virtues. In other words, the glory of God Himself is implicated in leading sinners along this way to salvation that we confess, possess, and know in Christ. To the extent that faith seeks to understand or fathom the way to salvation as the way of knowing the One who is the way, the truth, and the life, our catechism can give appropriate guidance. Questions that we might ask apart from Christ and His revelation in Scripture are futile and do not lead to reasonable answers.

Communion with Christ
There is no salvation apart from communion with Christ. The Catechism makes this very clear. Being saved is a matter of communion with Christ. It is "by a true faith" that one is "ingrafted into Him" (Q. 20). We also read in connection with baptism that one is "ingrafted into the Christian Church" through this sign and seal of God's covenant (Q. 74). In the sacrament of the Lord's Supper, we receive a sign and seal "that by the Holy Spirit we are ingrafted into Christ" (Q. 80). The same idea is expressed when the catechism speaks of being "implanted into Christ" (Q. 64). "It is impossible that those who are implanted into Christ by a true faith should not bring forth fruits of thankfulness." Through faith, or through the Holy Spirit, one becomes a member of Christ and "more and more united to His sacred body" (Q. 76).

These concepts are directly derived from Scripture. The vine and the branches in the parable spoken by Christ point to the bond that believers have with Him (John 15). Christ dwells in our hearts: "I live; yet not I, but Christ liveth in me" (Gal. 2:20). The New Testament offers plenty of textual material in this regard. The Reformation understood the significance of communion with Christ. In his tract on the Christian's freedom, Luther pointed out that the wonderful exchange granted to us through Christ's righteousness could only be realized in real union with Christ because He took over our sin and guilt. In this connection, Luther used the strongest possible terms: We form one body, one set of bones with Christ; we are one with Him—a single loaf of bread. In the core of Luther's theology, we encounter mystical union with Christ; justification takes place within this communion. This is where new life emerges, and this new life also becomes manifest in our relationships with our neighbors. In this connection, Luther did not hesitate to speak of a Christian's becoming a "human Christ" to his neighbor.

In the case of Bucer and Calvin, we encounter the same emphasis on communion with Christ. The expression Calvin uses in the opening of the third book of his *Institutes* is well known: everything that Christ has achieved for the salvation of the human race is useless to us and of no value "as long as Christ is outside us and we are separated from Him.... He must become ours and dwell in us, to share with us what He has received from the Father. We are ingrafted in Him and clothed with Him. What He possesses does not concern us until we grow together with Him in a single body." Calvin ascribes this mystic reality to the hidden work of the Holy Spirit.

Other Reformed theologians associate the appropriation of salvation with communion with Christ with the same conviction. The Catechism also uses clear language in this connection. It is only in close relationship with Christ that the riches of grace become our portion. This communion is achieved through true faith, described for us in the response to question 20. It stands in contrast to various forms of religiosity that superficially resemble true faith but that lack this living relationship with Christ. Before we can speak of sharing in the benefits of Christ, there must be this personal bond with Him, which is established through faith. This faith is the work of the Holy Spirit. It is for this reason that communion with Christ is described in this booklet of instruction as the unique and special work of the Spirit of Christ, who binds us to Christ through the Word. The testimony of Christ and that of the Spirit are intertwined. Where there is faith, there is the bond with Christ, and only then do we become partakers of the benefits of Christ. This sequence cannot be reversed: first His Person, then His benefits.

Here we also see an ecclesiological or ecclesiastical perspective: Ingrafting into Christ is also incorporation into His body, the church—meaning the church of Christ. A healthy mysticism forms part of a wholesome ecclesiastical life and vice versa. The Catechism can show us the way in this regard.

Faith: knowledge, assent, and confidence

In his description of faith, Ursinus captures the Reformation's interpretation of the term: confidence in the promise of the gospel. We come across a general definition of faith in a debate he led on August 12, 1572. The term "faith" refers to a certain knowledge that we acquire from a declaration by witnesses who we believe are not misleading us. The church refers to faith more specifically and distinguishes four kinds: historical faith, temporary faith, faith in miracles, and saving faith. Historical faith accepts as true what has been transmitted to us by prophets and apostles in the Scriptures. Temporary faith consists of knowledge of the teachings of the church coupled with a certain degree of happiness but without appropriation of the gracious promises and therefore without true conversion and perseverance to the end. Belief in miracles also displays a semblance of truth, to the extent that it reflects a certain awareness of God's will that allows for the possibility that miracles could happen.

Saving or justifying faith consists of knowledge whereby someone wholeheartedly agrees with the entire revealed Word of God. Through the Word, he ascertains that the promise of God's grace applies to him, for Christ's

Zacharias Ursinus

sake. Through confidence in God's favor towards him, he overcomes all sadness and fear. This confidence in the justifying God comes from the heart and the will. It consists of joy as a result of the assurance of God's grace towards us here and now, and it is coupled with the hope of future deliverance from all evil. As far as Ursinus was concerned, faith is not possible unless it leans on the revealed will of God. The Holy Spirit works this faith through the proclamation of heavenly teaching, and perhaps also through direct revelation. Since the former is usually the case, and God seeks to work and strengthen faith through preaching in church, everyone is obliged to heed and contemplate such preaching. Justifying faith is granted only in this life, and indeed only to those who have been predestined to life. This faith also includes historical faith. Even on the part of those who are most holy, it remains imperfect and weak in this life. Faith must fight a battle with doubt in the heart. One can nevertheless determine with certainty whether one possesses true faith. Only through the faith that appropriates the individual promises of grace do we receive righteousness before God and share in the communion with Christ and all His benefits. True repentance and the beginning of new obedience, in line with all commandments, cannot precede this faith but must always be part of it.

On the whole, in this explanation we encounter elements that also strike us in the Heidelberg Catechism. The prominence assigned to the knowledge of faith is noteworthy. The Catechism states that true faith is not only knowledge. However, the Reformation also sought to make clear that faith without knowledge does not exist. This emphasis was surely intended to dismiss the Roman Catholic practice of simply believing what the church believed. The Reformation insisted that there be knowledge. Justifying faith also included historical faith. But it far exceeded historical faith, and the knowledge that was meant here was also of a different nature.

For his definition of faith, Ursinus undoubtedly makes use of material from Melanchthon. In the latter's clarification of the Augsburg Confession, he points to faith that appropriates Christ's merits, through which we believe that we receive forgiveness of sin and justification for Christ's sake. This thesis offers assured comfort to a frightened conscience. Melanchthon writes that faith that justifies us does not merely consist of historical knowledge but includes appropriation of God's promise. This promise offers us forgiveness of sin and justification by grace for Christ's sake. Although faith is not viable without knowledge, it represents more than knowledge. It also constitutes assent and confidence. The expression "not only to others, but to me also" (Q. 21), is noteworthy; Ursinus apparently borrows it from Melanchthon,

John Calvin

who says, "I believe in the forgiveness of sins and eternal life. In true conversion this must be interpreted as follows: I believe that forgiveness of sins is not only granted to others, but also to me." According to Melanchthon, as well as Ursinus, knowledge is not just a matter of intellectual activity. It coincides with assent and has a very personal orientation: not only to others, *but to me also.*

That this understanding of faith was common among the Reformers can also be seen in Calvin's writings. In Calvin's first Catechism (1537), he describes true faith: "It should not be thought that the Christian faith consists purely of bits of knowledge of God or understanding of Scripture that swirl around in the brain without involving the heart, as usually happens with ideas that we entertain about things for one reason or another. Faith, however, is a firm and sure confidence of the heart, which makes us certain of God's mercy that has been promised to us in the gospel." In Calvin's view, therefore, there is a higher dimension of knowledge that manifests itself in a vibrant act of faith. According to him, it is based on the Word of God and originates in God's gracious promise. The promises of mercy that God offers to us are true not only all around us but also inside of us. We accept them in our inner self and make them our own. Calvin gives this definition of faith after a detailed description of its various components: "It is a firm and sure knowledge of God's benevolence towards us, which is based on the truth of

His promise in Christ which is full of grace and is revealed to our minds and sealed to our hearts by the Holy Spirit."

The knowledge that is involved here is indispensable to faith. It is revealed to our minds and simultaneously sealed to our hearts. Ursinus also focuses on this knowledge, which constitutes assent and at the same time proves its uniqueness in confidence. In his explanation of the Catechism, he uses the example of someone who is able to describe the taste of honey. It is something entirely different, however, to taste the honey. This is the experiential knowledge meant in the Catechism. This sure knowledge reminds us of the description that we find in the Gospel according to John: "And this is life eternal, that they might know thee" (John 17:3).

Knowledge and confidence both rest on the work of the Holy Spirit in our hearts through the proclamation of the holy gospel. The law does not operate as a means to acquire faith. The Spirit employs the gospel, which is the promise of God's gracious forgiveness. In this promise, God grants forgiveness of sins, eternal righteousness, and salvation.

Everything promised to us in the gospel
Lord's Day 1 of the Catechism provides us with a summary of the Christian faith from the point of view of our "only comfort." Lord's Day 7 offers us a description of faith that focuses on the gracious promise of God. The knowledge on which faith dwells is comprehensive: it includes everything that God reveals to us in His Word and everything that He promises to us in the gospel. The confidence of faith is no less extensive. It concentrates itself precisely on one point: redemption as it is granted by God in forgiveness, righteousness, and salvation. It is only in this way that faith fathoms the length, breadth, and height of God's love in Christ, which exceeds all knowledge. The comfort of faith is, in fact, all-inclusive. This starts to make sense to us when we place the emphasis on the essence of faith that is inextricably intertwined with the content of faith.

The Catechism subsequently inquires about the content of faith: What then is necessary for a Christian to believe? Everything that is promised to us—as many promises as there are, they all qualify to be known and trusted as the content of faith. This trust or confidence agrees with the nature of faith. The Reformation placed special emphasis on confidence. In his pastoral work, Luther encountered people who sought a basis for confidence that they were unable to find. He knew this searching only too well, and therefore he was able to speak of the essence of faith that is very personally and experientially appropriated by people. Melanchthon spoke of the necessity of faith from the point of view of disquieted consciences that seek repose, comfort, and certainty. Ursinus followed the same tack. He spoke of the knowledge, so rich in comfort, of losing oneself and knowing oneself to be the possession of the Lord Jesus Christ. A person focuses on his personal salvation, which enables him to live and also to die. This in no way represents a narrowing of the truth or a limiting of the fullness of the revelation to something that only a single person can experience, as is apparent from the necessity to believe everything that is promised to us in the gospel.

The gospel promises indicate the content of faith. This content cannot be discussed apart from *personal* faith. What is promised to us in the gospel cannot for a moment be separated from Him who promises and is faithful. Faith directs itself to the God who promises.

In question 23, the Catechism presents the content of professed faith. It is not a listing of a number of dogmas, which could equally well be presented separately or in a different sequence. It is a matter of faith in the Father, the Son, and the Holy Spirit. Knowing and trusting this Triune God constitutes eternal life.

In expounding each article of the creed, the Catechism highlights the comfort of knowledge and confidence. The Father of our Lord Jesus Christ is my God and my Father. He is at the same time the Creator and the Preserver of His creation. Through His work, He provides all that I need. The extensive manner in which Lord's Days 11 through 19 confess the person and work of the Lord Jesus Christ is completely in line with this truth. He is the Savior; those who receive Him with a true faith find in Him everything that is needed for salvation. In His threefold office, He carries out the work of redemption, of which we read in question 34: He is our Lord "because He has redeemed us, body and soul, from all our sins … and made us His own possession." He is the Mediator, who has suffered and borne the wrath of God. The necessity of atonement through expiation is brought out again here. Redemption constitutes deliverance from death. Faith continues to be assailed, but the theme of comfort keeps returning. In our most profound temptations we may "wholly comfort" ourselves that He has delivered us from "the anguish and torment of hell" (Q. 44). The aspect of comfort has been woven throughout all the questions: from those dealing with crucifixion, resurrection, ascension, and session at the right hand of God, to the confession of the comfort of His second coming. The essence of faith—as comforting knowledge and confidence—fully agrees with the content of faith, as it expresses itself from first to last in the confession of Father, Son, and Holy Spirit.

The three Lord's Days in which the Holy Spirit is explained also deal with comfort. Indeed, the Spirit is the Comforter who makes us partakers of Christ and all of His benefits by a true faith and thereby comforts us and abides with us forever (Q. 53). The church is also the work of Christ; He gathers, defends, and preserves it. It is the place where communion with Christ and all His treasures and gifts are experienced, and where, on the basis of this communion, we also serve one another. The expiation of Christ is the ground for forgiveness, the "not remembering" of sins. In the end, the theme of comfort returns doubly: first in connection with the resurrection of the body and then in the article concerning eternal life, which yields rich comfort.

Justified by faith only

The connection between Lord's Days 7 and 23 is obvious. The essence of faith is described in Lord's Day 7. The content of faith is discussed in Lord's Days 8 through 22. Lord's Day 23 outlines the implications of faith in terms of its essence, content, and profit. True faith is faith that justifies, as is evident in all aspects of Lord's Day 23. The distinction between the essence of faith, referred to in Lord's Day 7, and the well-being of faith, addressed in Lord's Day 23, can at times be drawn in pastoral work. There is a danger, however, that with this artificial distinction one of the most essential positions of the Reformation fades into the background. The belief in justification by faith has correctly been described as the article by which the church stands or falls. Ursinus referred to it as the most important point apart from and together with the confession of God Himself.

Question 59 introduces justification: "But what doth it profit thee now that thou believest all this?" The succinct answer is no diminution of the confession, but a total concentration on the crux of the matter. All perspectives of our confession intersect in this one article. In the terse response, the matter is expressed from three different points of view. Through faith I am in Christ. This is the communion of Christ in which the sinner receives everything. The Spirit unites us through faith to the Savior personally. In this communion that wonderful exchange takes place: what is ours becomes Christ's, what is Christ's becomes ours. In this way we become righteous before God, which constitutes the second aspect. In His divine judgment God has nothing more to require from us. Therefore the third element follows: we are heirs to eternal life. The Holy Spirit has already sought to reassure us in this regard, according to Lord's Day 1.

In Lord's Day 23, we hear the echo of other writings by the hand of Ursinus, as well as the discovery that was common among the Reformers as a whole. In his synopsis of Christian theology, Ursinus asks, "How are we justified by God in this life?" His answer is that we are justified "only through faith in Christ, since in His gracious mercy God forgives the sins of those of us who believe and imputes to us Christ's satisfaction as though we had achieved it ourselves, and therefore He accepts us without any merit of our own and grants us the Holy Spirit and eternal life."

A subsequent question calls attention to the connections between God's mercy, Christ's merit, and our own faith: "How can it be, as you say, that we are justified through God's mercy and Christ's merit, as well as through our faith?" His reply is illuminating: "All of these agree perfectly with each other. It is only through mercy that God accepts us as righteous, although we are unrighteous. We only please God because He imputes to us Christ's death and His righteousness. However, it is through faith that we receive Christ's righteousness that God grants to us."

The reply of the Catechism also connects faith with pure grace and Christ's atonement. *Sola fide* resounds: by faith alone. This faith is not a new work. It is nothing but faith in the promise of the gospel, whereby forgiveness is granted and imputed not only to others, but also to me. Imputation constitutes the manner in which we partake of it. Faith is the means worked by the Holy Spirit. Calvin points out that our salvation comes about only through God's mercy, and not through any merit of our own, or through anything that originates within us. Therefore it is appropriate for us to place our entire hope in this mercy, to root ourselves deeply in it, and to ignore any works of our own and not to put any hope in them. "And so it is the nature of our faith to prick up its ears, to close its eyes—that is, to focus entirely on the promise and to ignore all human worth and merit."

Faith and promise fit each other perfectly. They are mutually dependent. This is so much the case that Calvin says that the promise would be revoked and dissipated without effect if one were to trust in any way in one's own merit. "It is indeed fulfilled only for those who are fully convinced, without the least hesitation, that it will be fulfilled for them, or to say it with a single word: who believe in it. When faith collapses, the promise ceases to have any effect."

The only thing that remains is for us to embrace this benefit with a believing heart (Q. 60). The "inasmuch" in the formulation of our Catechism (i.e., "inasmuch as I embrace such benefit with a believing heart") does not refer to the extent of our faith, which in turn depends on the degree of our comfort. Obviously, great faith will receive greater comfort than little faith. But this is not the issue here. The Catechism means to say that only faith which accepts Christ's benefit can be viewed as faith that justifies. The German edition of

1563 reads, "if I only accept such a benefit with a believing heart."[1] The Latin text is even clearer. In translation it reads, "if only I accept these benefits with a true confidence of the heart." Without confidence in the promise, there is no assurance. Then the promise fades away and loses its power.

On the other hand, the Holy Spirit uses precisely this promise to bring about believing confidence in the heart. Then the Spirit overcomes the flesh, which always seeks to take into account one's own merits. In the tension of this struggle between the flesh and the Spirit, assurance is granted that Christ's merit is more than adequate to cause us to emerge from God's judgment as righteous because of the gracious imputation of Christ's righteousness. The Spirit then "beareth witness with our spirit, that we are the children of God" (Rom. 8:16). In this way, the doctrine of justification constitutes the work of the Triune God.

Signs and seals of the covenant of grace

The introduction to the discussion of the sacraments in Lord's Day 25 refers back to the main theme of the Catechism: only faith lets us share in Christ and all of His benefits (Q. 65). The reality of communion and mystical union with Christ is, according to Ursinus, crucial for salvation. We saw earlier that we only receive Christ's benefits in communion with Him: "only those who are ingrafted into Him, and receive all His benefits, by a true faith" are saved (Q. 20). This salvation coincides with the work of the Holy Spirit, concerning whom we confess in Lord's Day 20 "that He is true and co-eternal God with the Father and the Son" and "that He is also given me, to make me by a true faith partaker of Christ and all His benefits." The Spirit and faith go together, just as the gospel of the promise and faith belong together. It is only in the promise that salvation is granted to us. Faith, by the Spirit, makes us partakers of Christ. The Spirit works faith in our hearts.

In this connection there are two forms of mediation. The first one is the proclamation of the holy gospel, whereby faith is worked. Faith indeed comes through hearing and hearing through the Word of God (Rom. 10:17). The second form of mediation of salvation is the use of the sacraments. Who uses these sacraments? Not the believer, in the first instance—although he obviously is considered to be their user. In the first place, it is the Spirit who uses the sacraments to strengthen our faith. This is the case with preaching, which we must learn to make use of because the Spirit employs it. The same is true of the administration of the signs and seals of the covenant. We are not

---

1. "Wenn ich allein solche Wolthat mit glaubigen Hertzen anneme."

the first ones to employ these means; the office or ministry of the Spirit is to work faith in us and to strengthen it through the means mentioned here.

The description that the Catechism gives of a sacrament is also based on an important concept of this book of instruction, namely, the promise of the gospel. This means Christ and all of His benefits: Christ who comes to us in the garment of Holy Scripture, "cloaked in the promises of the gospel" (Calvin). As often as we receive the promise of the gospel with true faith, our sins are forgiven (Q. 84). Our book of instruction states the content of this promise. It embraces nothing other than God's granting us forgiveness of sins and eternal life through grace, on the basis of the one sacrifice of Christ accomplished on the cross. This gift takes place in the promise. The partaking of these benefits takes place by faith, through the Holy Spirit who works this faith. "Granting" and "being made a partaker" are expressions that we also encounter in the prayer following the Lord's Supper. There the church expresses thanks for the fact that God has given us His Son as a Mediator and sacrifice for our sins and has granted us eternal life. But it also gives thanks for true faith, through which we are made partakers of such benefits. These two perspectives coalesce: in the promise salvation is granted to us, and through faith in the promise we partake of salvation.

The salvation of God is summarized in the preaching of the cross of Christ: there the sacrifice has been made, and there lies — outside of ourselves —the only ground for our salvation. Our total salvation rests unshakably secure in the one sacrifice of Christ, accomplished on the cross. Thus everything in the doctrine of the sacraments comes down to what is also the sole content of preaching: the cross of our Lord Jesus Christ. This core of the promise of the gospel, Jesus Christ and Him crucified, is testified and sealed to be true in both baptism and the Lord's Supper, in different ways. This is the content of the Word of God. The Word is not supported by seven sacraments. The church administers two signs and seals to sinners to indicate that God is trustworthy in all of His promises, which are indeed yea and amen in Christ Jesus (2 Cor. 1:20).

The covenant and baptism

The objective of baptism is to strengthen faith. Indeed, the Holy Spirit seeks to strengthen faith through the use of sacraments, not only or even primarily by their administration, but particularly by the believer's being active with the sacraments by faith. Baptism concerns the washing away of sins. Leo Jud pointed out in his catechism that, strictly speaking, baptism itself does not wash away sins. In Scripture, the Holy Spirit commonly refers to outward

M. LEO IUD PASTOR ECCLESIÆ TIGURINÆ
AD D. PETRI AB ANO 1522 AD 1542

Leo Jud (painting by a contemporary)

signs as though they are the things that they represent. The Catechism refers to "external baptism with water" (Q. 72). But through this external sign and seal it is impressed on our hearts that only the one sacrifice of Christ, accomplished on the cross, is of real advantage to us. Outwardly we are washed with water; similarly, Christ's blood cleanses us from the impurity of sin through His Spirit. The Spirit works and strengthens faith through this sacrament.

To have been washed by blood and the Spirit implies two things. In the first place, it means the forgiveness of sins on the basis of the sacrifice accomplished by Christ on the cross. But there is no forgiveness without the renewal of the whole life. The Catechism says that we are "sanctified to be members of Christ" (Q. 70). Here again we encounter the idea of communion with Christ, or partaking in the body of Christ. It is only in communion with Him that we receive forgiveness of sins—never apart from this communion. But sanctification is also a consequence of communion with Christ. It is impossible to live in this communion and then not to "die unto sin and lead holy and unblamable lives."

The promise of the gospel is the only ground for the sacrament of baptism. It includes the promise that Christ will wash us with His blood and Spirit as certainly as we are washed by the baptismal water. However, a sacrament, simply as an outward sign, will never be able to strengthen us in the absence of faith; neither will faith acquire any strength apart from the promise of the gospel. In this promise, Christ Himself comes to us. As many as three promises are listed in question 71. In the first place, there is the great commission, which emphasizes the unconditional nature of the promise. We do not take the gospel to people who are particularly receptive or suited to it. It definitely will have an effect on people who have been predestined. But it does not come to people in their capacity as the elect. Lost sinners may hear the glad tidings, and the Spirit works faith where, when, and as He wishes. We need only obey His command: "Go ye therefore" (Matt. 28:19). The second promise establishes a close relationship between faith and baptism. Only through faith do we recognize the outward sign as a proof of what God seeks to work inwardly and, indeed, accomplishes. The third promise points to the relationship between baptism and regeneration in the washing away of sin. The guilt of sin in this respect is no less important than the pollution or power of sin. The guilt of sin is removed through forgiveness; the power of sin is broken through the power of the work of the Spirit.

Attention returns to outward cleansing with water in question 72. Outward cleansing itself does not effect the washing away of sin; only the blood and Spirit of Christ cleanse from sin. God does not speak in this powerful way without great cause. Not only does He teach us that blood and the Spirit wash away sin, He also assures us by a "divine pledge and sign" that what happens outwardly is inwardly accomplished by the Holy Spirit (Q. 73). And only faith, described in Lord's Day 7 and sketched in terms of its fruit in Lord's Day 23, shares in the rich blessing of being strengthened by this sacrament.

As would be expected of a book written in an era that witnessed all the fury of the fight against Anabaptism, the Catechism discusses infant baptism (Q. 74), with attention given to the covenant, the divine institution that connects the Old and New Testaments. Our Catechism is definitely aware of this covenant, even though its treatment of it does not match the refinement and elaboration achieved by Heinrich Bullinger and Leo Jud in Zurich. The Catechism, however, does represent the view that had become common among practically all Reformers. The covenant is not described here in terms of a theological model; at the same time, there is no doubt whatsoever that children belong to the covenant. They are included fully in God's covenant and His church. Although the covenant and the church cannot be separated from each other, they can be distinguished. God's promises pertain to both the covenant and the church, and both are subject to the promise of the ministry of Christ's blood and Spirit. These promises are not only to adults, but also to children. For this reason, children must be incorporated into the Christian church through the sign of the covenant and distinguished from the children of unbelievers.

Circumcision is the sign of the old covenant; baptism has been instituted in the place of circumcision. We read as much in the form for baptism: "Since, then, baptism has come in the place of circumcision, the children should be baptized as heirs of the kingdom of God and of His covenant." It is said here without any reservation that baptism replaces circumcision. It does not imply any theology that rejects Israel. It is merely a matter of the promise, which definitely has not diminished in force now that grace has abounded.

We rightly administer infant baptism. Do we also use it to teach an upcoming generation the richness of the blood and Spirit of Christ, of the covenant and the church?

The covenant and the Lord's Supper

The confession of the Lord's Supper is also dominated by the central idea that we encounter throughout the Catechism. However, the emphasis on the mystery of communion with Christ is particularly strong here. The issue of the Lord's Supper played a major role in the Palatinate's switch to the Reformed confession. The gulf between Rome and the Reformation involved not only the doctrine of justification by faith, but also the doctrine of the mass, in which the idea of sacrifice continued to play a role. From the point of view of the Reformers, the mass was eminent proof of the extraordinarily refined doctrine of works righteousness that stood in the way of the doctrine of *sola gratia*. The interpretation of the Lord's Supper separated the Reformed community from Lutherans in a different manner. The Reformed church placed the emphasis on the work of the Holy Spirit, who binds us to Christ. The main cause of disagreement was not the presence of Christ in the Lord's Supper, but how one could share in the person and benefits of Christ—which explains why these questions received a great deal of attention in the Catechism. They are immediately raised in the introductory question (Q. 75), which treats how we "partake of the one sacrifice of Christ, accomplished on the cross, and of all His benefits."

The answer points first of all to Christ's command. He said, "This do in remembrance of me." The answer points next to the promise, where the emphasis falls on the phrase "for me": "His body was...broken...for me, and His blood shed for me, as certainly as I see with my eyes the bread of the Lord broken for me, and the cup communicated to me." The acts of breaking and pouring that we witness with our eyes are outward signs that point to the certain promise of God. What happens inwardly? He "feeds and nourishes my soul to everlasting life as assuredly as I receive from the hand of the minister, and taste with my mouth, the bread and cup of the Lord as sure signs of the body and blood of Christ." Christ does this Himself, through His Spirit. Therefore, the Reformed Lord's Supper form tells us, we may "not cling with our hearts unto the external bread and wine but lift them up on high in heaven (*sursum corda*),[2] where Christ Jesus is, our Advocate, at the right hand of His heavenly Father."

Eating and drinking the Lord's Supper means that in order to receive forgiveness of sins, the believer accepts in his heart the entire suffering and dying of Christ, apart from which there is no forgiveness. Just as baptism brings Christ's sacrifice close to us, so that we may place our confidence in it through faith, so also the Lord's Supper proclaims to us the entire suffering and dying of Christ. The promise of forgiveness and eternal life is confirmed both at the table of the covenant and in baptism. But the Lord's Supper goes further. In a very special way it brings us to communion with Christ Himself. Of this mystery of the Lord's Supper, Calvin said, "If someone were to ask me in what way Christ is present, I would not be ashamed to confess that this mystery is too sublime to be understood by my mind or to be expressed in my words. And, to say it yet more clearly, I experience it more than I can understand. And thus I embrace without any struggle whatsoever the truth of God in which I may rest secure."

The bread and the wine do not change into the body and blood of Christ. Nevertheless, the Holy Spirit works in us in a special way, so that we partake of the body and blood of Christ as truly as we receive the bread and the wine in His remembrance. Here we encounter anew justification by faith: His suffering and obedience become as certainly ours "as if we ourselves had in our own persons suffered and made satisfaction to God for our sins" (Q. 79). The Lord's Supper therefore signifies and seals no other benefit than complete forgiveness, which is attained in communion with Christ. Even if this communion is an unfathomable miracle, it is no less true. It occurs, in fact, through the Holy Spirit, who dwells in Christ as the Head and in us as His members, Christ in heaven and we on this earth. But His Spirit seeks to dwell in us and to make us partake of the fullness of His suffering and dying.

At this central point, the threefold pattern of Christian comfort returns: misery, deliverance, and gratitude. One might ask if we can still partake of the one comfort in both life and death, if we cannot or dare not celebrate

---

2. *Sursum corda* means "lift up your hearts."

the Lord's Supper. The reverse of this question is equally legitimate. If we do not partake of the comfort of the Christian faith, can we nevertheless attend the Lord's Supper? In connection with these questions we must not forget, however, that the Lord's Supper was instituted to strengthen weak faith through participation. Knowledge of the three fundamental elements of comfort forms part of the wedding robe that we must wear to be able to sit at the table of the covenant.

The covenant and discipline

The church, whose image is sketched in the Catechism, assembles in this world around baptism and the Lord's Supper. This is how Christ's work becomes visible. The description in Lord's Day 21 provides something of the background: Christ gathers, protects, and preserves the church through the Word and the Spirit, in the unity of true faith and from the beginning of the world to its end. In so doing, He employs not only the Word, but also the sacraments. In a sense, both sacraments determine the structure of the church.

Within the Reformation there were different views concerning the structure of the church. In Zurich, the predominant view was that the government ruled the church. The Christian city therefore coincided with the Christian church. In Geneva, Calvin chose a model in which ecclesiastical discipline was emphatically differentiated from the juridical power of the state. Many could not agree with this model. It took until the middle of the 1550s be-

Evangelical worship service in which preaching, baptism, and the celebration
of the Lord's Supper take place (painting in the Roskilde Cathedral, 1561)

fore Calvin's vision was accepted by the Genevan government. Ecclesiastical discipline was exercised by the consistory, the institution appointed by the church for this purpose. In Heidelberg at this time, there was disagreement over whether the Zurich model or the Geneva model should be adopted. The Catechism indicates in Question 85, however, that ultimately the choice fell on the Reformed model of church organization, as was practiced in Geneva, France, Scotland, and the Netherlands. This reflects the influence of both Olevianus and Ursinus.

In a sense, the motivation for this choice was infant baptism. The broad nature of the covenant was maintained through the baptism of infants, but the church did not automatically admit children to the Lord's Supper. The church order that adopted the Catechism placed profession of faith between baptism and the Lord's Supper. We see here a confessing church that clearly emphasized the holiness of the covenant of grace. Through public profession of faith, one was admitted to the circle of believers who gathered around the Lord's Table. Ecclesiastical discipline was seen as a means to build up the church. Those who behaved as unbelieving and wicked persons were not admitted to the Lord's Supper, for God's covenant was not to be desecrated. According to the Reformed persuasion, this practice was in line with the command of Christ Himself and of His apostles that the keys of the kingdom must be administered to prevent God's wrath from being kindled against the entire church.

The primary use of the keys of the kingdom of heaven is in preaching, whereby the promise of the gospel is proclaimed to everyone. Whenever this promise is received in faith and repentance, there is forgiveness of sin. Forgiveness takes place only because of Christ's merits and by grace. Whenever people receive the promise in true faith, there is full salvation. On the other hand, the same preaching testifies that wrath and eternal judgment will remain on all those who do not repent and as long as they refuse to be converted. Employment of the same keys of the kingdom brings judgment or salvation. The testimony of the gospel is decisive. The seriousness of this matter is so great that the Catechism asserts that God will judge accordingly, both in this life and the next. It is scarcely possible to present the great seriousness of preaching in stronger terms. God acts according to the testimony of the gospel, which must be brought out in preaching.

In addition to proclamation, excommunication is also a means of grace, employed as a last resort. The consistory, in the name of Christ and on behalf of the congregation, has the responsibility to keep access to the Lord's Supper pure. The sequence of events concerning ecclesiastical discipline is outlined in Question 85. It is presented in greater detail in the church order of the Palatinate and contains elements that can still be recognized in Reformed canon law.

Atonement and renewal

The third element of the Catechism—gratitude—is presented from the perspective of Lord's Day 1. Comfort is brought about by Christ. Through His Holy Spirit, Christ assures us of eternal life. Through that same Spirit, He makes us willing and ready to live henceforth unto Him. Assurance is a gift that Christ imparts to us through the Spirit. This is the subject of Lord's Day 7 as well as Lord's Day 32. The assurance of forgiveness of sins rests entirely on the gracious nature of God's mercy. The certainty of forgiveness and eternal life, however, does not stand on its own; it is directly related to the renewal of life in gratitude. We live only through Christ, and our "life is hid with Christ in God" (Col. 3:3). The Spirit of Christ makes our hearts willing and ready for this new life.

These ideas resurface as the Catechism turns specifically to the gratitude owed to God for our deliverance. Question 86 is a clear summary of the foregoing material. We have been delivered from misery, which reminds us of the approach taken by the Catechism. Comfort reflects the certainty of deliverance, brought about undeservedly—or, to put it more strongly, without any merit on our part. As far as merit is concerned, there is no room for boasting. Deliverance comes *sola gratia*—by grace alone—entirely owing to God's mercy, precisely because He desired it to be this way. Question 86 summarizes these truths quite succinctly and then continues: "Why must we still do good works?" This question might reflect the objection that is commonly raised against the doctrine of free grace: Doesn't this doctrine make people careless and wicked? What difference do our works make? Do we really need to pursue and practice them?

The answer to question 86 focuses not on what we do or fail to do, nor on our diligence, but on what Christ has done and continues to do. The first point is that He has "redeemed us by His blood." This refers to atonement through satisfaction, and it has everything to do with the justification of the ungodly. Christ has purchased us and redeemed us through His death and resurrection; this truth constitutes the foundation. But that is not all. Having redeemed us in this manner, He "also renews us by His Holy Spirit after His own image." He comes to dwell in our hearts and makes us conformable to His suffering, death, and resurrection. Christ makes His Spirit dwell in our hearts, and the Spirit causes us to conform to Christ's image. Thus, atonement precedes renewal; Golgotha precedes the resurrection and Pentecost. The focus is not on our own activities, our own works, or even our own *good* works, but on the good work of the Lord Jesus Christ, in which atonement and renewal are connected, and which results in justification and sanctification in our own lives.

The purpose of the redeemed and renewed life is threefold. First, it brings praise and glory to God. Second, it assures us that our faith is true faith; putting it differently, it assures us that Christ, whom we confess, is indeed the crucified and risen Lord and Savior. He works faith *and* conversion in us; these two go hand in hand. Third, we are redeemed and renewed so that our neighbors may be won for Christ. A life of gratitude projects a persuasive power to win our neighbors over to Christ. When these three elements are lacking and life continues in sin, salvation can never be attained.

The life based on Christ is characterized by death and resurrection (Lord's Day 33). Through communion with Him we share in His suffering. We die to ourselves and to sin, but at the same time we live out of Him; His power works in us. Sincere sorrow of heart for sin and crucifixion with Christ mark the one side of this communion. Resurrection with Christ is on the other side and gives rise to a Christian life that is marked by the unspeakable joy that the believers find in reconciliation with their God and Father, and by a desire and love to live for Him, doing truly good works. Children of God possess a real wellspring, namely, a true faith. They know a reliable norm, the law of God. They also have a real goal, of which perhaps they are too seldom conscious: the honor of God. They do not live by personal insight or human ordinances, but by faith, according to God's law and for His honor. This makes a Christian's freedom real, for he has been justified and is sanctified in, by, and through Christ.

The role of the law in sanctification

In the Catechism, the law and the gospel are inseparable. The law functions as a schoolmaster that leads us to Christ. From it we learn the extent of our sin and misery. The Lord Jesus Christ has fulfilled the law. Through Him we can obtain deliverance from the curse of the law. In his Shorter Catechism, Olevianus explained that Christ has delivered us from the curse of the law and from as many thousands of curses as the sins that we have committed. Christ became a curse so that we may be filled with His blessing. Out of His hands we receive back the law as a norm for Christian living. Calvin interpreted the law not only as the Ten Commandments but also as the entire framework of religion given by God to Moses. This was the old covenant. The new covenant is ruled by the law of the freedom found in Christ. The commandments remain unchanged. But now that they are fulfilled in Christ, they serve as a guideline for life in faith. The Spirit no longer writes it on tablets of stone, but in man's innermost being.

The Catechism explains the commandments from two perspectives: negatively, in terms of what is forbidden, and positively, in terms of what remains the Christian's obligation. According to Calvin, this is how the law remains an instrument par excellence for teaching us the will of the Lord better and more clearly each day. Day by day we need to progress in an increasingly pure knowledge of the will of God. However, we do not only need instruction but also encouragement—an incentive that does not allow us to sit on our hands. In urging us to observe the law, the gospel finds its true purpose — namely, teaching us to obey the law out of gratitude.

In interpreting the law, the Catechism asks to what extent a Christian is able to "perfectly keep these commandments" (Q. 114). The answer has not escaped controversy, since it speaks of "a small beginning of this obedience." Doesn't this expression diminish the richness of grace? And when it is said of "the holiest men," what can be expected from Christians who dare not count themselves among the least of the holiest men? Even of them it is true that "he which hath begun a good work in [them] will perform it until the day of Jesus Christ" (Phil. 1:6). His work has a beginning. But there is more: it is a promise. His Word is a living seed; His Spirit is a power unto salvation. Do not underestimate this promise. Their lives reflect a beginning. They earnestly intend to live not merely according to some but according to all of God's commandments. The law in its entirety, as summarized by Christ in the double commandment to love, teaches us to recognize sin. Now it turns out to be a principle that seeks to practice the love of Christ in all aspects of life.

The following question cannot be avoided: why does God want "the ten commandments so strictly preached, since no man in this life can keep them" (Q. 115)? The reply presents another summary of the entire teaching of the Catechism. The element of misery resurfaces in the statement that we need to "learn more and more to know our sinful nature." Precisely when it comes to genuine gratitude for life in God's presence, the flesh proves to be strong and sometimes nearly all-powerful. It refuses to subject itself; neither is it able to do so. A life of gratitude is a life of struggle between flesh and spirit. But this struggle is also how the need for forgiveness and righteousness becomes clearer. They must be sought in Christ. At the same time, the desire grows to seek complete deliverance only in Christ and never apart from Him. Finally, the guidance of the Holy Spirit is more necessary than ever. It becomes absolutely essential "to pray to God for the grace of the Holy Spirit, that we may become more and more conformable to the image of God."

Here we encounter the word with which Calvin ended nearly all of his prayers: *until*. This word reflects impatience, hope for consummation, and anticipated perfection, which we are to attain one day. Then sin, misery, and our sinful nature will completely be things of the past. "After this life" there will be complete deliverance and total renewal, according to the image of God. In this life everything is imperfect, but beyond this life there will be perfect renewal and glory.

The most important aspect of gratitude
The interpretation of the Lord's Prayer may be seen as a summary of everything that the Catechism teaches to this point. All three elements of the Christian faith are clearly present. The focus is now on people who have come to know the comfort proclaimed by the gospel and, in a demonstration of the most important element of gratitude, come to the discovery that this comfort can only be received by way of sincere sighing and unceasing prayer. Our need and misery are never more obvious than when we fold our hands, bend our knees, and humble ourselves in the presence of God's majesty. This prayer identifies us as poor sinners, weighed down with misdeeds and subject to evil that always cleaves to us (Q. 126). Furthermore, we are so weak that we cannot exist for a single moment while we deal with deadly enemies that assault us unceasingly (Q. 127B).

In addition to misery, the Lord's Prayer also focuses on deliverance. Deliverance rests on solid ground—namely, that God hears our prayer for the sake of the Lord Jesus Christ, as He has promised us (Q. 129). The foundation of our prayer is childlike reverence and sincere confidence that God, through Christ, has become our Father (Q. 120). The miracle of atonement is evident in deliverance: for the sake of the blood of Christ, God will not hold our sins against us. Spiritual warfare remains, but the power of the Holy Spirit will preserve us (Q. 127). Finally, gratitude reveals itself in the Lord's Prayer in that we sanctify, glorify, and praise God in all His attributes. This happens when we arrange and direct our entire lives—our thoughts, words, and deeds—in such a way that the name of the Lord will not be blasphemed on our account, but rather praised and glorified (Q. 122). This prayer, as the Catechism explains, speaks of trust in terms of the smallest things of life. God, as our Father, provides for our body and soul. And thus we recognize all the elements of Lord's Day 1: belonging to the the Triune God with body and soul.

The Lord's Prayer is not merely a confessional statement but a powerfully experienced truth, as can be seen from the Catechism's final question. The "Amen" at the end of the Lord's Prayer is not just a pious closing. It means that this prayer is true and certain, and this certainty is a matter of conviction. First, there is the sense that we truly mean it. Our prayer is not simply a string of words, but it is a true desire of the heart. This element of experienced truth, or rather of experiential knowledge, permeates the entire Catechism. One cannot read Lord's Day 1 without noticing that it refers to real comfort, which is brought about by the gospel, granted by the Holy Spirit, and experienced in His power. Spiritual life, as it is described in the Catechism, is also a life in which there is hellish anguish and pain and extreme temptations, struggle, and affliction. It is a life filled with experiences and consequences. Even the final question focuses on the nature of a Christian's life. When he says, "Amen," he knows that he meant what he asked for. He feels in his heart that he truly desired what he prayed for. But the certainty that God has heard his prayer is not based on this feeling or experience. It is a matter of the Christian's faith in God's promise, which remains even when all other certainties vanish.

The Catechism of "the only comfort" deals explicitly with the greatest certainty. The Reformation retrieved the ultimate security that man can find in life: in Scripture alone, in grace alone, in faith alone, and all of this especially through Christ alone. Throughout the entire Catechism, we see nothing but the confession of what Christ has done, does, and yet will do, until He has totally completed His work and we come to the promised perfection after this life. Then God will "be all in all" (1 Cor. 15:28).

CHAPTER 5

The Heidelberg Catechism in the Netherlands

A. CATECHISM TEACHING FROM THE LATE MIDDLE AGES
by Wim Verboom

Religious instruction prior to the Reformation

We admit at the outset that it is rather difficult to paint a satisfactory picture of religious instruction in the Netherlands prior to the Reformation. We concentrate on the latter half of the fifteenth and the opening decades of the sixteenth century. Dioceses had various regulations in place—for example those pertaining to instruction that led to a person's first Communion, penance, and confirmation—but the question is to what extent these guidelines were followed in practice. The population was largely illiterate, which must have resulted, generally speaking, in a rather limited religious knowledge. Luther's complaint in his Small Catechism probably also applied to the Netherlands: "Help, dear God! How much misery have I witnessed: the average person knows virtually nothing about Christian doctrine, especially in the villages."[1] Nevertheless, we attempt to form an idea of catechism teaching and other religious instruction, seeking to do as much justice as possible to the reality of this period.

Family

When we focus initially on the family as a place of religious instruction, we must take into account that it was not the natural parents but the ecclesiastical parents (known as godparents) who brought a child to baptism in those days. They were also the ones who responded to the question about instructing the child in the doctrine of the church. Because their role was more theoretical than practical, one might expect little to have come of this practice. The catechetical situation in the Netherlands during the period prior to the Reformation was researched by A. Troelstra; he determined that despite

---

1. "Hilf, lieber Gott, wie manchen Jammer habe ich gesehen, dass der gemeine Mann doch so gar nichts weiss von der christlichen Lehre, sonderlich aug den Dörfen."

shortcomings, one could nevertheless identify situations in which families did take the religious instruction of their children fairly seriously. He points to parents who attempted themselves to introduce their children to church life and doctrine. Families used a booklet published in Gouda called *Die tafel des kersteliken levens* (Code for Christian Conduct). In this booklet we read in a "proper admonishment"[2] various matters concerning the responsibility of parents. We read that "parents must educate their children and teach them that they must bring to God their Creator innocence and purity...that they must also teach them the Lord's Prayer, the Ave Maria, the twelve articles of the holy Christian faith, the Ten Commandments."[3]

It further describes, with respect to the duties of children, "how they should pray in the evening and in the morning at their bedsides upon their knees."[4] Parents had the following responsibility: "Similarly, they shall be diligently taught to worship at mass, to attend mass."[5] And further: "Similarly, the parents are not only obligated to teach and admonish their children with words, but when necessary to correct them with sharp rods and constraint."[6] "Similarly, children are to be sent to school in due time and kept off the streets."[7]

The booklet contained the following material, which was to be taught to the children, especially in preparation for penance: the Lord's Prayer, the Ave Maria, the Apostles' Creed, and a detailed catalog containing the following categories: the five external and five internal senses, the four cardinal virtues, the four sins that cry to God for vengeance, the four last things, the seven deadly sins, the seven physical and seven spiritual works of mercy, the seven gifts of the Spirit, the seven sacraments, the eight beatitudes, the nine secret sins, and the Ten Commandments.

In reviewing this material, one gets the impression that this upbringing and instruction in the faith primarily envisaged devotion, godly living, and conscientious reception of the sacraments, as well as the ability to perform religious acts. Knowledge of doctrine thus supported the practice of religious

2. "scoen vermaninghe"

3. "Die ouderen sellen har kinderkijns opvoeden ende leren hem, dat si gode horen scepper offeren onnoselehyt ende reynicheyt...item men sal hem leren dat pater noster, Ave Maria, Die XII articulen des heylighen kersten ghelovens. Die tien gheboden."

4. "Hoe si des avons ende des smorghens beden sullen voer horen bedden op hoeren knyen."

5. "Item, men salse vliteliken leren ter misse te dienen, misse te horen."

6. "Item, soe en sijn die oudaers niet alene schuldich hoer kinderen mit woerden te leren ende te berispen, mer als tijt is met scarpen roeden ende mit besceydenheyt te corrigeren."

7. "Item soe salmen die kinderen goet tijts ter scolen setten ende van de straten bringhen."

living. It should be kept in mind that a child grew up in a world permeated with religion; the child breathed religion. Troelstra observed that "from the first to the last breath a son of the church was exposed to catechetical influences." The child saw the Stations of the Cross[8] in church; he imitated the crossing of oneself and the praying of the rosary. He learned to kneel in front of the altar and the images of the saints, and he was involved in Christmas and Passion pageants. Some families possessed the *Biblia pauperum* (Bible of the Poor) as well as picture books about biblical history, the teachings of the church, and the lives of saints.

School

The second place where a child could receive religious instruction in pre-Reformational times was in school. Several kinds of schools were available, including monastery, cathedral, and chapter schools. Education at schools was overseen by the church. In this connection we must keep in mind that most children did not attend school. We do read about the education of ordinary people, but as a rule only the children of the upper class of society went to school, and this usually was Latin school.

An interesting method was used to teach children the first principles of their faith. Religious education formed part of instruction in reading. The ABC booklets that were designed to teach children how to read incorporated church-related material, such as the Lord's Prayer and the Ave Maria. There were also books with stories from the Bible and portions of the lives of saints. In addition, children had to memorize Bible texts, learn to sing songs, and above all, learn to pray. One of the aims of this type of education was that children would learn how to serve the church, as choir boy or as altar boy.

Parish

There are no indications that the church itself provided religious instruction to children in the Netherlands during the period preceding the Reformation, at least not as a specific function. Concerning parochial instruction in the faith, we must especially consider practices associated with penance. For penance, a child was required to know certain truths concerning the faith, especially catalogs of sins, as a guide for confession to a confessor.

Children were expected to do penance from the age of discretion, which was about seven years old. The expression in the third baptismal question in the classical Reformed baptismal form, "when come to the years of discre-

---

8. The Stations of the Cross depict the stages of Christ's sufferings from the night of the Last Supper to His death.

tion," refers to this age. In the booklet entitled *Van de Seven Sacramenten* (Of the Seven Sacraments), we read, "And therefore one shall guide, teach and persuade the young, as soon as they gain adequate understanding and discernment between good and evil, to participate in penance, so that they will acquire this as a good habit and learn to distinguish between God and sin."[9]

In connection with the practice of penance, the church published confession guides, which were instruction booklets that discussed sins, virtues, and similar topics in question-and-answer format. During the Reformation, these guides evolved into catechisms in dialogue form.

There were also learning opportunities for adults in church. The preaching of sermons based on the lectionary was often interrupted for the presentation of catechetical sermons dealing with the classical doctrines of the church. Catechists, monks, and others were appointed to preach catechetical sermons. Less formal teaching sessions were referred to as *collations*.

Furthermore, church buildings were full of objects of catechetical significance. Even at this time, people were familiar with plaques of the Ten Commandments and the Apostles' Creed. In addition, there were Stations of the Cross, many different images—especially the image of Mary with little Jesus on her arm—as well as murals, woodcuts, and other forms of religious art. Let us not forget acts and rituals, which were all full of symbolism. Learning was an ongoing process.

When we consider instruction in the faith in its totality in the days prior to the Reformation, we conclude that this type of education had fallen by the wayside. Perhaps this situation also reflects the fact that the church of the Middle Ages was sacrament-oriented. The way to salvation was thought to consist not in personal knowledge of the Bible and the content of faith, but in the correct way of receiving the sacraments. One shared in the faith of the church. Reformers subsequently referred to this approach as *fides implicita* (implicit faith). The content of confession guides and similar material suggests that the principal aim of such instruction was the practice of godliness. Therefore such instruction did not have to ignore inner feelings.

Nevertheless, in this author's view, this instruction tended to dwell on outward aspects of the faith—namely, the awareness and practice of religious customs and church functions. Knowledge was limited. Everything points to the fact that radical renewal—the Reformation—was required.

---

9. "Ende daer om selmen den ionghen soe gheringhe ende gheraye als si verstant ende onderscheyt hebben tusschen goet ende quaet daer toe leyden, leren ende brengen, datsi biechten, opdat si daer van in goede ghewoenten comen ende gode ende die sonden leren ontsien."

Religious instruction of the Reformation

The reformation of the church also implied the reformation of catechism teaching and instruction in the faith. That the Reformed Church of the Netherlands took this responsibility seriously is obvious from the great attention that ecclesiastical assemblies paid to instruction in the faith. Such instruction was also highly necessary.

From the very beginning, the Reformed Church cultivated the catechetical system of instruction wherever it was practiced in the triad of family, school, and church. Wherever it was not practiced, every attempt was made to institute a catechetical approach through new guidelines.

That the Reformation attached such significance to instruction in the faith reflects a number of its theological principles. The covenant plays an important role in the experience of the church and of faith. Through baptism, by analogy with circumcision in Israel, the Lord establishes His covenant with the children of the church. They are included in God's covenant just as adults are (Heidelberg Catechism, question 74). The important thing is for children to learn to respond to the covenant through faith and conversion. Instruction in the faith fits into this framework. Through upbringing and education, the Holy Spirit seeks to bring children to the knowledge of God and profession of faith in Him. This type of learning involves the entire person: head, heart, and hands. Responding to the covenant is not a matter of one or more isolated acts but affects all of life.

In the church of the Reformation, learning was a lifelong experience. There was instruction within the family, at school, and in the church by means of worship services and profession of faith classes, and at another stage catechism classes for children. For adults, in addition to worship services, there were both public and private catechism classes, the latter signifying learning circles within the congregation.

Family

It is immediately obvious from the third question of the form for baptism that the responsibility of parents (not godparents) to instruct their children in the faith was considered to be very important. It asked parents, "Do you promise and intend to instruct these children, "when come to the years of discretion," in the aforesaid doctrine, and cause them to be instructed therein, to the utmost of your power?"

More broadly, we encounter numerous ecclesiastical regulations concerning this parental responsibility. An example is found in the decision of the 1572 Regional Synod of Edam: "That they are therefore charged with

A father enrolls his child
with the teacher at school
(woodcut from 1554–1555)

the responsibility to instruct their children and are committed to their godly upbringing."[10] The Provincial Synod of Dort in 1574 prescribed "that the family's evening prayers—which every father is required to offer up together with his family—are to be conscientiously practiced."[11]

The content of such instruction within the family contained standard components, such as faith, commandments, prayers, and sacraments. Once translated into the vernacular, even Scripture itself became accessible to families, so that the new generation could become acquainted with what the Bible said. In addition, sources made reference to psalms, songs, morning and evening prayers, prayers before and after meals, and so forth. A popular guide for such religious activities was the church's service book, incorporating Petrus Dathenus's Psalter, published in 1566. The National Synod of Dort of 1618–1619 determined that parents must bring their children to church and subsequently discuss the sermons, especially those based on the Catechism, with them at home.

However, it must be realized that actual practice did not always correspond to church regulations. We repeatedly come across complaints about parents who failed to meet these expectations.

---

10. "Dat men haer alzoo die sorge des kynts selven opleydt ende tot godsalygen opbringinge desselven verbint."

11. "Dat de huysghebeden des avonts—die een ieghelick huijsvader met sijn huijsghesin schuldich is te doen—te neerstigher onderhouden worden."

School education
(woodcut from 1524)

School

The start of the Reformation saw a deterioration of schools rather than an improvement, owing to the abandonment of Roman Catholic education, especially in the form of monastic schools. It took a while before Reformed educational institutions could be established. Since the government carried primary responsibility for education instead of the church, the Reformed church repeatedly put pressure on the government to reform existing institutions or, if this proved impossible, to establish new schools. For this reason, the Provincial Synod of Dort of 1574 decided that "with respect to schools it has been determined that the ministry with responsibility for all classes must first determine in which locations schools ought to be established."[12] To ensure the schools' adherence to Reformed principles, the church sought to wield its influence through a regular inspection of classes and by issuing directives for schools in collaboration with the government.

The schoolmaster was an important person. From a catechetical perspective, he held a key position. However, good Reformed schoolmasters were frequently unavailable. The church continually monitored this situation, especially since schoolmasters were well suited to act as readers in church services, among other ecclesiastical functions.

---

12. "Van den scholen is besloten, dat ten eersten de ministri van allen classen sorch draghen op welcken plaetsen schoolen behoeven te wesen."

Example of a *Hanenboekje* (Rooster Booklet)

Religious instruction figured prominently in school directives from the start. The Synod of Dort of 1618–1619 prescribed that religious instruction be given two days per week. The instructional content was usually identical to that pursued within families. The pre-Reformational practice of teaching children to read by means of catechetical material was retained. For this purpose they used the popular *Hanenboekjes* (Rooster Booklets).

The Synod of Dort advised schools to pursue three levels of instruction in the Christian faith. The youngest children were to learn the basics from the Rooster Booklets. The middle group was to be catechized with the help of *The Compendium* by Herman Faukelius. The oldest pupils had to learn the Heidelberg Catechism.

There is little information about how religious instruction took place. One can imagine that students had to memorize aspects of the faith, with older pupils helping younger ones. From time to time the schoolmaster might ask students to come forward to recite their memory work.

Every Sunday afternoon the schoolmaster attended the catechism service in the company of his students. This brings us to the third instance of catechism teaching: the church itself.

Church

The oldest form of catechetical instruction given by the Reformed church in the Netherlands was the Sunday afternoon catechism sermon. The former vesper services were transformed into services of instruction in the principles of Scripture for the congregation. There are early examples of catechism services in the Netherlands. In Amsterdam, Pieter Gabriël de Vlaming preached from the Catechism as early as 1566. Well-known synod meetings (Dort 1574, Dort 1578, and Middelburg 1581) issued regulations for the conducting of catechism services. The Synod of The Hague of 1586 required that the Heidelberg Catechism be used for catechism services. From that time on, catechism services focused exclusively on the Heidelberg Catechism. The Synod of Dort of 1618–1619 determined that the entire Catechism was to be covered once per year.

However, quite an effort was required to introduce catechism services. Many ministers were reluctant to conduct them, and the number of church-goers was small. It was not until the second half of the seventeenth century that it became a general custom for the Catechism to be taught in a separate Sunday afternoon service.

Catechism examination in church (from a copper engraving by Johann Dürer, 1630)

Regular catechism classes as we know them today did not exist for children or young people for a long time. As mentioned above, it was the custom for the schoolmasters to accompany the children to the catechism services. They had their special place in church. Some of the children would recite the Catechism questions and answers that they had memorized at school. The overall liturgy of the service of instruction was as follows:

1. Scripture reading.
2. Reading of the questions and answers of the Heidelberg Catechism.
3. Catechism sermon.
4. Recital of questions and answers of the Catechism by school children.

It was not until after the Synod of Dort of 1618–1619 that separate catechism classes were initiated in some locations. The motivation for this decision was that the catechism service was neither the only nor the most suitable way to teach children.

However, from the very beginning the church instructed persons who desired to make profession of faith. Profession of faith replaced confirmation and differed from it in three ways. The candidates had to give evidence of faith, they had to profess their faith, and they were given access to the Lord's Supper. Then an examination took place concerning the candidates' motivation for making profession of faith and their conduct of life. Making profession of one's faith was frequently referred to as joining the church or beginning to attend the Lord's Supper. Profession of faith was frequently made before the consistory or its representatives, although the profession might also take place in the midst of the congregation, as in the Dutch refugee church in London. The Synod of Dort, referred to above, stipulated that three to four weeks of instruction were required before profession of faith could be made. It became customary to use the period between two successive celebrations of the Lord's Supper for the teaching of the Catechism to candidates for profession of faith. Often these classes were taught not by the minister himself but by others known as catechists.

There is limited information about the age at which profession of faith was made in the Netherlands. It is our impression that at the start of the Reformation, young people made profession of faith at about age fourteen. Later the minimum age was raised to sixteen.

In addition, the Reformed church soon instituted separate catechism classes for adults. There were public as well as private catechism classes, depending on their accessibility. A precursor to this practice was the "prophesyings," at which the sermon preached on the preceding Sunday was discussed. These "prophesyings" are referred to by the Convent of Wezel (1568) and were held by the Dutch refugee church in London on Thursday afternoons.

The Acts of the Synod of Dort state that "the office of minister will also include approaching all those who are eager to learn, and, accompanied by an elder, to assemble a sufficient number of them from among the members of the church, as well as other adults, in someone's home or in the meeting room of the consistory, or in some other suitable place, on a weekly basis, in order to discuss the main aspects of the Christian religion and to teach them the Catechism to the extent of their ability, taking them through sermons on the Catechism and making every effort to give everyone a clear and concise understanding of the Catechism."

Finally, the church of the Reformation maintained the practice of reading portions of the Bible aloud in church services. Plaques with the Ten Commandments, the Apostles' Creed, or other catechetical texts hung on the walls of many churches. The Reformed church did not employ a great deal of symbolism. Existing images and murals were removed from church buildings. The focus was on the Word, which was expounded and applied to the congregation verbally in the preaching and visibly in the sacraments of baptism and the Lord's Supper.

Catechisms prior to the Heidelberg Catechism

As in the Palatinate, the reformation of religious instruction called for new textbooks. These appeared in due time in the Netherlands. The Heidelberg Catechism (1563) coupled with its Compendium (1608) became the most important book of instruction. But until Dathenus translated the Heidelberg Catechism into Dutch in 1566, a considerable amount of other material was used. Even after the translation, several other means of instruction remained in circulation, and we now take a closer look at the most prominent of them:

1. Calvin's Catechism (1542)
2. Łaski's Larger Catechism (1546)
3. Micron's Shorter Catechism (1552)
4. Micron's *Corte Undersoeckinge* (Brief Inquiry, 1553)
5. Marnix van St. Aldegonde's Compendium (1592)

Calvin's Catechism (1542)

This catechism, also referred to as the French Catechism, was used for catechism preaching in the Walloon churches. The National Synods of Dort (1578) and Middelburg (1581) prescribed the use of this catechism in the French-speaking churches. It must have been used extensively prior to the return of the Southern Netherlands to Catholicism at the fall of Antwerp in 1585. This book of instruction contains 373 questions and answers. Although the focus is largely on doctrine, this catechism also treats practical aspects of the faith.

A number of introductory questions concerning the purpose of life and the knowledge of God are followed by the standard components: (1) The Apostles' Creed, (2) the Ten Commandments, (3) the Lord's Prayer, and (4) the means of grace—the Word of God and the sacraments.

In distinction from the average Lutheran catechism, Calvin's catechism begins with a discussion of faith by means of the Apostles' Creed. That is followed by a review of the law, in which the focus is on the third use of the law (*tertius usus legis*)—that is, as a guide for the practice of faith. Calvin's view regarding the Lord's Supper comes through clearly. Consider, for example, question 355:

> Minister: Thou dost not mean to say that Christ's body is comprised in the bread, or His blood in the wine?
>
> Pupil: No. In order to appropriate the truth of the sacrament, we must lift up our hearts to heaven, where Jesus Christ is in the glory of His Father, and from where we expect Him to come to redeem us; we should not seek Him in perishable elements.

The discussion of the Lord's Supper is also combined with a treatment of discipline (Questions. 368–373).

Łaski's Larger Catechism (1546)

During his stay in East Friesland, Jan Łaski (1499–1560) produced a catechism that was translated into Dutch by J. Utenhove (1520–1565) in 1551 for use in the Dutch refugee church of London. The order for this church, *Christelicke Ordinancien* (Christian Ordinances, 1554), stipulated that older children must study this catechism before making profession of faith. The title of the booklet was *De catechismus oft kinderleere diemen te London, in de Duytsche ghemeynte, is ghebruyckende* (The Catechism or Instruction for Children Being Used in the Dutch Church at London).

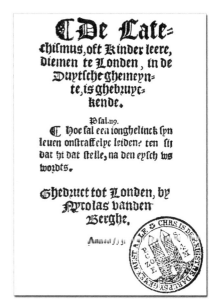

Jan Łaski's Catechism or
Instruction for Children

This catechism has 250 questions and answers, with an emphasis on practicalities. The first few questions deal with the purpose of life and knowledge of God. These are followed by other well-known subjects: (1) the Ten Commandments, (2) the Apostles' Creed, (3) the Lord's Prayer, and (4) the sacraments.

The discussion of the law precedes that of faith. The law is viewed as an expression of God's will for our lives. We cannot fulfill the law ourselves; it drives us to Christ and His redemption. Through faith in Him, the law becomes what it purports to be: the rule for daily life. It is further noteworthy that faith is described in the same way that Calvin describes it in the 1559 edition of his *Institutes* (III, 2.7): "Faith is a sure, certain and true knowledge of God's good pleasure and favor towards us" (Q. 118).

In this catechism, a good deal of attention is given to infant baptism (Questions. 233–239). Although its orientation is not polemical, in the background there is a clear rejection of the Anabaptist view of baptism. Much emphasis is placed on God's covenant, to which children also belong.

Micron's Shorter Catechism (1552)

The Christian Ordinances of the Dutch refugee church of London also stipulated that small children of this church must learn the Shorter Catechism of Marten Micron (1523–1559). Once they memorized this, they had to learn Jan Łaski's Catechism. Micron's catechism has 134 questions and answers, which are simple and personal. In content, this catechism resembles Łaski's. The sequence of the classical components is (1) the Ten Commandments; (2) the Apostles' Creed; (3) the Word and sacraments, as well as discipline; and (4) the Lord's Prayer. This booklet's view of the law agrees with that of Łaski's catechism.

It is interesting to read questions 92 and 93 concerning infant baptism. Here infant baptism is defended on the grounds that small children share in God's salvation, not as a reflection of their profession, but on the basis of God's Word. In this respect, they are considered to be equivalent to deaf or mentally handicapped adults. Consider the content of the following questions:

92. Q. Why was faith and its oral profession not equally demanded from the children of the church prior to baptism?

A. The church has far surer confirmation of its salvation from the Word of God than from the profession of adults. And congenital illness, as a result of which some persons can neither believe nor make profession, is not counted against them for Christ's sake, in whom they are blessed—that is, regarded as holy, righteous, clean, and faithful—no less than are other adult believers. The same must be thought with respect to the baptism of adults of the church who are deaf or mentally handicapped.[13]

93. Q. To whom then does Mark refer (Mark 10:14)?

A. Understood as referring to adults only, it was raised in vain as an argument against infant baptism, as though one wickedly and unjustifiably sought to damn children together with the deaf and the mentally handicapped as lacking faith.[14]

---

13. "Vraghe: Waerom wert het gheloove, ende de mondelicke belijdinge niet der ghelijcken van den kinderen der Ghemeynte gheeyscht, eer sy ghedoopt werden?

"Antworde: Overmidts dat de Ghemeynte van harer salicheyt veel sekerder ghetuygenisse heeft wten woorde Gods, danmen wt de belijdinge der volwassenen hebben kan. Ende haer aengeboren krancheyt—door welcke sy niet ghelooven, noch belijden konnen—die wert haer niet toegherekent om Christus wille, in den welcken sy ghesegent, dat is, heylich, gerechtich, reyn, ende gheloovich gheacht werden, niet min dan de volwassene gheloovige. Het selve moetmen ghevoelen van den doop der volwassenen dooven ende sotten der Ghemeynte Christi."

14. "Vraghe: Van wien dan is de plaetse Marci ghesproken?

"Antworde: Is 't dat sy verstaen is van den volwassenen alleenlick ghesproken te wesen, te vergeefs werdt sy teghen den kinderdoop voort ghebracht, t' en zy dat men de kinderen met de dooven ende sotten der Ghemeynte, ongodlick ende t' onrechte wille verdoemen, om des wille dat sy niet ghelooven."

Micron's Corte Undersoeckinge *(Brief Inquiry, 1553)*
Micron wrote his second catechism for adults who came from elsewhere, settled in London, and wished to join the Dutch refugee church. The title indicates that this catechism focuses on the examination of knowledge required for the profession of faith.

It is a small booklet comprising forty-one questions and answers, quite practical in nature and focused on personal faith. The booklet commences with a question concerning the assurance of being a member of Christ's church.

Question: How are you assured in your heart that you are a member of Christ's church?

Answer: The Holy Spirit testifies to my spirit that I am a child of God the Father through Jesus Christ, His Son and my High Priest, who through the holy sacrifice of His body and shedding of His blood has cleansed me from my sins. I further feel that I am being stirred up through God's Spirit to obedience to God's commands.[15]

This question is followed by well-known subjects: (1) the Ten Commandments; (2) the Apostles' Creed; (3) the Word and the sacraments, as well as discipline; and (4) the Lord's Prayer.

The relationship between the law and faith in this booklet is similar to that of both preceding works. It is noteworthy that the epilogue concerning profession of faith is practically identical to that of the subsequent *Compendium* by Herman Faukelius, which suggests that Faukelius borrowed this text from Micron. This document gives us a good impression of the profession of faith employed at the start of the Reformation. The text states that "when someone wishing to join the church has confessed these beliefs, he is asked if he entertains any doubts with respect to these doctrines, so that these might be cleared up. If so, attempts are made to set him at ease. But if he is comfortable with them, he is asked if he is resolved to forsake the world and lead a new Christian life."[16]

---

15. "Vraghe: Hoe sydy in u herte versekert dat ghy een lidtmaet der Ghemeynte Christi syt?
"Antworde: Vut dien dat de heylighe Gheest tot mynen gheest ghetuycht, dat ick een kint Gods des Vaders sy, doer Jesum Christum synen Sone ende mynen opperste priester, de welcke my, doer de heylighe offerhande syns lichaems ende wtstortinghe syns bloets, van myne sonde ghesuvert heeft. Ick ghevoele oock boven dien dat ick doer den gheest Gods, tot ghehoorsaemheyt der Goddelicker gheboden, gheroert werde."
16. "Als de ghene, die hem tot de ghemeynte begheven wilt, dese hooft stucken beleden heeft. So vraeghtmen hem oft hy yeverst inne, der leeringhcn halven, eeneghen twyfel heeft, opdat men hem ghenouch doen mach. Indien hy seght Ja, so souckt men hem te voldoen.

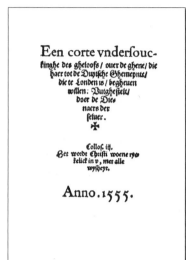

Title page and opening page of *Een corte vndersouckinghe* (A Brief Inquiry)

The candidate is finally asked if he is prepared to submit himself to Christian discipline. If so, he is admonished to maintain peace, love, and harmony with all people, and to seek reconciliation with anyone with whom he might have a quarrel.[17]

Marnix van St. Aldegonde's Kort Begrip (Compendium, 1592)

Although the Heidelberg Catechism had for several decades been the official book of instruction of the Reformed Church in the Netherlands, the catechism by Philip Marnix van St. Aldegonde (1540–1598) was used for a long time, especially in the northern provinces. It comprises 223 unnumbered questions and responses that are personal in nature, practical, and brief, but at times quite polemical against Rome. The booklet opens with a discussion of creation according to God's image, after which the basic subjects appear in the following order: (1) the Apostles' Creed, (2) the sacraments, and (3) the Ten Commandments.

It is noteworthy that prayer—specifically, the Lord's Prayer—is not

---

En is 't dat hy gherust is, so vraecht men hem, of hy voer hem ghenome heeft de weerelt te versaken, ende een nieu Christelyck leven te leyden."

    17. "Ten eynde vraechtmen hem oock, of hy hem der Christelicke straeffue wilt onderwerpen. D'welck hy ghedaen hebbede, so vermaent men hem tot vrede, liefde ende eendraechticheyt met alle menschen, ende tot vredemakinghe, indien hy met iemant eenich wtstel heeft."

Philip Marnix
van St. Aldegonde

covered. However, polemics directed at Rome repeatedly come to the fore-
ground, as is obvious from the following questions and answers.

Question: Where does this God dwell?
Response: In heaven.
Question: Does He not dwell in the church of the papists?
Response: No, He does not.
Question: Is the church of the papists then not God's house?
Response: No.
Question: Who then dwell in the church of the papists?
Response: Idols.
Question: What are these idols?
Response: Large dolls.
Question: What are they then?
Response: Dumb blocks.[18]

Conclusion

Glancing back, we obtain a global impression of religious education in its

---

18. "Vraghe: Waar woont dese Godt? Antwoort: In den hemel.
"Vraghe: Woont hy niet inder Papen kercke? Antwoort: Neen hy.
"Vraghe: Is dan der Papen-kercke Godt's huys niet? Antwoort: Neent.
"Vraghe: Wat zijn dese Af-goden? Antwoort: Groote Poppen.
"Vraghe. Wat synt dan? Antwoort: Stomme blocken."

entirety in the days preceding and during the Reformation. We see that in the period prior to the Reformation, knowledge of the Bible and the church's faith were, generally speaking, quite minimal. This instruction took place in three spheres: the home, school, and church. Education was primarily aimed at the practice of devotion and the ability to perform religious obligations. Only the upper class of society was in a position to send children to school. It was therefore a relatively small group that possessed any knowledge of the faith. In church itself, instruction took place principally in connection with penance, or the guidelines for confession. Apart from this, there was no regular instruction. Whatever was learned was acquired spontaneously, in a culture that was steeped in religion.

As a result of the Reformation, religious education changed profoundly. Hereafter it was based on the idea of God's covenant, which includes children. The purpose of instruction was to encourage children to respond to this covenant in their profession of faith, which replaced confirmation. Although learning was a lifelong engagement, the bulk of it had to take place during childhood. The Reformation retained education within the triangle of family, school, and church and assigned to it an entirely new content. Schools were now open to all children. Their structure reflected a theological and ecclesiastical orientation. The starting point was baptism, followed by education and catechism teaching, which brought children to profession of faith. Thus, they became members of the church and were admitted to the Lord's Supper. Subsequently, they were exposed to various forms of education for the rest of their lives. We realize, however, that this was less predictable in reality than these principles suggest.

Educators and families employed catechisms for instruction. Although these booklets contained their own biases, on the whole they all comprised the following components: faith (the Apostles' Creed), commandments (the Ten Commandments), prayer (the Lord's Prayer), and the sacraments. Usually the catechisms had a practical rather than a doctrinal orientation. Sometimes they were polemical in nature (e.g., Marnix van St. Aldegonde). To some extent, these booklets took into account the children's age. The concentric approach of teaching ranged from basic principles to more detailed explanations and from simple truths to more complex realities. After the Heidelberg Catechism was introduced to the Netherlands by Dathenus in 1566, followed by its *Compendium* by Faukelius, the earlier material permanently faded into the background. However, this shift also brought about greater uniformity, a change that was extremely beneficial to all.

B. ECCLESIASTICAL RECOGNITION OF THE CATECHISM
by Teunis M. Hofman

The Reformation in the Netherlands
Because the Reformation in the Netherlands emerged from a confluence of events and developments that took place in the sixteenth century, consideration of the Reformation should not be restricted to the religious dimension. Furthermore, it is important to realize that the time that preceded the Reformation was one of enormous influence.

Political situation
A study of the Reformation in the Netherlands must take into account the political situation of this region in the late fifteenth and early sixteenth centuries.

In many documents from and about this period, the uniqueness of the region played an important role. There is frequent reference to the special relationship that evolved over time between the sovereign and his people. In his documentation, the historian Emanuel van Meteren went well back in time to search for the origin of political privileges in the Netherlands. He paid much attention to the remarkable independence of the Dutch counts. For example, they delegated authority over parts of their counties without having to seek approval from any foreign authority. Van Meteren traced this practice back to the Roman Empire, to the days of Julius Caesar. The Low Countries did not have kings or judges then, but wise, experienced, and knowledgeable men ruled "according to ancient customs and origins."[19] According to Van Meteren, this must be taken into account when considering the special relationship between the sovereign and his region. For example, in Brabant and Holland the sovereign had to honor a certain "agreement," a situation that resulted in a stable form of government in the Netherlands for many centuries. The "overlords" were bound to various regulations, and the prince swore to maintain these stipulations and laws. This special relationship was expressed in terms of the relationship between a father and his children or between marriage partners.

Restricted freedoms
To understand why the Reformation took root in the Netherlands, we must recognize that the sovereign sought to centralize power. It is undeniable that the policies of Charles V and his son Philip II concerning the church in the Netherlands and the repressive measures of these rulers against the move-

---

19. "nae haer oude ghebruyken ende herkomen"

Charles V

ment of the Reformation was met with firm resistance from the councils of the Seventeen Provinces. Perhaps there were practical reasons for such a policy, like the greater effectiveness of a centralized bureaucracy. On the other hand, personal ambitions may have played a role; the sovereign may have wanted a tighter grip on power.

In this process, the church in the Seventeen Provinces was not spared. Charles V and his successor consciously strove to gain increasing control over the church. Their attempts to exercise greater influence over church appointments also reflected a pecuniary interest in that they imposed financial obligations on the clergy. At the same time, they sought to curtail the church's financial control over society by limiting ecclesiastical assessments, challenging the tax-exempt status of the clergy, and constraining the steadily growing real estate holdings of the church. This should not be viewed primarily as a policy to reduce the financial burdens of ordinary citizens, but rather as an attempt by the central government to enhance and consolidate its power. It sought to foster greater loyalty and acquire new revenue to cover its chronic financial shortfalls. It was partly through this interference in ecclesiastical and spiritual affairs that many residents of the Netherlands felt robbed of their traditional freedoms. When overlords start to lord over the common folk, resistance can be expected.

A great deal of the pamphlet literature associated with the subsequent Dutch Revolt suggests that nonreligious factors should not be overlooked

in a review of its causes. It is difficult to disentangle the political and economic factors. Consider, for example, the economic consequences of the
imposition of taxes by the sovereign. What could the provinces do about this
situation? Weren't they increasingly sidelined by the demands of the central
government? The Seventeen Provinces were, generally speaking, quite prosperous—with Antwerp playing a key role as a financial center.

Representatives of the Dutch Further Reformation have also written
about the period of the Dutch Revolt and have explicitly identified "personal
freedoms" as an important factor. For example, in *Zions Basuyne* (Zion's
Trumpet) and *Zephaniae waerschouwinge* (Zephaniah's Warnings), Willem
Teellinck referred to "acquired freedom and liberty, rights, justice, privileges, well-being, and prosperity."[20] In his *Coopmans Iacht* (Merchant's Quest,
1637), Godefridus Udemans advocated free navigation and the associated
trade. He pointed out that the Lord God particularly blessed the Netherlands
through its location beside the sea. He defended the right to free navigation
and recalled the role played by our "blessed ancestors," who did not allow
themselves to be robbed of blessings "which God had given to our country
by way of nature and opportunity."[21]

Fiscal and economic factors
In connection with freedoms, the authority to levy taxes was an important
consideration. Could the sovereign adjust tax rates entirely on his own, or did
he have to get permission from representatives of the affected regions? We
are reminded of the system of *beden* (petitions for funds) levied by the sovereign. In all agreements between the sovereign and the Provincial Council
of Holland, finances played a key role. The sharply increasing fiscal burden
associated with centralization and the enormous expense of warfare did not
escape the attention of the general population of the Netherlands. The growing influence of central government bureaucrats on cash flow exacerbated
conflicts of interest. The costs incurred by the sovereign were financed to a
large extent through borrowing. The associated interest burden increasingly
claimed the available funds. Another source of income to the central government came from crown or domain assets. Because of ongoing financial
shortfalls, portions of these assets had to be liquidated continually, resulting
in steadily decreasing annual revenues.

---

20. "vercreghen vryheit ende liberteyt, rechten, gerechtigheden, privilegien, welstant
ende prosperiteyt in neeringhe ende wel-varen"
21. "salige voorouders...die ons God door de natuere ende geleghenheyt van ons lant,
gegeven heeft"

Philip II (engraving by
Hieronymus Wierx, 1586)

In 1542, the central government approached the state assemblies of the Dutch provinces with proposals for new levies. The regions successfully resisted plans to levy a tax of one percent on luxury goods. The Province of Holland fought especially hard against the planned taxation of exports and trade; trade was to remain unencumbered. The representatives of the cities in this region strongly defended this philosophy. Resistance to such taxation measures proved successful; consequently, the great shortfalls of this time could not be made up. The government increasingly resorted to state loans with interest. In those days, the system of government borrowing enriched the wealthy. They enjoyed free trade and generally realized high interest earnings. By means of local levies, they made the general population contribute to the costs associated with government debt. Many consumer goods were increasingly heavily taxed at the local level. The general population was well aware of this situation. Wage increases fell considerably short of price inflation, which resulted in a loss of purchasing power. However, increasing prosperity and a consequently growing demand for labor offset the loss in income of enterprising families.

Personal freedom

The personal freedom of Dutch citizens was also affected. A series of relevant measures in the realm of jurisprudence can be traced through the first half of the sixteenth century. The central government also expanded its influence in this area. On one hand, ecclesiastical law was curtailed; on the other hand, new structures were implemented to shore up the policies of Charles V and Philip II with respect to religion and their opposition to the Reformation. The threat of an increasingly intrusive central authority thus began to affect the personal freedoms of ordinary citizens. The national sovereign increasingly sought to bypass the restrictions imposed on him, while the provincial councils resisted this tendency with all their might.

Matters that Emperor Charles V found difficult to accept proved outright unacceptable to his son. Philip increasingly acted contrary to the established freedoms of the Low Countries. He aimed to seize complete and absolute power. When General Alva arrived on the scene, a total demise of Dutch freedoms appeared imminent. In 1572, the Provincial Council of Holland took up arms at Dort to defend these freedoms, and war was declared to Alva. The Dutch Revolt became reality. The Northern Netherlands proceeded to remove from King Philip the title of "count" as a result of the Pacification of Ghent (1576) and the Union of Utrecht (1579). The declared reason was violation of the laws of the land. Justification for abjuration is sometimes referred to as *ab violas Imperii leges*, the violation of the country's constitution.

Suppression of religious freedoms

Biblical research was greatly stimulated during this time, partly because of the influence of humanism. Lutheran, Anabaptist, and Calvinist Reformation movements left deep tracks in large areas of Europe. Because of the integration of church and state in those days, the new world of theological thought was not only important to believers in their church and personal lives; it also touched all of reality, including public life. However, Charles V and his successor were not prepared to relinquish the old faith, either in their personal lives or as a foundation of stable government for their entire realm.

The sovereign's personal faith also guided his quest for unity in the Netherlands. Charles V had gained the support of a significant portion of the clergy by manipulating them. In turn, the clergy assisted him in the implementation of his government policies at the local level. In 1559, Philip II established an independent ecclesiastical province in the Netherlands that resulted in a realignment of dioceses and fulfilled a longstanding dream of his father, Charles V.

The Netherlands was influenced by Luther from the very beginning. The ground had been prepared in various ways. We have in mind the influence of Modern Devotion and humanism, as well as the role played by early Bible translations.

The Reformation movement encountered a steadily growing resistance from government. The national government decreed increasingly drastic measures to effect repression.

However the actual extent of the Inquisition (the so-called "black legend") and jurisdictional conflict in the Netherlands is evaluated, it is undeniable that it caused major upheaval to the inhabitants of these regions. The national government made efforts to pursue unity in as many areas as possible; these attempts eventually led some of the regions of the country to break away. While official policy turned increasingly severe, local magistrates and judicial powers tended to have great difficulty with this harsh approach and sought to moderate its impact on their constituents. It is entirely appropriate to consider the role played by the lower nobility in the Dutch Revolt. In addition to persons such as Hendrik van Brederode, Lord of Vianen, "the great sea-beggar," we can mention Catharina van den Boetzelaer, Lady of the Castle of Aalter. She had a warm heart for Protestantism and clearly demonstrated it within her own jurisdiction. Family ties with the Northern Netherlands also played a significant role, as did the close connection between Protestantism and the social upper crust in the neighborhood of Aalter. Deep-seated religious beliefs on the part of the nobility and prosperous citizens cannot be ignored. When the tide turned against Protestantism around the region of Aalter in the Southern Netherlands, important figures from the entourage of Catharina van den Boetzelaer, such as court clerk Simon Stalpaert, Adrian of Maldreghem, and John of Dendere, were condemned. They remained faithful to their Calvinist convictions unto death. The testimony of Guido de Brès at the time of his imprisonment and execution reveals the spiritual power and eloquence of his deep faith.

Refugee churches

The repression of the Protestant faith in the Netherlands of the sixteenth century left deep scars in society and politics. Government repression also had grave economic consequences for the Southern Netherlands because many people were driven from their homes. Most considered these hardships worth suffering for the sake of the faith. They sought a safe haven abroad to escape judicial punishment and to confess and practice their faith in freedom.

Refugee churches emerged, particularly in England and Germany, that were often fertile ground for Reformed ecclesiastical practices.

Refugee churches played an important role in the emergence and impact of the Heidelberg Catechism. Partly because of trade connections, many Dutch immigrants settled in the Rhineland region of Germany, in such places as Calcar, Goch, Xanten, Emmerich, Duisburg, Aachen, and Frankfurt. Part of the London church had found refuge in Frankfurt, and in 1544, the Frankfurt city council decreed that all Protestants would be welcome. Petrus Dathenus arrived there from Emden and clashed with the Lutheran ministers of the city. Subsequently, the Church of Reformed Low Countrymen found refuge in the monastery of Frankenthal, near Worms, through the mediation of Frederick III, Elector of the Palatinate. This settlement also held great significance for developments in the Seventeen Provinces of the Netherlands.

One of the links in the establishment of the refugee churches was Petrus Dathenus. As early as 1559, in the spirit of Calvin he persuaded his fellow believers in Flanders and Antwerp that resistance to the government could be legitimate as long as it was initiated by *magistratus inferiores* (lower level authorities). In 1561, the various consistories were divided over the right of revolt. People became more and more agitated. Thus, Calvinism became an increasingly significant political factor. For example, as presidents of the

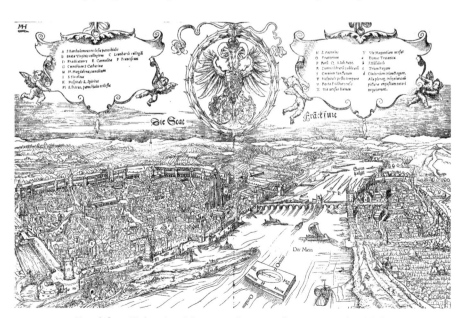

Frankfurt (Sebastian Münster, *Cosmographiae Universalis*, 1550)

Synod of Ghent in 1566, Herman Moded and Petrus Dathenus discussed the possibility of raising three million gold guilders to purchase religious freedom for the Netherlands from the king. It was further decided to engage in armed resistance if this transaction were to fail. In the latter case, the amassed funds would be utilized to raise troops in Germany for an army to be commanded by Hendrik van Brederode. However, this expedition of Toulouse, a city in southwest France, eventually ended in disaster.

At a later stage, Dathenus was actively engaged in the spiritual and political situation in and around Ghent. During this period, catechism teaching received a significant boost. A great deal was invested in a system of education, with a professor being attracted from Heidelberg. The political and practical application of Calvinistic principles led to a steadily growing conflict between Dathenus and Prince William of Orange.

Assessment

Any analysis of the Netherlands over the period leading up to the breakthrough of the Reformation—and also during the Dutch Revolt—calls for a broad sociopolitical framework. In pursuing centralization and a concentration of power, Charles V and his son Philip were continually confronted with the unique position of the Netherlands within their realm. Although each province had already developed a strong regional consciousness, there was also a growing sense of solidarity among the provinces, as was obvious from an institution such as the National Parliament. The practices employed by the central government frequently had unintended consequences and contributed to a growing estrangement between the Netherlands and its sovereign. In this political and economic context, the religious dimension could not be ignored. At this time the refugee churches made significant contributions to further augment the Reformational heritage in the Netherlands. The role of the Heidelberg Catechism in this process is clearly evident.

The Catechism in the Netherlands

There continue to be unresolved issues concerning the Dutch text of the Heidelberg Catechism. Doedes distinguishes among four early translations by 1565. The first translation appeared in 1563, bearing the vignette of the Emden printer Gillis van den Erven. This version was based not on the first German edition but rather on a revised edition. That same year, a second translation was produced by Petrus Dathenus and printed by Michael Schirat of Heidelberg. A third Dutch translation also existed; it was printed at Emden in 1565, but it departed from the 1563 Emden translation referred to above.

The first Dutch edition, Emden 1563   The Emden edition of 1566

At Emden, two more Dutch translations—namely, those of 1566 and 1567—were published. A fourth Dutch translation of the Heidelberg Catechism, not by Dathenus, is found in the church order of the Palatinate; it does not specify a printer or a location. According to Doedes, this version represents a blended Dutch translation.

The history of the Dutch text of the Heidelberg Catechism is complex. Its lineage was traced through the work of both Dathenus and Faukelius. Dathenus's 1563 translation was based on the second, revised German edition, as is obvious from the answer to question 80. In 1566, the same printer published a reprint that differed somewhat from Dathenus's 1563 edition. The 1566 edition was published in combination with Dathenus's Psalter. To date, it has proved impossible satisfactorily to account for the significant differences between the 1563 and 1566 editions. Nevertheless, the 1566 edition constitutes the basis for the Dutch text that has been the most enduring. The Middelburg text, produced by Herman Faukelius, is largely based on Dathenus's 1566 edition. Caspar van der Heyden also provided a Dutch edition of the Heidelberg Catechism, printed in Antwerp by Gielis vanden Rade in 1580. An improved edition appeared in 1591, printed in Middelburg by R. Schilders.

Ecclesiastical involvement in the development of the Dutch text

The Synod of Veere (May 17–27, 1610) decided, among other things, that "it is believed to be good and advisable that the 37 articles of our Confession be printed correctly following the Catechism as well as by itself."[22] In the Acts of the Classis of Middelburg on October 14, 1610, we find the decision of the Regional Synod of Veere to have the Belgic Confession of Faith and the Heidelberg Catechism printed "anew and correctly,"[23] in combination with a number of forms for prayers and the like. The acts of the classis next reported that "this assembly has thus instructed and authorized Gillis Burs to arrange with the printer to provide this classis with two hundred copies."[24]

In 1611, Herman Faukelius published a Book of Forms through the printer of the Provincial Council of Zeeland, Richard Schilders of Middelburg. Over a period of years, both confessional documents had been adapted and expanded to such an extent that a revised edition proved necessary.

Despite the involvement of the National Synod of 1618–1619 with the Heidelberg Catechism, an official Dutch church text was subsequently established. To date, the Dutch translation of Middelburg (1611), which is largely due to Dathenus, is considered to be the most authentic text since 1619. These facts constitute sufficient justification to pay extra attention to the personalities and work of both Petrus Dathenus and Herman Faukelius.

Petrus Dathenus, translator and Psalm versifier

The man whose name is invariably connected with the translation of the Heidelberg Catechism deserves closer attention. He was born in 1531 or 1532 at Cassel, which at that time formed part of the Southern Netherlands; today it belongs to northern France. In the final phase of his life, he also referred to himself as Pieter van Berghen or Petrus Montanus. He passed away on March 17, 1588, at Elbing, in the neighborhood of Danzig.[25] In his early youth he joined the Carmelite monastery of Ieperen. By 1550, he supported the Reformation and was active as a preacher. For this reason, he had to flee to England, where he was soon called to the ministry. How his calling came about and where he served is not clear. It cannot be confirmed that Dathenus

---

22. "Het wort goet ende raetsaem ghevonden, dat de 37 artickelen onser Confessie achteraen den Catechismus, ende oock alleen, correct geprent worden."

23. "van nieuws ende correct"

24. "Soo is van dese vergaderinghe Gillis Burs last gegeven ende gemachticht om van tweehondert exemplaren voor dese classe met den drucker overeen te commen."

25. Danzig is modern-day Gdansk, Poland.

Petrus Dathenus

studied at Geneva, but he corresponded with Calvin on November 2, 1555, and met with the Genevan Reformer in Frankfurt am Main in 1556.

In Frankfurt, Dathenus served the Low German refugee church beginning in 1555, when many had to leave England because of the persecution of Bloody Mary. This task was not easy for Dathenus, considering the nature of the work and the need to build up the church. The church in Frankfurt was experiencing friction with Lutheran ministers. Although Dathenus was prepared to go further than Caspar van der Heyden was in seeking a compromise with Lutherans, he nevertheless had to leave Frankfurt in 1562. Dathenus and his church were warmly received in Frankenthal, in the Palatinate. Here Dathenus enjoyed the confidence of the elector, who engaged him as an envoy in religious discussions. In this way, Dathenus established many contacts with other representatives of refugee churches, such as the one at Jülich.

For Dathenus's trip to Flanders in the fall of 1566, the elector provided him with a letter of recommendation to the Count of Egmont. From then until the spring of 1567, Dathenus preached in Flanders (Ghent) and Zeeland (Flushing, Zierikzee, and Middelburg). In Ghent, he attended a synod that offered the king a sum of three million guilders in exchange for religious freedom. He also spent much of his time preaching and attending ecclesiastical assemblies, and he initiated political activities in Flanders. He sought support for the cities of Doornik and Valenciennes. Following the defeat of Wattrelos, in French Flanders, Dathenus went through Antwerp to Vianen to offer his services to Brederode, and subsequently he went to Amsterdam. Dathenus was compelled to return to the Palatinate in the spring of 1567, when troops that supported the Dutch Revolt were defeated. In the fall, he traveled to France to provide support to the Huguenots as counselor and army chaplain in the company of Johann Casimir of the Palatinate.

Following the Peace of Longjumeau on March 23, 1568, the Prince of Orange sent Dathenus to Basel, Bern, Zurich, and Schaffhausen to provide financial support for the Dutch Revolt. Dathenus was chairman of the Convent of Wezel, after which he was finally able to work for approximately one

Frederick III welcomed the Calvinists expelled from the
Netherlands and in 1572 founded for them the new city of Frankenthal
(nineteenth-century print from an old painting)

year in the church in Frankenthal. During this time, an especially cordial bond had grown between Elector Frederick and Dathenus. Dathenus was probably appointed court chaplain prior to January 1570, and he moved from Frankenthal to Heidelberg. He continued to look after the interests of the Dutch church with the same zeal as before. Along with Olevianus, he promoted the Calvinist form of church discipline in the Palatinate. In 1571, at the request of the elector, Dathenus played an important role in religious discussions between Frankenthal and the Anabaptists.

For the next two years, Dathenus was preoccupied with political activities. In the fall of 1572, he traveled to Holland and Zeeland as commissary of the prince, mainly to reorganize church property. In the course of this business, he visited Dort in October and Delft in November of 1573. Activities on behalf of the elector of the Palatinate took Dathenus to Switzerland and England in 1573.

A year later, Dathenus accompanied Louis of Nassau on his military campaign, although he probably missed the defeat near Mook. In various religious and political matters, he was consulted by both the elector and the landgrave of Hesse. Dathenus played an important role in the marriage between William of Orange and Charlotte de Bourbon. The prince called him in 1575 as court chaplain, but Dathenus remained the court chaplain of Elector Frederick until the latter's death on October 26, 1576, although he spent very little time in Heidelberg.

At the time of the changing of the guard in the Palatinate, Dathenus's connection with the court came to an end. The new elector, Louis VI—a strict Lutheran—had no use for Dathenus and consequently dismissed him. Johann Casimir, who also inherited part of his father's territory, sympathized with the refugees from Holland and took Dathenus along on a military campaign to France. In May 1577, Dathenus resumed his ministry in Frankenthal. At this time, Dathenus may have traveled to the Netherlands. At any rate, in June 1578 he was nominated by the churches of the Palatinate to be their delegate to the Synod of Dort, where he was chosen as chairman. Shortly thereafter, he visited Antwerp, Kortrijk, and Utrecht. He also ministered in Amsterdam and in the Church of Saint Bavo in Ghent.

The prince wanted Dathenus in Antwerp rather than Ghent. Difficulties emerged in Ghent when Dathenus took up a position that was opposed to that of William of Orange. From the pulpit, the preacher accused the prince of having neither God nor religion; he claimed that the prince switched religious convictions as readily as clothing. On several fronts, Dathenus worked at cross purposes with the prince. Differences in political insight at the local, national, and international levels played an important role in this regard. According to Dathenus, the government should have promoted the Reformed religion, a view that ran counter to the freedom of religion that the prince supported. In December 1578, freedom of religion was also introduced in Ghent, and Dathenus was forced to leave. His relationship with the prince had been permanently damaged, despite the hopes and attempts of individuals and ecclesiastical assemblies to reconcile the two.

In August 1579, Dathenus returned to work in Frankenthal. Various shadows fell across his subsequent years. His health deteriorated. Beginning in January 1582, he made efforts to be released from service. After initial refusal by the consistory, approval was granted in May. Many doubt that Dathenus was really as worn out as he wanted people to believe. Did he perhaps seek to free up time for political pursuits?

Following a stay in Frankfurt, Dathenus returned to Ghent in December 1583. His sojourn there ended in a political fiasco because of differences of opinion regarding France. Following his departure from Ghent, he increasingly clashed with regents and provincial councils of the Northern Netherlands as a result of his political pronouncements from the pulpit, as occurred in Gouda. It is from this perspective that we should view an order for his imprisonment. Dathenus spent time in custody in Vianen, Vreeswijk, and Utrecht. On December 28, 1583 or 1584, he was released from prison after a lengthy hearing in Utrecht; from there he traveled via Amsterdam to northern Germany.

The concluding phase of Dathenus's life is veiled in uncertainty and obscurity, probably for two reasons. It was a period of great instability for Dathenus in a political and social as well as a theological and spiritual sense. Furthermore, information about this phase of his life is limited and has been variously interpreted. He earned his living under the pseudonym Petrus Montanus, probably in Husum and Elbing as a physician and general practitioner and a grammar school teacher. After mid-1585, he lived in Staden near Danzig. It is believed that during this time, Dathenus entertained the ideas of the Anabaptist leader David Joris (1501–1556). Rumors to this effect circulated in the Netherlands and were subsequently investigated by the Synod of The Hague (1568). Dathenus attributed this thinking to severe illness and disappointment over the manner in which he had been treated in the Netherlands.

Nevertheless, Dathenus continued to bear testimony to God's grace. His doctrinal return to the Reformed confession led to his desire to resume his former profession, to the extent that his health allowed. There initially appeared to be an opening for him in England, but Dathenus turned down this request. Subsequently, he was asked to help establish a refugee church at Danzig, where the local magistrate appeared prepared to make available a church facility to those of the Low German Reformed persuasion. In view of the opposition from the citizenry, Dathenus considered it advisable to decline this position also.

In the end, Dathenus settled in Elbing. He was respected by his fellow citizens, lived in relative poverty, and eventually died there.

Herman Faukelius, author of the Compendium

Herman Faukelius was born around 1560 at Bruges, where his father held citizenship rights. It appears that his parents were already members of the Reformed Church. Nothing else is known about his youth. In 1580, Faukelius attended the preparatory school in Ghent. He began studies at Leiden on June 28, 1583. On October 22, 1584, he registered at the University of Heidelberg. Petrus Dathenus registered there the following day, but it is unclear in what capacity. It is possible that Faukelius and Dathenus already knew each other in Ghent.

In 1585, Faukelius received a call from the Dutch church in Cologne. He left the University of Heidelberg in September 1585, and he was present for the first time at a classis meeting in Cologne on October 8. We know this information from the acts of the classis meeting that was held at Aachen on April 16, 1585. At the latter meeting, the examination of Faukelius was brought up by the Dutch church of Cologne. It was reported that this matter

Herman Faukelius

had been pending for half a year already, with the result that Faukelius was not yet authorized to administer the sacraments. Classis then determined the procedure to be followed. The municipal church and the Walloon church would each appoint two ministers to attend his trial sermon "and determine the result of the examination on behalf of the entire synod."[26]

Faukelius made personal notes of how this examination of July 31, 1586 transpired. The municipal church was represented by its ministers of the Word accompanied by two elders. The Walloon church had sent its minister accompanied by two elders, and the Dutch church had sent two elders and a deacon. Following the presentation of his trial sermon, Faukelius was examined and deemed qualified to serve as minister. The following day, August 1, 1586, he was inducted into the church at Cologne by Johannes Badius. We know from the acts of classis (Aachen, April 8, 1587) that Faukelius was instructed to write to the University of Leiden to identify a suitable person to fill a vacancy in the area of Münster. Faukelius preached a sermon to the brethren at a meeting in Aachen on September 30, 1587. It was thoroughly discussed "and necessary improvements were brought to his attention by the chairman Johannes Badius, in a friendly manner."[27] At the synod meeting in Aachen on March 15, 1589, Faukelius was chosen as assessor (committee member-at-large).

Faukelius was called to Middelburg in 1594, but it was not until 1599 that the Cologne consistory released him. He was subsequently able to serve Middelburg for over 25 years. He was gifted in many areas and made the most of those gifts. In 1604, he became army chaplain for Prince Maurice. As an opponent of Arminius, Faukelius was involved in a preparatory meeting held at The Hague in 1607. There he declared himself opposed to a revision of the Belgic Confession of Faith and the Catechism, entirely in line with the position of the churches and the Provincial Council of Zeeland.

Faukelius served the church in various capacities: as a Bible translator, as an apologist attacking Anabaptists and Arminians, as a delegate and assessor of the Synod of Dort in 1618–1619, as a publisher of the Belgic Confession of Faith, and as an author of catechetical texts. He was also responsible for the management of matters pertaining to the East India churches. He remained fully active in the church virtually to the very end of his life. He died on May 9, 1625.

Faukelius's connection with the Catechism goes back to an early date. As

---

26. "ende wijder die examination ende confirmation in namen des ganschen Synodi hiermedt soude opgeleght werden"

27. "ende wat daerin te verbeteren van noode was, is hem door den praesident, Johannes Badius, vriendlick angeseydt worden"

early as March 2, 1583, he defended eighteen theses derived from the Heidelberg Catechism at the illustrious preparatory school in Ghent. Faukelius's edition of *Kort begrip der Christelijke Religie voor die sich willen begeven tot des Heeren Heilig Avondmaal* (Compendium of the Christian Religion for Those Who Seek Admission to the Lord's Supper) appeared in 1608. For this work, Faukelius drew on earlier work done by Caspar van der Heyden. This booklet was first used in Middelburg, and it was officially introduced in Zeeland in 1611. Faukelius's work on the publication of the Heidelberg Catechism (Middelburg, 1611) is of definite importance.

At the Synod of Dort of 1618–1619, Faukelius presented himself as a moderate person with an infralapsarian view, a perspective that was not appreciated by everyone. Some believe that it was because of his influence that the Canons of Dort were not worded quite as strongly as they might have been. Faukelius frequently worked together with Antonius Walaeus.

In Middelburg in 1621, Faukelius published *Babel, dat is verwerringhe der Wederdooperen onder malkander* (Babel, or Confusion among Anabaptists). The author appreciated the Anabaptist emphasis on the sanctification of life, and from this perspective he held them up as an example. Although he advocated tolerance towards them, he rejected their doctrine after thorough study.

Ecclesiastical recognition of the Catechism

To understand properly the ecclesiastical recognition of the Heidelberg Catechism, it is necessary to trace the decisions made by the various Reformed synodical assemblies that were held principally in Holland and Zeeland in the sixteenth and seventeenth centuries. This string of events began in Wezel (1568) and ran through Emden (1571) to Dort (1619). Again, we recognize the crucial role of the refugee churches in providing leadership.

Wezel 1568

In recent years, the Convent of Wezel has returned to the center of attention, especially over whether it was indeed held in the German town by this name. This council produced articles that deal with the Heidelberg Catechism; its third chapter is dedicated to the subject. Article 2 leaves open the question of whether catechism teaching should be based on the Geneva Catechism, for the Dutch and Walloon churches, or on the Heidelberg Catechism, for the German churches. "However, we leave this up to these churches until the next synod." In these articles, much attention is given to the catechetical instruction of young people.

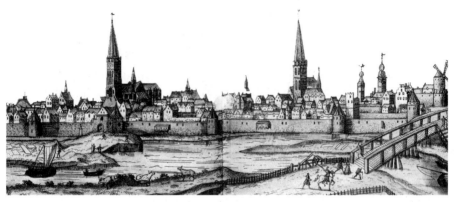

Wezel (Braun and Hogenberg, *Civitates Orbis Terrarum*, 1572)

Emden 1571

The Synod of Emden (1571) followed the spirit of the Convent of Wezel in addressing the use of the Catechism in French- and German-speaking churches (article 5). For churches using the Low German language, the Heidelberg Catechism was recommended but not mandatory.

Dort 1574

In the Acts of the Synod of Dort of 1574, we find a further clarification regarding the use of the Catechism. Having read the articles of Emden, the synod decided on June 16, 1574, "that a single catechism be used in all churches of the province; furthermore, that this be the Heidelberg Catechism; thirdly, that formally only this catechism be memorized, and that ministers should also present the Brief Inquiry [Micron, 1553] in its main points."[28] This meeting also discussed a catechism and a church order produced by Godefridus van Winghen and presented to synod, to be printed following approval. The churches decided "to retain the usual catechism and order published with the Psalms."[29] The Synod of 1574 also determined that after a celebration of the Lord's Supper, a catechism sermon would normally be preached in the afternoon. This synod also recognized that ministers of the Word were to ensure that schoolmasters endorse the Belgic Confession of Faith, subject themselves to the church order, and teach young people the Catechism.

In 1574, the synod was also presented with a question from the Classis of

---

28. "Datmen eenerlei Catechismum in allen Kercken der Pouincie houden sal. Ten anderen dat dit sal wesen de Heidelbersche [sic] Catechismus. Ten derden datmen desen Catechismum alleen opentlicken sal leeren, ended dat de Dienaers in het besondert t'cort Ondersoeck den sommighen voorhouden mueghen."

29. "bij de 'ghewoonlicken Catechismo ende ordeninghe bijden Psalmen ghedruckt te blijuen"

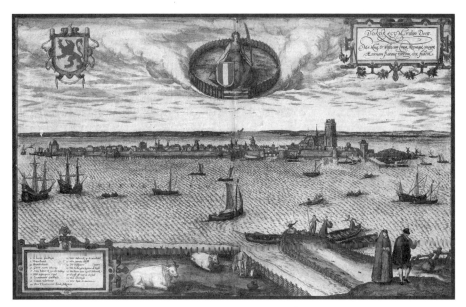

Dort (Braun and Hogenberg, *Civitates Orbis Terrarum*, 1575)

Walcheren: Is it a good idea to produce printed sermons on the Catechism? Synod appeared to support such a practice. Ministers were to take turns expounding one or two questions of the Catechism; this practice would sharpen the mind and thus enhance the quality of catechism preaching in the churches. Reference was also made to the "brief inquiry for those who join the church of Christ, prepared by Marten Micron, to be used for the instruction of children depending on people's needs."[30]

Dort 1578
The Synod of Dort of 1578 also addressed doctrine, the sacraments, and ceremonies. Great importance was attached to unanimity in doctrine. In this regard, the Belgic Confession of Faith, which had been republished in 1578, played an important role. Its thirty-seven articles had to be endorsed by ministers, professors, and elders. Chapter 4, article 2, of the acts of this synod refer to the use in German churches of the Heidelberg Catechism and the Psalms translated by Petrus Dathenus. The Walloon churches used the Catechism published with the French Psalms. Synod also gave the German churches permission "to use the Brief Inquiry concerning faith based on the

---

30. "corte ondersoeck der ghener die hen tot the Gemeente Christi begeuven, door Martinum Micronium gemaeckt, in de plaetse der kinderleere nae geleghenheyt des volckx te gebruycken"

Catechism"[31] that was printed with the Psalms of Dathenus for the instruction of those "who join the church."[32]

Concerning the administration of the Lord's Supper, the Synod of Dort decided that preaching on the basis of the Catechism would take place during the afternoon service. It adopted the approach of the 1574 Synod of Dort and determined in chapter 4, article 16: "But in the afternoon the usual sermon based on the Catechism will proceed."[33]

Middelburg 1581
In 1581, the Synod of Middelburg published "Particular Questions," which underscore the approach adopted by the 1578 Synod of Dort for the use of the Catechism in public worship services. There are small textual differences in the language of the two synods. The 1581 Synod of Middelburg decided that the catechism of Caspar van der Heyden should no longer be used. The *Corte Memorien* (Short Summary) of the Middelburg synodical acts mention a task for Jeremias Bastingius and the Classis of Walcheren. The latter "will prepare exegetical sermons on the catechism of our churches."[34] This approach is somewhat different from the one taken by the 1574 Synod of Dort in response to the question from the Classis of Walcheren about printed sermons. Concerning regulations regarding the Lord's Supper, the Synod of Middelburg took a less stringent position regarding catechism preaching than did the 1574 and 1578 Synods of Dort. Brabant had asked about retaining the former policy, and synod now indicated that in the afternoon service of thanksgiving, one could profitably preach on something other than the Catechism. Thus, churches were left free in this regard.

This synod was also asked by Haarlem and Overijssel if it would be advisable "to produce a summary of the Catechism, as Olevianus had done."[35] For small children at Latin school, the Middelburg Synod recognized an effective middle ground: the summary of the Catechism written by Theodore Beza and published in both Greek and Latin. But this pedagogical recommendation probably still caused the little children quite a few headaches!

The Hague 1586
The 1586 Synod of The Hague recognized a role for consistories in the su-

---

31. "het corte ondersoeck des geloofs wt den catechismo to same ghetrocken"
32. "die hen totter ghemeynte begheuen"
33. "Dogh na den middag salmen met de ghewoonlicke predicatie ofte catechismo voortvaren."
34. "sullen maecken exegemata ouer den catechismum onser kercken"
35. een summa des catechismi te maecken, als Oleuianus gedaen heeft

pervision of schoolmasters (article 19). This provision pertained not only to reading and writing, "but also godliness and the teaching of the Catechism."[36] In article 61, this synod also dealt with the place of the Heidelberg Catechism in the afternoon service, in which ministers had to explain briefly the summary of Christian doctrine contained in the Catechism and adopted by the Dutch churches. At this synod, the churches of South Holland expressed a need for what the 1581 Synod of Middelburg had in mind with the *Exegemata supra Catechismus* (exegetical sermons on the Catechism), and they put pressure on the synod of 1586 to promote this work.

Dort 1618–1619
In the years leading up to this synod, some theologians and politicians advised a revision of the confessional documents. Arguments on the side of the Remonstrants were usually cloaked in a veil of obfuscation that was purposely maintained by prominent people such as Hugo Grotius and Van Oldenbarnevelt.

Remonstrant objections
The Synod of Dort now demanded clarity of content from the Remonstrants. On December 21, 1618, the Remonstrants submitted a document dealing with the Belgic Confession of Faith; one week later, they submitted another concerning the Heidelberg Catechism. Synod explicitly inquired about the relationship between these concerns and those submitted earlier to the Provincial Council of Holland. The chief issues raised earlier were now presented in greater detail. The Remonstrant objections primarily concerned the general role of confessional documents. How much authority did they have relative to Scripture? How much leeway was there in interpreting the confessional documents, and how could one prevent a slavish adherence to them? Remonstrants sought a solution to their questions through relativization and obfuscation of the confessional statements. They submitted a long list of reservations about the Heidelberg Catechism. A number of delegates from abroad, however, were not impressed with this list. The questions pertained to the creation of man according to God's image and the essence, implications, and knowledge of sin—questions that implied important differences with the Catechism. The delegate from Heidelberg requested a copy of the Remonstrant objections; this was understandable, because his town was the cradle of the Catechism.

---

36. maer oock die selfde inder Godtsalicheyt ende inden Catechismo onderwijsen

The opening of the National Synod at Dort in 1618, according to a drawing by François Schillemans

This, in fact, settled the matter. Procedural questions continued to be discussed until the Remonstrants were expelled from synod on January 14, 1619.

Ecclesiastical examination

At the request of Parliament, the Catechism was examined and reviewed at the 147th and 148th sessions of synod, as had previously been done with the Belgic Confession of Faith. Both sessions were held on May 1, 1619, in the morning and the afternoon, respectively. The examination focused on the conformity of the Catechism to God's Word. All questions and answers of the Catechism were read, and everyone was encouraged to express his views. In the afternoon session, there was great unanimity among both national and international theologians concerning the agreement of the Heidelberg Catechism in every sense with the Word of God. There appeared to be no need to change anything.

The acts of the synod contain laudatory statements concerning the content, character, and usefulness of the Heidelberg Catechism.

Focus on catechism teaching

It may easily be forgotten that the Synod of Dort did not occupy itself only with doctrinal questions. According to the acts, catechism teaching received ample attention, beginning with the fifteenth session on November 28, 1618. National and international theologians participated in discussions on catechetical matters. The Heidelberg Catechism received considerable praise on more than one occasion. In their view, it contained a wealth of material for reflection on catechism teaching and its place at home, at school, and in worship services. Didactic advice was offered on age categories, the partition of lengthy responses, the need for repetition, incentives for encouragement, the need to maintain order in church services, and so forth. The important role of parents in religious education was highlighted, as were the role of magistrates and the importance of giving a good example. In preparation for marriage, the presentation of children for baptism, and the celebration of the Lord's Supper, the content of faith was to be tested and discussed. The Emden delegates referred to the historical background of the Catechism; it reminded them of the catechetical work of Jan Łaski.

In its seventeenth session on November 30, 1618, the Synod of Dort made decisions regarding catechism teaching. Synod made reference to a shorter catechism for the youngest children and a short one for children in the next age group, as was prescribed in the Palatinate and in the churches of Middelburg. Several ministers (Gomarus, Polyander, Thysius, Faukelius, Lydius, and Udemans) were appointed to draft this short catechism.

In the acts, we read a report of the 177th session at which proposals for both of these abridged catechisms were discussed. The shorter of the two, for the youngest catechism students, was read and had to be expanded at certain points. The other catechism, intended for the intermediate age group, was not read aloud because it would have taken too long, according to the chairman. The synod decided to leave the use of the various catechisms open "so that the churches could either use these, or the one that had been produced and published by the church of Middelburg." The latter was a reference to Faukelius's *Compendium*.

Assessment

Initially, delegates raised the question of which catechism ought to be used. For the German-speaking churches, this eventually became the Heidelberg Catechism. Other catechisms, such as that of Caspar van der Heyden, stood no chance. The name of Dathenus was closely connected with the publication of the Heidelberg Catechism; his influence must have been decisive in determining that it was the catechism of the German-speaking region and not that of Geneva that prevailed.

Reflection on the preaching of the Catechism was an important theme of the early Reformed synods. Thus the Synod of The Hague of 1568 pronounced itself explicitly in favor of preaching on the Heidelberg Catechism in afternoon services, in the form of an annual cycle. In part because of a request of Parliament, the Synod of Dort (1618–1619) made an explicit pronouncement concerning the scriptural nature of the Heidelberg Catechism, and it reviewed in great detail the importance and practice of catechism teaching on the basis of the Heidelberg Catechism. This established a trend for the subsequent centuries.

Use and impact of the Catechism

We cannot do justice to ecclesiastical recognition of the Heidelberg Catechism by merely summarizing the outcome of the various Reformed synodical assemblies. We also must consider regional and local details to sharpen the image. We review such aspects as catechism teaching at church and at school, the Catechism as a form of unity, and criticism of the Catechism in the doctrinal fight between Remonstrants and Contra-Remonstrants.

Catechism teaching in church and school

It is obvious from the acts of early classis meetings in the Northern Netherlands that decisions concerning the Catechism made at national synods were not conscientiously implemented in local churches as a matter of course.

At a meeting held in Gorinchem in October 1573, the Classis of Dort considered whether the Heidelberg Catechism was actually being taught in all churches. The answer was encouraging: for all the churches represented there, the Catechism was invariably being taught. It probably was not without cause that at subsequent classis meetings this topic kept resurfacing and the necessity of teaching the Catechism to young people was continually emphasized.

The classis meeting at Schoonhoven, held on August 3, 1574, brought up catechetical instruction in schools. All the brethren confirmed that this was indeed taking place. Furthermore, they made reference to the examination of students from the pulpit, although in this respect there appeared to be less conformity. Nevertheless, the classis recommended that such examinations be strictly maintained.

During a classis meeting at Dort in 1575, the church at Gouda appeared to be out of step in this regard. The magistrate had dismissed the schoolmaster, "with the result that catechism teaching had ground to a halt." The classis admonished the Gouda ministers to carry on with catechism preaching "even if they might have only a single child respond."[37] In this way, the classis underscored the importance of the preaching and teaching of the Catechism. At subsequent classis meetings in 1576–1578, local practice remained on the agenda. During this period, the observations at classis remained largely positive. For example, according to the Classis of Dort in May 1578, everything in this regard "went reasonably well."[38]

How accurate was this picture? At the classis meeting at Strijen in June 1579, a different story was told. The familiar question about faithfulness in Sunday catechism preaching was answered with these words: "Well, in some cases, it has not been done for a long time."[39] Although the affected brethren were in a position to identify the causes, the classis unanimously decided that in the future, every church was to use the Heidelberg Catechism. Practices at Westmaas and Zwijndrecht were unsatisfactory in this regard. In Sliedrecht and Wijngaarden, there was not even a church; no alms were collected, and there was no school. There, the Heidelberg Catechism must have remained largely unknown.

The acts of the classis meeting held at Dort on July 22, 1597, offer insight into the situation surrounding catechism preaching. We come across relevant information in a visitation report. Visits had shown "that on Sunday afternoons no instruction occurred in some places,"[40] even where residents showed an interest. The classis subsequently admonished preachers among the brethren "to preach on the Catechism on Sunday afternoons, even if they might only be addressing five or six people."[41] The classis indicated that catechism preaching might be a problem in multipoint parishes.[42]

The Classis of the Lower Veluwe that assembled in Putten on April 25, 1598, and at Elburg on July 18, 1599, undertook to introduce catechism preaching in rural areas. This classis was continually preoccupied with former Roman Catholic priests who refused to accept the teachings of the Heidelberg Catechism. These cases proved to be long, drawn-out affairs, as was the situation involving Peregrinus van Heerde (also known as Pelegrinus or Pilgrim), who was a parish priest at Vaassen.

Interest in catechism preaching at classis meetings also focused on trial sermons. On December 3, 1612, Reverend Gualterus Busius presented his

37. "of sij oock maer een kint tot antwoorden mochten hebben"
38. "gaet overall redelijcken toe"
39. "Ja, doch bij sommigen een tijt lanck nyet"
40. "dat des sondags namiddach in sommige plaetsen niet geleert wort"
41. "den catechismus des namiddags te prediken, al souden zij oock voor vijf ofte ses menschen leeren"
42. In a multipoint parish, a minister served more than one community.

A Protestant church service (Pieter de Bloot, 1624)

sermon proposal at the Classis of Middelburg; it was decided that at the next meeting of classis, Reverend Jac. Walaeus of Meliskerke would speak on question 57, which deals with the resurrection of the dead. At the opening of the Classis of Middelburg on November 2, 1620, Ephraim Wante presented his sermon proposal on questions 86 and 87 of the Heidelberg Catechism. His sermon met with the approval of the brethren. At the conclusion of the meeting, it was decided that Paesschier de Meester would present a sermon proposal on the next questions of the Heidelberg Catechism.

Beginning in September 1619, the Classis of Deventer sought agreement for "a definite, common date to begin catechism preaching,"[43] in line with the decision of synod. On July 18, 1620, this classis decided that catechism preaching should commence in all churches on August 13, 1620. This preaching was to be preceded by a special notice, one week prior to this date, "to ensure its success."[44] When questioned at the meeting of October 10–11, 1620, the brethren indicated that they had held to the agreement "and that they also discerned the Lord's blessing in this necessary and Christian

43. "eenen seeckeren dach op denwelcke men die cathegismum tegelijcke anvange te predicken"
44. "updattet mit merdere frucht moge affgaan"

work."[45] The churches were expected to carry on this work and realized that the decree so frequently promised by the authorities unfortunately appeared to be delayed. This implied a role for delegates to synod. At this particular session, Reverend Johannes van Alcmade pointed out that as a result of a required trip, he would be unable to preach on the Catechism for a stretch of time. Classis accepted this as a legitimate reason.

The organization of the teaching ministry
On December 3, 1591, the Classis of Dort made reference to "the reading of the Shorter Catechism"[46] (possibly Micron's Brief Inquiry) prior to the "morning service"[47] and to preaching on the Catechism in weekday services. The classis clearly offered some flexibility in this regard: "All are encouraged to do their best and to see how God will bless such efforts."[48] In 1592, this classis considered the question raised by the church at Breda of whether the examination of young people on the Catechism could also be performed by an elder or a schoolmaster. This practice was not considered to be inappropriate,[49] but the minister could not be left out of the picture entirely. Permission was granted "so long as one or two of them would recite their memory work to the minister for the sake of uniformity with other churches."[50] Thus, instruction of children in the faith retained an important place in a church's worship service.

The Classis of the Lower Veluwe, which met at Harderwijk on April 13, 1594, mentioned that the traditional practice of children's reciting the Catechism in church ought to be reestablished. At the classis meetings of May 20 and September 23, 1595, the church at Harderwijk was admonished to conform to this practice.

The Classis of Dort, which met on July 16–17, 1619, at Maasdam, considered the question of whether the text of Holy Scripture ought to be read first in services of instruction, or only the relevant passage of the Heidelberg Catechism. It was decided that classis should be guided "by what synod shall reject or approve."[51] The Regional Synod of Leiden, which met during the summer of 1619, achieved unanimity for South Holland on this point by

---

45. "ende dat sie ock den segen des Heren in dit notigh ende christelick werck spueren"
46. "het lesen des cleynen Catechismi"
47. "des voormiddags"
48. "Is een iegelick bevolen sijn beste te doen en te besien, wat vruchten Godt geven wil."
49. "niet onstichtelijk"
50. "mits dat een oft twee voor den predikant reciteren om de gelijckformicheyt met andere kerken"
51. "nae 't geene dat het synodus sal arresteeren of goet vinden"

means of article 84, which provided that "first a suitable passage of Holy
Scripture that corresponds to the question and answer will be read, and only
then the question and answer that is to be expounded."[52]

Schoolmasters and the Catechism

The Classis of Dort decided on September 6, 1583, that if there were no
qualified local schoolmasters, ministers should take charge of teaching the
Catechism to young people, to the extent that their workload permitted. One
had to make the most of limited resources and time. This assembly was conscious of the necessity of instruction "in the fear of the Lord."[53]

Schoolmasters did not universally appreciate having to teach catechism
classes. In 1587, tensions arose in Hendrik-Ido-Ambacht and Rijsoord. The
schoolmaster there even stood to lose students "because he intended to teach
the Catechism."[54] The classis meeting at Dort instructed Gillis Tavenier to
admonish the parents in this regard.

A meeting of the Classis of Rotterdam on November 24, 1586, saw a
role for government in the promotion of catechism teaching at school and in

---

52. "Eerst een bequaem text der H. Schriftuijre, waerop de vrage ende antwoorde
passen, sal voorgeleesen worden ende daerna eerst de vrage en antwoorde, die verclaert sullen
worden."
53. "in der vresen des Heeren"
54. "overmits hij se wil de Catechismum leeren"

A school class in the seventeenth century

church. This is precisely what Anabaptists sought to prevent for their children. From the Classis meeting of June 27, 1594, we learn that brethren from Delfshaven were admonished to provide good education, including instruction in the Catechism, "since the school is unlikely to send children to church and to have them recite the Catechism."[55]

Problems associated with the Remonstrant view of the Belgic Confession of Faith and the Catechism were encountered in connection with some teachers. The classis meeting held at Hillegersberg on January 6, 1620, mentioned such problems with schoolmaster Sebastiaen of Hillegersberg. Having been questioned at this meeting, this teacher admitted that he had difficulty with question 60, which concerns justification. For this reason, he could not subscribe to the Acts of Synod (Canons) and the Catechism. The classis took note of this and documented his refusal.

The Classis of South Beveland, which met on January 7, 1585, instructed brethren De Volder and De Smet to admonish the schoolmaster of Serraeskercke, a task that was done successfully: "He desires to execute the duties of his office with respect to the reformation of the school and the teaching of the Catechism with greater diligence than he has done to date."[56]

At Middelburg on April 28, 1610, the Classis of Walcheren raised the need to address the supervision of instruction in the schools at the upcoming Regional Synod of Veere on May 15. Objections from schoolmasters to catechism teaching could not be tolerated. The same classis considered questions raised by the Classis of Tholen over the approach to catechism teaching, such as a shorter catechism for the instruction of children. However, they did not want to tamper with Sunday afternoon catechism preaching.

The Veluwe region frequently had trouble with sextons and schoolmasters who were reluctant to accept Reformed doctrine. This situation hindered the teaching of the Heidelberg Catechism, as evidenced by the acts of the June 2, 1596, meeting of the Classis of Harderwijk. Problems were mentioned in connection with Oldebroek and Nunspeet.

For many years the Classis of the Lower Veluwe had to deal not only with the rector of Vaassen mentioned earlier, but also with the local schoolmaster, a Jesuit. According to the acts of classis that cover its April 12–13, 1608, sessions, Pastor Peregrinus and the schoolmaster led both young and old into superstition and sin.

---

55. "also aldaer weijnich ordre is in de schoole om de kinderen ter kercke to brengen ende den catechismum op te zeggen"

56. "Hy wil syn officie in 't reformeren der schole ende in 't leeren van den catechismo neerstelicker uutvoeren dan hy tot noch toe ghedaen heeft."

The Classis of Nijkerk, which met on June 3–4, 1612, dealt in great depth with the desirability of good education. The discussions repeatedly mentioned instruction in the Heidelberg Catechism. If catechism teaching were to fail in the schools, it would have grave consequences for ecclesiastical instruction.

Schoolmasters reprimanded

Since it is found that young people are very much hampered in instruction unto godliness through neglect by inept and ignorant schoolmasters, especially in rural areas, this Christian classis admonishes ministers of the Word and consistories to pay close attention to schools, in accordance with the decisions of various national and provincial synods, endorsed by the highest levels of government. Young people should be instructed by their teachers not only in languages and the fine arts, but also in the Christian Catechism, in order to be able to recite the latter in church on Sundays. If there are any ignorant parents who do not wish to see their children thus instructed and for this reason trouble the schoolmasters, the latter must seek to persuade such parents with solid reasoning, or to accompany them in visiting their ministers to be further enlightened by them. And if there are found to be any schoolmasters who frequently dispute the Catechism in person, despising or rejecting it, or who otherwise through neglect cause the Catechism not to be taught to young people in the schools, as a result of which its use, and also its recital in front of the pulpit in church, would diminish or disappear altogether, the consistory concerned will take corrective action and, if this will not improve the situation, report this to the highest level of government so that the school will be provided with better and more qualified school functionaries. In this regard, a number of written complaints have been lodged against the schoolmasters of Nijkerk on behalf of the local church. Both of them, having been summoned and having been read the rules twice, have promised classis with a handshake to do their best and their utmost in this regard.

From the Acts of the Classis of Nijkerk, June 3–4, 1612

A form of unity

In connection with classical examinations, the Acts of the Synod of Dort refer to agreement with and subscription to both the Belgic Confession of Faith and the Heidelberg Catechism. Such agreement was also expected from ministers transferring from another classis. We wonder whether all those affected actually knew what they agreed with. For example, in November 1607, a candidate for examination, Cornelis Hanecop, was called to Brandwijk; he had never yet read the thirty-seven articles of the Belgic Confession of Faith. He was given another month to do so. In July 1608, it appeared that a candidate named Celosse had never even seen them. Classis was quite disturbed about this. We read, "The question is raised whether, when those who are newly admitted to the service of the church are given time to read the 37 articles and the Catechism on reception as members by this classis, they should not much rather read the same within the time span of 14 days during which they prepare themselves for the examination."[57]

The Classis of Dort

In the Classis of Dort, it was noticed towards the end of 1610 that questions about four newly admitted ministers were being raised as to "whether they themselves intellectually and emotionally, in common with the church, are comfortable with the Christian Catechism and the Belgic Confession."[58] If they entertained different views in this regard, they had to promise "to communicate this to the brethren in hopes of setting at ease those who were ill at ease with this."[59]

In connection with the examination of three candidates in July 1611, the Acts of the Classis of Dort report in considerable detail the questions asked of two brethren who were admitted to the Christian ministry concerning their agreement with and subscription to the Belgic Confession of Faith and the Catechism. At the same time, close attention was given to the potential for diverging views in the future. Explicit assurances regarding pure doctrine were built in at the time of admission to the Christian ministry.

The line of agreement with and subscription to the confessional statements at the time of examinations and similar occasions is subsequently readily traceable in the Acts of the Classis of Dort.

Even following the Synod of Dort, the Classis of Dort had trouble persuading every minister to subscribe to the two confessional statements

---

57. Is voorgestelt een sekere vraege of men diegene die tot den dienst der kercke van nieus opgenomen worden, sal tijt vergunnen om de 37 artyckelen ende den catechismum te lesen als sij in de classe worden opgenomen tot lidmaten derselver, of sij niet veel meer deselve behooren te overlesen binnen den tijt van die 14 dagen in dewelcke sij haer praepareren tot het examen.

58. of sij haerselven niet gerust en vinden in 't verstant ende gemeyn gevoelen der kerke over den christelijcken catechismum ende Nederlansche confessie.

59. met de broeders te communiceren op hope van de ongeruste gerust te stellen.

referred to above. This did not primarily concern the content of the Belgic Confession of Faith, the Heidelberg Catechism, and the Canons of Dort, but mainly the Acts of the Regional Synod of South Holland. Some ministers, such as Abraham van der Mijle of Papendrecht in November 1619, requested time for reflection on the acts. Timothy Wijckentoorn, minister at Mijnsheerenland, initially indicated having a problem with the acts of the regional synod, but he belatedly subscribed to them. Subsequently, the Classis of Dort made sure that those absent from the crucial meeting signed in due time. The classis was still engaged in this process at the time of the meeting held at Klaaswaal in April 1620. There appear to have been a number of ministers who were not prepared to subscribe to the form prescribed by the national synod; their problem concerned this particular form and not the content of the confessional statements themselves. They appealed to special exceptions and exemptions purportedly granted to them at an earlier date by the classis or its committee members. These exceptions were not recognized by the Classis of Dort at this time or at any time in the future, and the synodical requirement was maintained.

The Classis of Rotterdam
Initially, the Acts of the Classis of Rotterdam/Schieland refer to subscription by ministers to the Belgic Confession of Faith only; such a reference was made as early as July 4, 1581, at the meeting at Charlois, and again in November 1584. Subscription to the Belgic Confession of Faith was at issue in the transfer of a minister from another classis and also following the examination and admission of new candidates. It is noteworthy that in this classis, no reference was made to subscription to the Catechism between 1581 and 1584. The acts of this classis present a consistent picture in this regard. Ministers and candidates subscribed only to the thirty-seven articles; in this connection, the church order and the classical regulations—for example, those dealing with the care of widows—were nearly always included. Thus, ministers also committed themselves to contribute to the well-being of widows.

Only after April 1605 do we notice in the Acts of the Classis of Rotterdam that subscription to the Catechism began to play an explicit role. Then all brethren were requested to declare "that they remain steadfast by the doctrine of the Catechism and the 37 articles, signed by all of them."[60] The importance of the matter appears, among other things, from the following special meeting of this classis at Rotterdam on May 17, 1605. The matter of

---

60. "dat zij blijven volstandich bij de leere des catechismi ende den 37 artickelen by henlieden allen onderteekent"

subscription to the Catechism and the Belgic Confession of Faith arose again. It appears, however, that there was more at issue from the decision made by this classis. As an exercise in the chapters on Christian doctrine, two ministers were asked to formulate theses that were to be discussed and evaluated at classis. Even the tone of the exercise was prescribed: They "must proceed in all friendliness."[61] We read in the same acts that "our very own doctors sometimes disagree on these matters."[62] At the level of classis, commitment to the Catechism received increasing attention, in part due to the problems that emerged at the Leiden Academy between Arminius and Gomarus.

In connection with the tumultuous and contested examination of Simon Episcopius, conducted on September 27–28, 1610, during sessions of the Classis of Rotterdam, reference was made only to subscription to the Belgic Confession of Faith. In this examination, tensions mounted so high that delegates from five concerned churches left the meeting. When Episcopius, who entered the ministry at Bleiswijk, was granted membership in the classis on January 3, 1611, it was "on condition that he subscribe to the Belgic Confession and accept responsibilities similar to those of other brethren of the classis."[63]

Lack of clarity regarding the status of the Catechism within the Classis of Rotterdam lasted well into 1619. The classis meeting at Delfshaven on September 3, 1619, left little room for doubt when two ministers were admitted, namely, Reynout Sergerz. Donteclock of Poortugaal and Cornelis Jacobsz Pelanus of Charlois. We read that they both promised "to abide by the resolution of synod, in line with the teachings summarized in the Catechism and the Confession, and further to help bear the responsibilities of classis."[64] We see even greater precision in the formulations concerning subscription at the meeting of classis on October 7, 1619. The minister called to Rhoon was admitted as a member of classis on promising "to subscribe to the Confession, the Catechism, as well as the canons of the national synod held most recently at Dort."[65] At the same time, he was to share in all of the responsibilities of classis.

It is noteworthy that the Acts of Classis of 1620 revealed that subscription

---

61. "'t welc met alle vriendschap sal geschieden"
62. "doordien onse doctores daerin somwyle discorderen"
63. "mits conditie dat hij de Nederlansche confessie sal onderteekenen, ende draghen ghelycke lasten neffens andere broeders des classis"
64. "Beloovende beijde haer te dragen naer de resolutie des sijnodi, naer de leere sommierlyck vervatet in den catechismus ende confessie, ende voorts de lasten des classis te helpen dragen."
65. "de confessie, catechismum, mitsgaders de canones synodi nationalis laetst tot Dordrecht gehouden te onderteeckenen"

Simon Episcopius
(engraving by D. Petri, 1615)

to the Three Forms of Unity (the Belgic Confession of Faith, the Heidelberg Catechism, and the Canons of Dort) had not yet been fully implemented in all respects.

Critical examination

The recognition of the Catechism as a standard for pure doctrine was not achieved without pain. Although more than one classis explicitly referred to the role of the Catechism on a par with the Belgic Confession of Faith as early as 1605, actual subscription to the Catechism did not become common practice until after the Synod of Dort in the course of 1619.

The Classis of Dort

In order to bring the criticism leveled at the Heidelberg Catechism into sharper focus, we will follow the controversy surrounding this confessional statement in greater detail.

At times, criticism was limited to the way the Catechism was organized. For example, at the meeting of the Classis of Dort in April 1597, it was observed that "there are some unfortunate subdivisions of the Catechism into sections."[66] It was decided to bring this to the attention of the regional as well

---

66. "eenige quade affdeelinge zijn in den Catechismo"

as the provincial synods, to see "whether it might be worthwhile to request the general synod to do something about this."[67]

At the request of the regional synod, the classis meeting at Dort in November of 1606 sought to come up with a more substantial question concerning the Catechism: "whether they feel that there is anything that needs to be changed as far as the foundation and substance of its doctrine is concerned."[68] They were unanimous in their agreement with the Catechism and the Belgic Confession of Faith, and they saw no reason to change anything. Still, everyone was assigned the task of checking for anything that might have to be changed in "any way of speaking,"[69] and to bring this to the attention of classis at its next meeting. At the same meeting, Episcopius was instructed to write to Breda about the questions concerning the Catechism and the Confession of Faith indicated above.

At the classis meeting held in Westmaas on April 24–26, 1607, the brethren again declared that they could not identify anything that was in conflict with basic doctrine. However, two ministers—Abraham Costerus and Philippus Nisius—did have something of substance to report to classis. Costerus identified "some problems with Scripture references,"[70] and Nisius saw "an apparent conflict between questions 1 and 36."[71] They were instructed to submit any additional issues in writing to the next meeting of classis. Both ministers presented their remarks as requested. The submissions were to be reviewed and studied by classis representatives and ministers at Dort. Subsequent acts of classis reveal that Nisius was not comfortable with the views of the brethren. He indicated that he "would not press his views unduly,"[72] but he would be pleased to receive further clarification. Costerus openly declared that he had nothing fundamental against the Catechism or the Belgic Confession of Faith. At the meeting of December 1608, Nisius did not hide his desire that it was time his objections were addressed. Pastors Dibbetz and Lydius were asked to prepare notes on the issues raised by Nisius, and the latter was to appear at the January 1609 classis meeting "to confer with them."[73] Otherwise he was free to consult with members of the provincial

---

67. "off niet noodich en waer dat zulx het generaell synodus aengedient zoude worden om daerin te voorsien"

68. "Oft sij yet daerinne bevinden noodich omme verandert te sijne, den gront ende substantie der leere belangende."

69. "eenige wijse van spreken"

70. "eenige allegatiën der Schriftuerplaetsen"

71. "eenich discord so hem dunct tussen de eerste ende 36 vrage"

72. "niet hardelick te willen sijn voorstellinge dringen"

73. "met hem te confereren"

council; some correspondence to that effect was being considered by classis. As for potential objections, Nisius was advised to "send these to their lordships in a sealed envelope."[74] At the provincial council, such letters were saved up to be passed on to the regional synod in due time. It is noteworthy that in December 1608, the Classis of Dort raised objections about this practice of the provincial council. Their motivation was clear: "In our view the right of churches was thus very much compromised."[75] In line with synodical decisions, complaints had to go through classis, and the latter wished to adhere to this procedure.

A discussion on January 7, 1609, left Nisius unconvinced. Classis representatives felt that he was unable to substantiate his claims; nevertheless, he was unwilling to change his opinion. A conversation with him in the afternoon did not lead him to abandon his view. It was then decided to transfer the matter to the provincial synod. He received a reply by return mail that "he was forbidden to raise the issue from the pulpit or to discuss it with anyone either in private or in public."[76]

The ecclesiastical meetings made continued attempts to keep relations between churches and government authorities in the open. Thus the Classis of Dort (September 10–18, 1618) requested the provincial council to bring any objections lodged with it by certain ministers against the Catechism and the Belgic Confession of Faith to the Regional Synod of Delft to be held on October 8. It may be viewed as an amusing detail that the authorities in The Hague asked Joh. van Oldenbarnevelt in writing where these documents might be located. Van Oldenbarnevelt replied that he had received such objections, but that as a result of moving and some renovations he did not know precisely where they had been filed away. He indicated that they should be searched for in one of his three offices.

The Classis of Rotterdam

In its meeting on April 23, 1607, the Classis of Rotterdam focused on synod's decision "that everyone be obliged to report any concerns with respect to the Christian Catechism and the Belgic Confession."[77] The classis charged all brethren to bring their views to the next meeting. Concerning the meeting

---

74. "in besloten missive aan Haere Edele over te seynden"

75. "Overmits onses bedunckens daermede het recht der kercken seer wert gecrenct."

76. "Hem is oock verboden dese questie op den predicstoel te brengen ofte met ymant daervan te spreken in 't heymelijck oft in 't openbaer."

77. "dat een igelijck sal gehouden sijn in te brengen, of hij iet heeft over den chr. catechismo ofte Nederlantsche confessie."

of June 18, held at Rotterdam, we learn that "the brethren have unanimously declared to have no objections to the teachings of the Catechism and the Confession."[78]

More tension emerged in the meeting of this classis held at Rotterdam on May 12, 1609. This meeting addressed synod's request as well as a letter from the provincial council concerning possible objections. When asked, ministers Nicolai and Cupus refused to indicate if they had any objections; they simply stated that they were well aware of the procedure for lodging objections. Pastor Matth. Adriani indicated "that he also had some reservations."[79] We further read that "the remainder declared to have no objections."[80]

At a special meeting held at Rotterdam on February 15, 1611, this classis dealt with the invitation issued by the delegates of both Regional Synods of Holland. On February 22, a meeting was held at Amsterdam to prepare for the upcoming conference. The Rotterdam Remonstrant minister Franciscus Lansbergius was chosen to attend. He was provided with a letter in which classis indicated that it was prepared to cooperate in ensuring peace among the churches. The classis explicitly allowed the five points raised by the Remonstrants to speak for themselves. In contrast with others, classis had no desire to prejudge these articles "as unscriptural, and contrary to both the Catechism and the Confession."[81]

However, the Amsterdam meeting refused to recognize Lansbergius as a delegate because his credentials were judged to be inadequate. In the end, Lansbergius had no alternative but to return home. The acts of classis reveal the resistance that he offered. At the same time, we notice that others from the district of Rotterdam who had severed themselves from classis on their own initiative sent Acronius to Amsterdam and provided him with credentials. The legality of this situation was challenged by Lansbergius in Amsterdam. The latter considered the conduct of the meeting in Amsterdam to be an insult to the Classis of Rotterdam; therefore, the Classis of Rotterdam lodged an official protest against Amsterdam on March 1, 1611. At the same time, they sent three ministers to the provincial council in The Hague to provide them with an official report and to complain about the treatment of the Classis of Rotterdam at the meeting in Amsterdam.

---

78. "De broeders hebben eendrachtelick verclaert nyt te hebben tegen de leere van de catechismus ende de confessie."

79. "dat hy oock enige bedenckinge heeft"

80. "de reste heeft verclaert daer niet tegen te hebben"

81. "voor onschriftmatich, ende beyde den catechismo ende confessie niet gelyckformich"

It appears that a conflict sharpened over the years concerning the position of the Remonstrants and their efforts to validate their Five Articles against Scripture, the Belgic Confession of Faith, and the Catechism. The opposing camps increasingly parted ways.

Government interference

Local authorities made attempts at various levels to mediate among the various ecclesiastical camps. At the classis meeting in Rotterdam on March 7, 1616, this mediation was done with a decree of tolerance. The local authorities, including the Grand Pensionary Hugo Grotius, persuaded classis to adopt the resolution of the provincial council. Reference was made to "a revision of the Confession and the Catechism, in which an extract of the office of mayor was at issue."[82] In this meeting there appeared to be many absences, among them Schiedam, Delfshaven, and Poortugaal. More than the weather was responsible for this.

At the meeting of classis in Rotterdam on October 18, 1618, local authorities weighed in by means of a letter from the Provincial Councils of Holland and West Friesland. The classis was urgently invited "to submit in writing to the current synod at Delft all of its possible reservations with respect to the Confession and Catechism in terms of each and every doctrine as well as their formulation, together with any reasons why it would be of the view that any of these formulations ought to be revised or further clarified."[83] The classis was also asked to present its views clearly regarding the articles of the conference held in Delft in 1613, in order to bring out any differences.

At the classis meeting held in Delfshaven on July 20, 1620, all criticisms and reservations surrounding subscription to the confessional statements (Belgic Confession of Faith, Catechism, and Canons of Dort) dissipated. All those present heard the act of subscription read and subsequently signed it.

At its meeting in Harderwijk on May 19, 1606, the Classis of the Lower Veluwe also had to deal with an act of Parliament concerning objections to the Confession of Faith and the Heidelberg Catechism. In the formulation of this decree, one senses a careful search for the proper role of churches. They

---

82. "van het revideren van de confessie ende catechismo, waerby is een extract van het ampt van de burgemeesters in dese saecke."

83. "alle haere bedenckingen die zy mogen hebben over ofte tegen de confessie ende catechismum soo de substantie van alle ende een yder leerstuck van dien als de maniere van spreecken derselver angaende aen de jegenwoordige synode tot Delft schriftelyck over te seynden met deductie van de redenen waerom zy souden meynen dat in de voornoemde formulieren eenige veranderinge ofte nader verklaringe soude noodich zyn."

could review any possible objections and submit them through the regional synod to the national synod.

According to the Acts of the Classis of Harderwijk (April 24–26, 1610), the doctrinal differences that had emerged were not lost on the stadtholder of Gelderland. A letter from the principality and county sincerely encouraged classis to keep in mind God's honor, the advancement of His Word, and the bond of unity. Mutual love and purity of doctrine were of the greatest importance in ensuring that the church was built up "and all innovation"[84] thwarted. To honor this request of the authorities, classis decided to have all ministers and elders present subscribe to the Heidelberg Catechism and the Belgic Confession of Faith. Nearly everyone present did so, and the result was duly reported to the civil authorities.

At the beginning of 1617, the local authorities of Gelderland and Zutphen also addressed the emerging doctrinal differences. As requested, classis sent delegates to a meeting of the local legislative assembly in connection with doctrinal issues that had arisen in Nijmegen. The delegates received clear instructions from classis that it wished to abide by the adopted Reformed doctrine. In this connection the forms "of unity"[85] are mentioned, namely, the Belgic Confession of Faith and the Heidelberg Catechism, "as well as the subsequent union of Barnevelt and the Acts of the Synod of Gelderland of 1612."[86] The Classis of the Lower Veluwe recommended that a national synod be held.

In the Classis of Deventer on July 6, 1619, confusion arose over the adherence of some ministers to the Belgic Confession of Faith and the Catechism as a consequence of the wily behavior of the reeves of Salland and Raalte. The ministers had signed resolutions presented by the reeves, but according to their own declaration, these brethren had merely sought to proclaim "sound and ancient doctrine"[87] to their people. They confessed their offense against classis, and the assembly generally admonished that such subscriptions should be avoided in ecclesiastical matters so that the freedom of classis and good order would not be impaired.

Assessment
Ecclesiastical assemblies of the Northern Netherlands committed themselves

---

84. "ende alle niuwicheyt"
85. "van eendracht"
86. "neffens die naerder unie van Barnevelt ende Acti des Gelderschen Synodi van anno 1612"
87. "gesunde und uralte lehr"

with great determination to the use and the implementation of the Heidelberg Catechism in both church and school. Subscription to the Catechism was pursued in order to safeguard purity of doctrine and unity of the churches. We observe local variations in the implementation of this commitment, especially where Remonstrant leanings were evident.

It is noteworthy that ecclesiastical demands to adopt the Catechism as a binding confessional statement were accompanied by government interference at various levels. The ecclesiastical assemblies sought to safeguard "the rights of the church."[88] Partly because of the pronouncements of the Synod of Dort of 1618–1619, the authority and acceptance of the Heidelberg Catechism in the Northern Netherlands were further strengthened and considered to be indisputable for a long time.

---

88. "het recht der kerk"

CHAPTER 6

The Heidelberg Catechism
in Preaching and Teaching

A. THE CATECHISM IN PREACHING
by Willem Jan op 't Hof

Catechism preaching in practice

When it comes to ecclesiastical matters, most secular and some church historians delight in pointing out the discrepancy between the ideal world prescribed by ecclesiastical assemblies and historical reality. In the case of catechism preaching, it may well be that provincial synods issued a universal decree that during the second service on the Lord's Day the Catechism was to be preached, but was it really put into practice? Were all churchgoers, who were generally quite ignorant, taught the doctrine of godliness by means of the Catechism?

As far as we can tell, it was generally the case that these synodical instructions were followed or had already been implemented spontaneously. In various places, catechism preaching in the second service on the Lord's Day was already common practice, such as in Delft in 1573, Dort prior to 1574, Naaldwijk in 1581, and Amsterdam in 1586. In some places, the Catechism was presented in weekday services. It was characteristic of the early and widespread introduction of catechism preaching that as of 1583, the Classis of Dort prescribed that a theology student was to present two sermons at every classis meeting: one based on Holy Scripture and one based on the Catechism.

The 1624 diary of the Reformed schoolmaster David Beck of The Hague indicates that he attended a catechism service every Sunday afternoon. He recorded for many Sundays the date, church, minister, and the catechism questions that were preached on. On January 7 of that year, prior to the Sunday afternoon service, he and his artist friend Herman Breckerfelt read from the latter's copy of the first edition of the well-known explanation of the Catechism by Gellius de Bouma of 1621.

Neglect

Historical research has nevertheless demonstrated that towards the end of the sixteenth century and at the beginning of the seventeenth century, the Catechism rarely, if at all, served as preaching material in a surprising number of churches. This situation arose for largely practical reasons, the most important of which was that in rural regions, many ministers had to serve more than one community. In such multipoint charges, the minister would preach in one village in the morning and another in the evening. Obviously, such a minister would not preach catechism sermons twice, if at all. It was recorded concerning Johannes Lydius that prior to his arrival in Oudewater in 1603, he had never yet preached from the Catechism. Sometimes the reasons were entirely different: in one church no afternoon service was held because farm responsibilities took priority, and in another church the catechism service was skipped because the herring fleet was departing.

It is also known that people sometimes felt a need for preaching material other than the Catechism. For example, at Assendelft in 1610, Henricus Geesteranus, having just gone through the entire Catechism, was given permission by his consistory to go through a book of the Bible in the afternoon services.

A more substantial reason for neglecting the Catechism was resistance on the part of both pastors and churchgoers. Under the influence of Dirk Coornhert and David Joris, Herman Herberts objected to the content of the Catechism and refused to preach from it, first at Dort and subsequently at Gouda. It was probably due to Herbert's influence on churchgoers that attendance during catechism services declined. In Gouda in 1597, this decline even led to the cancellation of the catechism sermon during the afternoon service! It was not until after the National Synod of Dort of 1618–1619 that the catechism service was restored.

In the seventeenth century, the Remonstrant ministers in particular purposely neglected catechism preaching. During an investigation by the Classis of Leiden in 1609, it was discovered that two ministers were guilty of such neglect: Jan Bors of Leiderdorp and Isaac Frederici of Noordwijk. In his capacity as delegate from Utrecht, Frederici subsequently spelled out his objections to catechism preaching at the Synod of Dort. In the Classis of Delft there was also a sympathizer of the duo mentioned above: Hendrick Bleyenburg of Zoetermeer.

There is no doubt that the Synod of Dort tremendously advanced the use of the Catechism during afternoon services. Not only were conscientious objectors to the Catechism expelled from the church by synod, but the synodical decree to discuss the Catechism during the second service on the

Lord's Day was not without effect. Nevertheless, the practical reasons listed above meant that, even after the Synod of Dort, far from all church members were exposed to Reformed doctrine through the Catechism. For example, in the Classis of Leiden some churches only conducted morning services on the first day of the week.

The second service on the Lord's Day was a widespread problem in the Province of Friesland. During the 1670s and 1680s, there were at least four ministers in every Frisian classis who never conducted an afternoon service and, consequently, never preached catechism sermons. It is therefore not surprising that the teaching ministry was a matter of continual concern at Frisian ecclesiastical assemblies. In 1667, the Classis of Woudster expressed the fear that because of negligence with respect to catechism preaching, "our Frisian people will perish like the Jewish people for lack of knowledge." At the Synod of Friesland three years later, the Classis of Dokkum proposed that the chairman ask all those present, one by one, whether they carried out their duties in this respect, and that in every synod and classis meeting this matter be regularly addressed. In 1675, a regulation to this effect was adopted in collaboration with other provincial synods. In order to ensure the practice of catechism preaching, even the assistance of the provincial council was requested.

Interior of the Great or Saint Odulphus Church at Assendelft,
viewed from the choir towards the west (Pieter Jansz. Saenredam, 1649)

In the Ommelanden region of the Province of Groningen, the situation was actually much worse. There, government pressure was required to persuade ministers to present Lord's Day 1 of the Catechism on November 11, 1621. The outcome was not surprising. A year later, an investigation of thirteen churches by the Classis of Loppersum revealed that in ten churches, the experiment had quickly fizzled out: attendance in four of them had declined to zero, in another four churches to two, and in one church to three. For one church, no figures were available. In three churches where catechism preaching continued, very few people attended two of them; church attendance remained high in only one church. Around 1640, government posters achieved greater success, but as late as 1680, complaints continued to surface that catechism preaching attracted no audiences.

In 1627, the Provincial Synod of Drenthe decreed that no minister, for whatever reason, was permitted to omit presenting the Catechism during the second Sunday service.

Seventeenth century
On the whole, the introduction of catechism preaching was a long, drawn-out affair in a large number of regions. The general impression was that catechism preaching in cities was more popular than in rural areas.

A striking example of success was the city of Amsterdam. In the Old

Franciscus Ridderus

Church, the Catechism was used for preaching right from the start. In 1592, it was decided that the Catechism would be presented for one year in the Old Church and the next year in the New Church. Starting in 1632, this practice was followed in both churches simultaneously. This book of instruction was so popular here that at the request of the various churches, it was decided in 1641 to offer catechism services in the South Church and the West Church.

Another seventeenth century source confirms that catechism preaching established deep roots in the cities: during 1664–1666, the Rotterdam Pietist minister Franciscus Ridderus (1620–1683) published a three-way conversation among Mary, Martha, and Lazarus in which he captured the feelings of ordinary church people. This dialogue constitutes a window through which we, as twenty-first-century people, are given a picture of the thinking of churchgoers in the last quarter of the seventeenth century. In producing this work, Ridderus undoubtedly had in mind his own congregation in Rotterdam. Mary and Lazarus interpreted the views of the serious and active church people, but Martha was presented as the mouthpiece of superficial church goers who largely attended church out of habit. The proportion represented by the latter may have been considerable in a large city such as Rotterdam.

It is interesting that the second dialogue of the first volume of 1664 opens with the subject of catechism preaching. The text of this passage, which is reproduced in a separate box below, makes clear not only that catechism preaching during the afternoon service was a regular practice of the Rotterdam church but also that it was attended by people on whose behalf Martha spoke. Such services were therefore not attended solely by sincere believers or people who took things seriously. But do not ask how such lukewarm Christians passed their time; like so many after them, they took a nap.

It is interesting to hear the personal view of the Marthas of those days concerning catechism preaching. Having had the Catechism explained for years on end, they knew it all too well. There was no longer anything new coming from the pulpit; this stale bread was no longer savory. At the same time, they were unhappy that in the afternoon services the minister kept on preaching from the same Catechism year after year. They sneeringly pointed out that they could well understand this practice, because ministers then did not need to spend so much time preparing their sermons. People, including ministers, preferred to take it easy! In fact, this is precisely the theme that emerged in the foregoing section: people enjoy variation.

In Lazarus's defense, it should be noted that to well-intentioned church-goers of those days, it was good that no new things were preached from the pulpit; innovations came from heretics. Catechism preaching was meant to strengthen members of the church in true doctrine. It was considered to be a solid buffer against false teachings of various kinds and was well appreciated.

Sunday afternoon

Martha: We went to church again and heard the minister preach from the Catechism. It was the same old story: I have listened to catechism preaching so often that I am nearly sick of it. I just napped. Ministers like to take it easy these days; this way they won't need much time to prepare their sermons. It would be great if they could preach on something other than the Catechism.

Lazarus: Well now, Sister Martha, what are you saying? Don't you know that this is the practice of all of our churches? You should not put it this way. Synods have established this order with great care, so that we can hear our entire set of doctrines again every year. Or would you prefer to hear something new every time? Don't you know how many false spirits there are, and how easily and slyly Satan can cause people to err? The Catechism is preached so that the truth may be retained, "that we henceforth be no more children, tossed to and fro, and carried about with every wind of doctrine, by the sleight of men, and cunning craftiness, whereby they lie in wait to deceive" (Eph. 4:14).

Franciscus Ridderus, *De tafel des Heeren ofte drie-weeckse samenspraek, tusschen Lazarus, Maria en Martha, Over de Voor-beryeding tot des Heeren Heylige Avontmael* (The Table of the Lord, or Three Weekly Dialogues among Lazarus, Mary and Martha concerning Preparation for the Lord's Holy Supper), Amsterdam, 1715, 1:26.

Whereas Ridderus assumed above that all Marthas attended the afternoon services on Sundays, in another publication, he painted a more somber picture of reality in which people devoted the remainder of the day to eating, socializing, and recreation.

It is surprising that in the second half of the seventeenth century, criticism was leveled at catechism preaching not only by uninterested churchgoers, but also from the perspective of the Dutch Further Reformation. We read about this in the most important publication of those days, namely, the program description of the Further Reformation, published in 1678 by Jacobus Koelman (1631–1695) under the pseudonym Cristophylus Eubulus, entitled *De Pointen van Nodige Reformatie* (Aspects of a Necessary Reformation). Koelman resisted the iron law of synods that required the teaching of the Catechism

A church service circa 1660
(painting by Emmanuel de Witte)

during afternoon or evening services. It was Koelman's view that ministers ought to have the freedom to cover other material in their sermons. The connection with Koelman's well-known criticism of the use of forms in worship services becomes clear when he labels catechism sermons "worn-out form sermons." At the same time, he agreed with the criticism by Ridderus's Martha, who accused ministers of laziness.

> Sunday meals ought to be special, i.e., better than on weekdays or preferably in the style of the Jews who eat their best meals on their Sabbath Days: then they stuff themselves to satiation. In the afternoon one rarely goes back to church. People think: it is only *the Catechism*, the same old lesson that has been heard a thousand times. People say: what would I do in church? I would go to sleep anyway. What then? One can take a nap at home, or remain at the table; or go for a walk, or engage in some other sinful pleasure, and so forth. Those who do end up going back to church, fall asleep because they have eaten their fill. When they return home, they carry on as before, having fun, indeed passing the time lightheartedly, playing cards, games, and so on. And especially in the evening they have another good meal! People enjoy having two good meals on a Sunday, but consider a single sermon to be more than enough.
>
> Franciscus Ridderus, *Nader Bedenckinge over den Dagh boven den Dagh* (Further Thoughts on the Day above All Days), Rotterdam, 1670, 184–185.

Jacobus Koelman

Koelman had another arrow in his quiver of reproach: in the service of instruction, Holy Scripture was crowded out or was displaced altogether. In most cases, the material of the Catechism was discussed with the help of a passage from Scripture, but it was done in such a way that the passage was hardly allowed to speak for itself. In some churches, they presented the Catechism without a text from the Bible and without reading a chapter from Scripture. In support of his views, he presented a detailed quotation from a work of the English Puritan, William Ames, who from 1622 to 1633 taught at the University of Franeker in the Northern Netherlands as professor of theology. In the quotation, Ames held that Holy Scripture, and not the text of the Catechism itself, should be the starting point for catechism preaching. Finally, Koelman demonstrated that someone of the caliber of the Dutch Reformed theologian Gisbertus Voetius agreed with Ames's point of view.

In accordance with synodical decrees, the Catechism is preached throughout the year, and in their Sunday afternoon sermons ministers are not at liberty to discuss other material in line with the situation and condition of the church and God's providence, so that those catechism sermons turn into worn-out form sermons, thus making preachers lazy. The Catechism is explained in such a way that the corresponding Bible text is barely mentioned. Indeed, in some places the Catechism is preached without a text from Scripture. First the Ten Commandments are read, and then the text of the Catechism, as is done in Middelburg. They might as well preach from the Apocrypha. Ames put it well when he said: "Although the Catechism must be impressed upon people with all due diligence, nevertheless a distinction should always be made between such a human form and Holy Scripture. It is therefore not appropriate for the Catechism to be presented in church as though it were equivalent to Scripture, when Scripture itself ought to be read. It is therefore most advisable, in deference to Scripture, in recognition of the efficacy of the proclaimed truth and in view of the risk of provocation, that selected Scripture passages be presented as the foundation of catechetical instruction, and that the teaching of the Catechism be drawn from these as the teaching of Scripture." In defending this view of Ames, Voetius indicates in his writings that this approach is more profitable, more appropriate, more secure, and more edifying.

Jacobus Koelman, *De Pointen van Nodige Reformatie* (Aspects of a Necessary Reformation), Vlissingen, 1678, 105–106.

Two years later, Koelman reiterated his view in *De weeg-schaal des heyligdoms, omtrent de feest-dagen der Gereformeerde Kerk in Nederlandt* (The Weigh Scales of the Sanctuary, Focusing on the Holy Days of the Reformed Church in the Netherlands, 1680). In it he reacted to the polemic that Ridderus had published against his *Reformatie Nodigh omtrent de feest-dagen* (Reformation Required with Respect to Holy Days, 1675). In his writing, Koelman advocated the abolition of Christian feast days. A passage is reproduced below.

Koelman raised several new arguments. First, the service of thanksgiving that followed the Lord's Supper in many churches had been superseded by the catechism service. Until shortly before this time, a thanksgiving service had been customary in Middelburg, the capital city of Zeeland. Permission for this service had been given by the National Synod of Middleburg in 1581.

In the second place, he saw a connection between catechism preaching and Roman Catholic laxness about preaching.

> As far as catechism sermons are concerned, in my view, they should not have to be given steadily throughout the year, without taking any liberty, depending on the occasion and the needs of the church, to preach about something else as directed by the Lord, upon reflection. Basic truths definitely must be preached; but nonetheless it should not have to be predetermined what a minister ought to preach about, because frequently there might be something else that would perfectly suit the occasion. When the Lord's Supper is administered in the morning, sermons of thanksgiving ought to be preached in the afternoon, but in many places these are omitted, and the Catechism is presented instead. Not so long ago this was precisely the traditional and unchangeable custom in Middelburg in Zeeland; the Catechism could not be interrupted. The national synod held at Middleburg in the year 1581 gave permission to omit trial sermons as well as sermons associated with the Lord's Supper, either in the morning prior to its administration or in the afternoon by way of thanksgiving, and to preach instead from the Catechism. Synod said nothing about the omission of sermons for feast days; nevertheless this would have been altogether more reasonable. Such catechism sermons turn into worn-out form sermons, making people lazy. If one were to add sermons on papist dominical texts, which continue to be preached by many pastors in certain provinces of our country and beyond, one would imitate all the more the laziness and worldliness of papists and neglect to proclaim the entire Word. This is earnestly warned against by Ames, *Exeg. Confess,* pp. 93–94 and Voetius, *Polit. Ecles.* part. lib. 2. pp. 607ff.
>
> Jacobus Koelman, *De weeg-schaal des heyligdoms* (The Weigh Scales of the Sanctuary), Amsterdam, 1680, 2:70–71.

In the same work, Koelman provided an example of bad catechism preaching: "I have heard that someone who had been called on the carpet by the magistrate concerning the practical application in one of his catechism sermons said that he had presented his sermon in this manner for over thirty years."

Eighteenth century
The experience with catechism preaching in the eighteenth century must have

Middelburg

been similar to that in the second half of the seventeenth century. In most churches, catechism preaching was well established. But in rural areas, especially in regions where Reformed doctrine and the Reformed Church had never become firmly established, there must have been exceptions to the rule.

Whereas the foregoing quotations feature criticism of catechism preaching, the positive impact of catechism preaching is emphasized by the recently published eighteenth-century diary of Pieter Morilyon. By profession, he was chief accountant for the West India Company, and he was actively involved in church life in his home town of Middelburg. He was born there in 1704 and breathed his last in 1783.

On Sunday, June 12, 1729, Morilyon listened to the catechism sermon preached by the Middelburg minister Henricus de Frein, who presented Lord's Day 30. This sermon deeply touched Morilyon.

> In the afternoon I submitted myself to the ministry of that faithful ambassador of Christ, Mr. De Frein. He preached on Lord's Day 30. To my great horror, I heard him present the secrets of Antichrist, but also the true characteristics of the genuine participant in the Lord's Supper. He asked: "Should a doubting soul be permitted to sit at the Lord's Supper? That is, someone who cries within his heart: 'Lord, why art Thou afar off? Why hidest Thou Thy face in times of disquiet?' May such an insecure soul indeed sit at the Lord's Supper?" "Oh," he said, "I am shocked when such tender souls are knocked over the head. Indeed, indeed, they must come. How could such a hungry person, whom the Lord has given such precious promises, be left to languish?" And he proceeded to cite that sweet verse, Psalm 22:29: "All they that be fat upon earth shall eat and worship [those only? Oh no]: all they that go down to the dust shall bow before him: and none can keep alive his own soul."

Oh, this is precisely how I experienced it myself. Such an empty, naked and poor person I was. With this thought in mind the generous, complete offer of Jesus rose up before me, so that my soul melted profoundly towards heaven, and became obsessed with a deep longing for Jesus. Oh, how I longed for the Lord's Supper. If it had then been such a festive day, I believe that I would have hastened to that table among the very first. This particular afternoon I frequently had to suppress my tears so as not to disturb those around me. To my great distress there was someone who closely observed my face. It bothered me to no end.

This faithful ambassador threw many sweet seeds into my heart. He said that a fake Christian permits grace to lean against him, but a truly devout person says: "Even if all ministers and God-fearing people would tell me: 'Friend, thou possessest grace,' then I would reply: 'None of this can help me. I cannot believe it. God must reassure me. Through His Spirit He has to place His message in my soul.'" This was a sweetly refreshing word to me. I was glad that the Lord had brought me under this ministry this very afternoon. It had been quite some time since I had sat through a public worship service with so many favorable impressions and such softening of the heart.

S. D. Post, *Mij zal niets ontbreken. Uit het leven van Pieter Morilyon* (I Shall Not Lack Anything. From the Life of Pieter Morilyon), Houten, 2003, 93–94.

This was not the only time that a catechism sermon offered fruit for Morilyon's soul. If the sermon on Lord's Day 30 had encouraged and comforted him, a sermon on Lord's Day 4 preached by the Middelburg minister Jacobus Glay was the means by which he recognized his uncleanness and pleaded for a new heart. "In the afternoon I listened to the sermon of Evangelist Glay based on the fourth Lord's Day. While singing, praying, and weeping I was granted to confess, profess, and bemoan my despicably unclean nature, pleading for a new heart on the basis of Psalm 51:2, 3, and 5. It perfectly suited my spiritual frame of mind."

Once in a while, a member of a "conventicle," or house church, would report being spiritually blessed by a catechism sermon. For example, at a gathering led by Morilyon at his country residence on Friday afternoon, June 28, 1771, a woman spoke of being spiritually blessed during a sermon based on Lord's Day 25. "We were all given open hearts and mouths to speak of the ways of the Lord. Everyone was given an opportunity to do so."

Nineteenth and twentieth century

In the nineteenth century, resistance to catechism preaching gradually gained momentum. Ministers, consistories, and church members felt increasingly uncomfortable with the teachings of the Catechism. Typical of these feelings was the fruitless request of the Zuidhoorn Ring, submitted to the Synod of 1831, to be permitted to replace Sunday catechism sermons with Scripture readings. The underlying developments eventually persuaded synod to eliminate the requirement to preach catechism sermons in 1860. This decision engendered so much opposition that it was reversed a year later. But these events reflected the spiritual atmosphere that gradually emerged in the Reformed Church and that subsequently would become even more pronounced.

Sunday catechism preaching became increasingly restricted to those of the Gereformeerde Gezindte (Reformed persuasion) within the national Hervormde Kerk (Reformed Church), which continues to be the case today. Outside the Hervormde Kerk, this practice has always been honored by churches that had their origin in the 1834 secession known as the Afscheiding. Within the Gereformeerde Kerken, which originated in the 1886 secession known as the Doleantie (the word means "mourning"), catechism preaching rapidly fell by the wayside following the Second World War. Other churches having their origin in the Doleantie tended to be more conservative, but they followed the lead of the Gereformeerde Kerken with some lag. In fact, Sunday catechism preaching has become an exclusive characteristic of the Reformed persuasion in the broader and interdenominational sense of the term.

Collections of sermons on the Catechism

From the very beginning, Reformed ministers in the Netherlands published sermons in diverse formats and of various lengths. It would have been strange if catechism sermons had not been included. Over a period of more than two centuries (1576–1801), fourteen collections of sermons on the Catechism were produced. Most of these were republished at least once and in some cases many times. It is noteworthy, however, that prior to the eighteenth century, only three such collections appeared.

Below we discuss exclusively Dutch publications that cover the entire Catechism. We omit catechetical and doctrinal treatises. The best-known example in the latter category is *Het Schat-boeck der Christelycke Leere* (The Treasure Book of Christian Doctrine) by Zacharias Ursinus. Of this work, no fewer than fifteen editions appeared in the seventeenth century alone, while

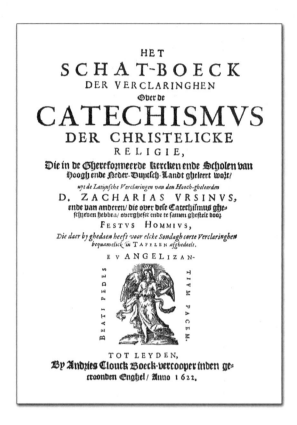

HET
SCHAT-BOECK
DER VERCLARINGHEN
Ober de
CATECHISMVS
DER CHRISTELICKE
RELIGIE,

Die in de Ghereformeerde kercken ende Scholen van
Hoogh ende Neder-Duytsch-Landt gheleert wort/
wyt de Latijnsche Verclaringen van den Hooch-gheleerden

D. ZACHARIAS VRSINVS,

ende van anderen/ die over dese Catechismus ghe-
schreven hebben/ overghefet ende te samen gheftelt door

FESTVS HOMMIVS,

Die daer by ghedaen heeft voor elcke Sondagh corte Verclaringhen
bequamelick in TAFELEN afghedeelt.

EV ANGELIZAN-

TOT LEYDEN,
By Andries Clouck Boeck-vercooper inden ge-
croonden Enghel/ Anno 1 6 2 2.

Title page of the commentary by Ursinus on the Catechism

in the eighteenth century this number was increased by one. We similarly leave aside those publications that only discuss a limited number of Lord's Days of the Catechism, even if they are based on sermon material. Finally, we omit commentaries on the Catechism based on discussion group exercises. The best-known and most important publication in this category is the commentary by Justus Vermeer, namely, *De leere der waarheid die na de godtzaligheid is, voorgestelt, bevestigt en toegepast in 85 oefeningen over den Heidelbergschen Catechismus* (The Doctrine of Truth in Godliness, Presented, Confirmed and Applied in 85 Sermons on the Heidelberg Catechism) in two volumes, 1749–1750. This commentary by a Utrecht elder and lawyer was written in the style of the Dutch Reformed theologian Gisbertus Voetius (1589–1676) and was republished a few years later.

The table below presents the number of Dutch catechism sermon collections published over a period of more than two centuries (1576–1801), subdivided into intervals of twenty-five years.

YEAR	FIRST PRINTING	TOTAL NUMBER OF PRINTINGS
1576–1601	1	2
1601–1626	1	3
1626–1651	0	1
1651–1676	0	0
1676–1701	1	6
1701–1726	3	10
1726–1751	4	21
1751–1776	1	15
1776–1801	3	12

Although some "catechism commentaries" were published in the sixteenth and seventeenth centuries, they did not gain much popularity. The low point occurred during the second and third quarters of the seventeenth century, when only a single publication appeared. The last quarter of the seventeenth century saw a renewed interest in these sermon collections, with a total of six publications.

Sixteenth century
The first collection of catechism sermons in the Netherlands appeared in 1588: *Vier ende vijftich predicatien, over den christelijcken ende in Gods Woord ghegronden Catechismus* (Fifty-four Sermons on the Christian Catechism Based on God's Word). It was written by Balthasar Copius, minister in the Palatinate, and translated from German by Johannes Gerobulus. Gerobulus was an interesting individual; on the one hand, some of his views and practices did not agree with those of the Reformed faith. For example, he was a fervent opponent of the customarily strict and public disciplinary procedures of that time—probably because he once had a painful personal encounter with them. He was also a proponent of far-reaching government involvement in ecclesiastical matters. Gerobulus was first in defending Sunday catechism preaching publicly in writing, judging by his *Censuren ofte berispinghen over den chr. Catechismus* (Criticisms or Reproofs of the Christian Catechism,

1588). His plea ignited the wrath of Coornhert, which resulted in the latter's publication of *Dolingen des Catechismi* (Errors of Catechisms). Coornhert's publication of criticisms was annexed to the Fifty-four Sermons translated by Gerobulus. Within twenty-five years, this work was reprinted at least three times. For those early days, this was unusually frequent. It probably meant that ministers used this collection of sermons on a large scale for the preparation of their own Sunday afternoon sermons.

Seventeenth century

In 1594, the catechism sermons of Philippus Lansbergen of Goes were published in Latin at Middelburg. By 1595, these sermons had become very popular in Germany. A second edition was published in the Palatinate in 1620 and 1621, followed by two other Latin editions in Germany. In 1616, a Dutch translation of the same work achieved two reprints. This was the first writing of this kind produced by a Netherlander.

The third and final work of the seventeenth century was not only written by a Netherlander, the Leiden minister Petrus van der Hagen (1641–1671), but was also published in the Netherlands. Although this collection of sermons was not published until after his death (1676), it achieved unusual popularity. This work saw no fewer than twelve editions in the seventeenth and eighteenth centuries. It was the only catechism sermon collection that experienced widespread international popularity. At Bremen, a German edition appeared in 1693.

Petrus van der Hagen

What is the explanation of the enormous popularity of this work by Van der Hagen, not only among ministers but especially among churchgoers? At the time that this commentary was published, when Cocceianism became quite strong, Voetianism continued to have many adherents. The attractiveness of Petrus van der Hagen's commentary on the Catechism was that the Cocceian theology that he practiced was hardly mentioned and was combined with Voetian ethics. In other words, he must have caught the attention of large groups of people in both camps. He was the first in history not to employ the text of the relevant Lord's Day of the Catechism as his starting point, but rather a corresponding passage from the Bible.

Eighteenth century
There is no century during which as many sermon collections on the Catechism were published as the eighteenth century. Whereas the sixteenth century saw only two printings and the seventeenth century ten, in the eighteenth century the number of printings increased to at least fifty-eight. The second quarter of the eighteenth century alone produced twenty-one printings.

In the first quarter of the eighteenth century, three new publications appeared. In 1710, a catechism commentary was authored by the Cocceian minister Matthew Gargon of Vlissingen, followed by three reprints within a span of twenty years. In 1717, the well-known Dirksland minister Johannes van der Kemp published a similar collection of sermons that would far outdistance all other collections in terms of popularity. This work was entitled *De christen geheel en al het eigendom van Christus* (The Christian Entirely Owned by Christ), and no fewer than nineteen editions are known to have existed during the period under review. It must have been present in countless homes. It is known, for example, that this work was included in no fewer than sixteen percent of estate inventories in The Hague. In 1725, the catechism sermons of the Cocceian Solomon van Til were presented to the reading public of the Netherlands. This publication was a translation; the original had been written in Latin. It was considerably less successful than Van der Kemp's collection; only a single reprint appeared.

In the second quarter of the eighteenth century, four new commentaries were added, three of which were published after their authors' deaths. Three of the four were written by Middelburg ministers, all kindred spirits. In 1736 and 1737, the posthumous sermon collection of the rationalistic minister Hermanus Reiners appeared; this two-volume collection was reprinted once. In 1739, a collection was authored by the Voetian Carolus Tuinman. This posthumous commentary enjoyed considerable popularity among church people, and four reprints were brought out over a period of more than twenty-five years. The third collection, also posthumous, appeared in 1742, authored by Tuinman's Middelburg colleague Bernardius Smytegelt. This one was even more loved by the reading public; in almost forty years there appeared five printings. In 1746, the first volume of a two-part sermon collection on the Catechism was authored by Henricus de Frein, their colleague in Middelburg. The second volume did not appear until 1753. These sermons differed from the others in that they had been preached on weekday evenings rather than on Sundays. This commentary turned out to be less popular and enjoyed only a single reprint.

In the third quarter of the eighteenth century, a single new collection of catechism sermons was published posthumously in 1774. Its author was Johannes Beukelman. No reprints appeared during this interval.

In the last quarter of the eighteenth century, three new commentaries appeared on the market. All three consisted of more than one volume, and over this twenty-five-year period, each enjoyed only a single printing. The first, a four-volume collection of sermons by Hermanus Ferree, minister in Dreischors, was posthumously published in 1785–1786. Similarly, catechism sermons by the Cocceian professor Petrus Curtenius of Amsterdam were published posthumously in four volumes in 1790–1792. The last collection in this series, by Johan Carel Palier, professor at 's-Hertogenbosch, was brought out in 1792 in two volumes.

The Experientially Reformed Community

It was pointed out earlier that the eighteenth century was the age of printed catechism sermons. This phenomenon cannot be explained by demographics, because the population of the Netherlands was only marginally larger in 1800 than in 1700. The degree of development and the level of prosperity must have been somewhat higher in the eighteenth century than in the seventeenth century. Nevertheless, these general factors cannot adequately account for the great discrepancy between these two centuries as far as the number of published collections of catechism sermons is concerned: ten compared to fifty-eight. There must have been other factors at play.

The catechism commentary that turned out to be the most popular, written by Johannes van der Kemp, can perhaps point us in the right direction. Judging by the nature of his sermons, the reading public must have been ordinary church members. This conclusion is consistent with the fact that the publisher who took care of the first four printings was Reiner van Doesburg of Rotterdam. Van Doesburg was known as a publisher for the experiential

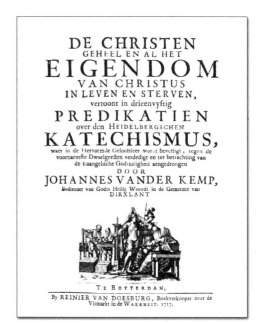

DE CHRISTEN
GEHEEL EN AL HET
E I G E N D O M
VAN CHRISTUS
IN LEVEN EN STERVEN,
vertoont in drieenvyftig
P R E D I K A T I E N
over den HEIDELBERGSCHEN
K A T E C H I S M U S,
waer in de Hervormde Geloofsleer word bevestigt, tegen de
voornaemste Dwaelgeesten verdedigt en ter betrachting van
de Euangelische Godtzaligheit aengedrongen
D O O R
JOHANNES VANDER KEMP,
Bedienaer van Godts Heilig Woordt in de Gemeente van
DIRXLANT

TE ROTTERDAM,
By REINIER VAN DOESBURG, Boekverkooper over de
Vismarkt in de WAERHEIT. 1717.

Title page of the catechism commentary by Johannes van der Kemp

segment of the Reformed community. Although experientially Reformed believers could be encountered in all strata of Dutch society, the overwhelming majority of them were found among ordinary church members. The subsequent publishers of Van der Kemp's catechism commentary had audiences similar to those of Van Doesburg.

There is yet another factor. It is known that Van Doesburg maintained close contact with kindred colleagues in various other provinces, and his publications therefore enjoyed a national reach. That the ninth through the eighteenth editions of Van der Kemp's catechism commentary were published in both Rotterdam and Amsterdam suggests that the experientially Reformed community of the entire nation was served by these publications.

But didn't these experientially Reformed believers listen to a catechism sermon Sunday after Sunday? Did they feel a need to read catechism sermons as well? There is historical proof that the latter question can be answered in the affirmative.

Morilyon, referred to above, wrote in his spiritual autobiography that on Sundays, following the last church service, he assembled his family to close the day. First his wife read aloud a sermon dealing with the Lord's Day of the Catechism that had been presented in church, and then he discussed with his family members what they knew about these things from personal experience and how they were to act with respect to the Lord. This domestic religious gathering was closed with the singing of psalms.

> On Sundays, following the worship service and the enjoyment of a cup of tea for our refreshment, my family members are once again called together. My wife reads out loud a sermon by father Smytegelt, Van der Kemp, or someone else on the material of the Catechism covered at church. I ask the members of my family a few pertinent questions, especially to ascertain and probe their feelings towards the Lord, and to see what they might know of these things from personal experience, or to determine what they must do to act appropriately towards the Lord.
>
> Then we close once again with the singing of psalms, according to the time and situation allotted.
>
> S. D. Post, *Mij zal niets ontbreken. Uit het leven van Pieter Morilyon* (I Shall Not Lack Anything. From the Life of Pieter Morilyon), Houten, 2003, p.162.

The reading of a catechism sermon served not only to reflect back on sermons preached but also as preparation for catechism preaching, as we see in the spiritual diary of a minister's daughter by the name of Jacoba van Thiel. The diary covers the period from 1767 to 1770, during which time she lived with her sister, Anna Catharina van Thiel, who was married to the Reformed minister of Overschie, Petrus Isaäcus de Fremery. On Saturday, July 9, 1768, Jacoba started reading the sermon by Johannes van der Kemp on the Lord's Day of the Catechism that was to be presented the following day. Since she had to look after guests, she was unable to finish reading this sermon until after the guests had departed. Other places in her diary indicate that she read this work by Van der Kemp while sewing, usually in the morning. Not only did she read from this work while performing household duties, but she also read it aloud to her sister or her sister read it to her. In January of 1769, she recorded: "During mornings I was usually occupied with ironing starched articles, while my sister read Van der Kemp off and on, as I did myself." On July 25, 1769, a similarly minded guest, their cousin De Fremery, naturally joined the sisters Van Thiel in their daily routine of reading aloud. That day the three women finished reading "in turn the portion by Van der Kemp on the Lord's Day that had been preached on." In the winter of 1768, Jacoba read Van der Kemp's catechism commentary even twice per day, morning and evening, which suggests that she read this work bit by bit. During these times, too, she read aloud to her sister. The diary entry of December 3, 1768, suggests that this practice of reading to one another gave rise to a mutual discussion of the reading material: "In the evening I first read from Van der Kemp, at the same time having a useful discussion with my sister." That this was not an exception is supported by the diary entry of October 30, 1768: the reading out loud of the sermon collection of Johannes van der Kemp "repeatedly gave rise to discussions beneficial to the soul."

The diary style of writing has the advantage that personal impressions and emotions are also recorded. In reaction to an illustration contained in a sermon by Johannes van der Kemp, Jacoba noted on December 7, 1768, that "for a moment it was as though the man had looked into my heart." A woman like Jacoba also immortalized her criticism, which she directed not at the content of Johannes van der Kemp's work but at its style. On February 27, 1768, she remarked on one of the sermons in this collection: "It occurs to me that this author is very concise but edifying with respect to this Lord's Day." In contrast, on April 29, 1769, she found the sermon on the fourth commandment "not concise enough." On January 26, 1768, she considered one of the sermons that discussed prayer to be nice, "only it surprises me that he answers the first question in the Catechism last."

Although Jacoba attended church faithfully and therefore submitted herself without fail to catechism preaching, she evidently also felt a need to absorb the material through personal reading. Van der Kemp's work turns up in her diary by far the most frequently. There are solid grounds for concluding that, during the week before or after the presentation of a Lord's Day of the Catechism in a church service, she read the corresponding sermon in Van der Kemp's commentary. She must have read this work at least once per week and completed reading it in its entirety once per year. It is an intriguing question whether she read this book year after year. It can reasonably be concluded that she did so twice in a row over the short period covered in her diary.

Jacoba van Thiel was certainly not the only one to make such intensive use of a catechism commentary. The spiritual journal kept from 1799 to 1801 by another minister's daughter, Johanna Maria Nahuys, reveals that she, too, regularly read the sermon collection by Johannes van der Kemp.

The catechism commentary by Vermeer mentioned above was a collection of group exercises that did not take the place of Sunday catechism preaching but were intended to complement and deepen one's understanding. It is not unreasonable to suppose that many thousands in those days felt the same need as Morilyon, Jacoba van Thiel, Johanna Maria Nahuys, Vermeer, and the members of his circle.

The nineteenth-century church historian G. D. J. Schotel serves as a witness here. Referring to a tradition with which he was personally familiar, he reported that in the eighteenth century most families read aloud a brief portion from a catechism sermon every afternoon. Although the phrase "most families" is probably an exaggeration, this testimony indicates that printed catechism sermons played an important role in everyday family life.

Whereas to Vermeer and his followers, home group discussions had become an important element of church life, they became an alternative to formal church attendance to a growing number of people, especially in the eighteenth century The reason for this shift was that preaching ceased to be orthodox, or it became so theoretical that the experientially oriented Reformed believers no longer received food for their souls. Whether collectively or individually, many of these unchurched people must have found the catechism commentaries to be pure in doctrine and edifying in nature.

Historical information strongly supports the hypothesis that the experientially Reformed believers were the prime readers and users of the Catechism. Many of the collections of catechism sermons, especially those of the eighteenth century, were published only after the deaths of the ministers who preached them. Included here are sermons by ministers Van der Hagen, Reiners, Tuinman, Smytegelt, Beukelman, Ferree, and Curtenius. Why did the publishers see the light so belatedly? It was because church people asked for them!

Overview of seventeenth- and eighteenth-century (re)printings of the fourteen collections of sermons on the Catechism

1. B. Copius, *Vier en vijftich predication* (Fifty-four Sermons), 1588 (1590, 1604, 1611)
2. Ph. Lansbergen, *Catechismus* (Catechism), 1616 (1645)
3. P. van der Hagen, *De Heydelbergsche Catechismus* (The Heidelberg Catechism), 1676 (1678, 1684, 1689, 1693, 1699, 1710, 1716, 1731, 1736, 1743, 1761)
4. M. Gargon, *De eenige troost* (The Only Comfort), 1710 (1713, 1718, 1729)
5. J. van der Kemp, *De christen geheel en al het eigendom van Christus* (The Christian Entirely Owned by Christ), 1717 (1720, 1722, 1724, 1726, 1731, 1733, 1736, 1742, 1745, 1750, 1754, 1758, 1763, 1768, 1773, 1779)
6. S. van Til, *Kerk-redeningen over den Heydelbergsche Catechismus* (Church Orations on the Heidelberg Catechism), 1725 (1731)

7. H. Reiners, *Gods onfeilbare waarheden* (God's Infallible Truths), 1736–1737 (1760)
8. C. Tuinman, *De toevlucht en sterkte van het ware christendom* (The Refuge and Strength of True Christianity), 1739 (1744, 1751, 1765)
9. B. Smytegelt, *Des christens eenige troost* (The Christian's Only Comfort), 1742 (1747, 1756, 1766, 1780)
10. H. de Frein, *Hondert and zeventig oefeningen* (One Hundred Seventy Sermons), 1746–1753
11. J. Beukelman, *De leere der waarheid tot godzaligheid* (The Doctrine of Truth unto Godliness), 1774
12. H. Ferree, *Verhandeling van den Heydelbergschen Catechismus* (Treatment of the Heidelberg Catechism), 1785–1786
13. P. Curtenius, *Leerredenen over den Heidelbergschen Catechismus* (Sermons on the Heidelberg Catechism), 1790–1792
14. J. C. Palier, *Leerredenen over den Heidelbergschen Katechismus* (Sermons on the Heidelberg Catechism), 1792

It would be in line with the explanation given earlier to conclude that the collections of sermons on the Catechism that were well received by the reading public were a combination of orthodox, Reformed doctrine and experiential-practical applications. Such was indeed the case. The most popular collection, that of Van der Kemp, perfectly met these criteria. The next most successful collection, that of Petrus van der Hagen, seemed to depart from these standards, but this departure was more in appearance than reality. He was indeed a Cocceian, but an experiential Cocceian who adhered to Voetian ethics and did not stress typically Cocceian elements of doctrine.

The other authors whose commentaries on the Catechism were published in the eighteenth century were also convinced Voetians or preachers who supported a synthesis of Voetianism and Cocceianism. At any rate, they were experientially and practically oriented. This is true of the Cocceians M. Gargon, C. Tuinman, and B. Smytegelt. There are only two exceptions that test the rule, as the saying goes: the Cocceian Van Til and the Cartesian-oriented Reiners. In this connection, it is noteworthy that their writings only achieved single reprints.

Nineteenth and twentieth centuries
At the beginning of the nineteenth century, the phenomenon of catechism preaching gradually lost significance in most of the Hervormde Kerk (Dutch Reformed Church). Since then, collections of new catechism sermons have

appeared alongside reprints of earlier catechism commentaries; the new sermons have had an exclusively Reformed orientation and have been written by authors from both inside and outside the Netherlands.

In the twentieth century, these publications came especially from ministers who belonged to church denominations that originated in the secessions from the Dutch Reformed Church in 1834 (Afscheiding) and 1886 (Doleantie). In the past few decades, there has been a definite increase in published catechism sermons preached by ministers of church denominations originating in the 1834 Afscheiding.

There are other publications that prove that the experiential wing of the Reformed persuasion deeply loves the Catechism as a comforting treasure book of the church. Although this may appear old-fashioned and otherworldly to outsiders, it is nothing to be ashamed of before the Lord God or in front of those who think differently. The Reformed persuasion considers it a privilege to safeguard this precious possession entrusted to it, and it does so faithfully and willingly.

B. THE CATECHISM IN CHURCH EDUCATION
by Marinus Golverdingen

As early as 1568, the Convent of Wezel, the first official Reformed church assembly in the Netherlands, prescribed a uniform approach to catechism teaching at home, at school, and in church. But in large areas, a thorough and reliable catechism teaching program did not get off the ground. It is for this reason that Willem Teellinck (1579–1629), the father of the Dutch Further Reformation, painted quite a somber picture of the general lack of knowledge. In his *Huys-boecken* (Booklet for the Home, 1618), he likened most grown-up Christians to babies who failed to receive adequate milk. In their youth they were not fed by their parents, guardians, or companions with the wholesome milk of God's Word. They did not receive instruction in the basic elements and principles of the Christian religion. This deficiency made it very difficult for them to acquire good judgment and a thorough knowledge of the truth. In *Noodwendigh Vertoogh* (Necessary Discourse, 1627), he referred to thousands of children who had been baptized but were never instructed in the significance of their baptism.

The curriculum of the Synod of Dort
Three forms of Catechism teaching
This general lack of knowledge in average men and women explains the great interest with which the Synod of Dort addressed "renewed catechetical instruction of young and old." Having obtained written advice from theologians in the Netherlands and abroad, it established clear guidelines for catechism teaching in the November 30, 1618 Friday morning session. According to this decree, catechism teaching from now on would take a three-pronged approach "so that Christian youth, from an early age, would be diligently instructed in the foundations of true religion, and might be filled with true godliness":

1. *domestica*: in families by parents as preparation of young children for school education;
2. *scholastica*: in schools by schoolmasters;
3. *ecclesiastica*: in churches by ministers and elders. Synod indicated that readers of Scripture lessons and visitors of the sick could be authorized to offer catechetical instruction as non-office bearers.

Catechism teaching as preparation for profession of faith as is commonly practiced today was not yet envisaged. Synod determined that three or four

Engraving of the
Synod of Dort of 1618

weeks before the administration of the Lord's Supper, those who desired to
join the church should "be repeatedly and diligently instructed, so as to be all
the more equipped and prepared to give an account of their faith."

In ecclesiastical thinking about the religious instruction of young people,
catechism teaching by the schools took center stage. On at least two days per
week, schoolmasters had to give their students an opportunity to memorize
the Heidelberg Catechism and help them understand its content. Their responsibility also included accompanying the youth of the school in attending
the catechism sermon at church on Sunday afternoons. It was a general practice that relevant questions and answers, which the children had memorized
at school, would be recited by a few talented students either before or after
the sermon. It was also the responsibility of the teaching staff to engage the
children in discussion to ascertain what they had learned in church.

Ministers were instructed to pay frequent visits to schoolmasters, accompanied by an elder. They were to encourage the schoolmasters to take
catechism teaching seriously and were to support them with demonstration
lessons and good advice for the children. Synod gave clear evidence of pedagogical insight. Ministers had to address and question children in a friendly
manner. In the process they were to encourage children to practice diligence

and godliness through "holy admonishments and praise." To promote the study of the material, they were to hand out small prizes "to be obtained from the magistrate."

Ministers were expected to preach "reasonably short" catechism sermons in public worship services, understandable to both young and old. They were encouraged to repeat their catechism sermons, especially in rural areas. It was also their task, in collaboration with an elder, to schedule weekly meetings for all "those who were eager to learn": church members and other adults with little or no education. They were to assemble these people in the consistory meeting room, in someone's residence, or in another suitable location to instruct them in the main areas of the Christian religion and to recapitulate their catechism sermons. The aim of this program of instruction was to provide everyone with a "clear and concise understanding of the Catechism." The minister was to supply "suitable questions and answers adapted to everyone's level of understanding." According to synod, this was the best approach to catechism teaching. These meetings were to be opened and closed with prayer and edifying admonitions.

In this description, we recognize our own system of catechism teaching by office bearers. The Synod of Dort, however, envisaged catechism teaching solely for young adults and older people. Catechism classes for baptized members of the church, as we know them today, did not yet exist. At the time of the Synod of Dort and thereafter, catechism classes and catechetical instruction were much broader concepts than is the case today. They encompassed instruction in Christian doctrine within families, schools, and churches.

Three textbooks

For catechetical instruction in schools, "three forms of the Catechism," or three versions of catechism instruction booklets, had to be used, targeting the various age ranges and varying degrees of comprehension on the part of students. It was generally agreed that a special booklet was needed for the youngest age group. Called the ABC Booklet, it presented the alphabet and was used to teach children to read. It became widely known as the *Hanenboekje* (Rooster Booklet), its name deriving from a rooster printed on the back of the title page. Above the rooster was the invitation, "Children, learn your lesson well." Underneath the rooster was a short verse:

> Early in the morning the rooster proves his zeal.
> Young people, study hard so you too may be praised.[1]

---

1. 's Morgens den haan zijn ijver vroeg bewijst, / Leert jonge jeugt dat men u ook so prijst.

The Rooster Booklet contained the Apostles' Creed, the Ten Commandments, the Lord's Prayer, and a few short prayers. As prescribed by synod, the booklet also contained the "institution of the sacraments and ecclesiastical discipline," a few simple questions about the three divisions of the Heidelberg Catechism, and a number of important Bible texts that were meant to encourage children to practice godliness. The booklet remained in use for several centuries and was reprinted as late as 1827.

For intermediate students "who had advanced to some extent in the foregoing material," synod prescribed a summary or compendium of the Heidelberg Catechism. Although the Compendium by the Middelburg minister Herman Faukelius had been available since 1608, synod decided to put together a smaller catechism on its own. A committee consisting of three professors and three ministers was charged with this task.

There was unanimous agreement about older students "who have progressed further in terms of age and knowledge." For them, synod specifically reiterated on May 1, 1619, during its 148th session, that the Heidelberg Catechism was the ideal book of instruction.

Role and significance of the Compendium

The committee assigned by synod to reflect on the preparation of a summary of the Catechism presented two proposals during its 127th session on Mon-

A school class in the seventeenth century

day afternoon, May 27, 1619. Only the smaller of the two booklets was read aloud at the meeting. The chair proposed that the other booklet not be read because it was quite long. Judging by the terse reference in the acts, there was scant enthusiasm for either booklet. In addition to the Heidelberg Catechism, two new booklets would have to be published on behalf of synod. This situation might have given the false impression that there were doubts about the Heidelberg Catechism, which had been viciously attacked by Remonstrants but which had been unanimously adopted by synod as a confessional statement. Synod desired to avoid giving this impression, according to Th. Heijncius of Amsterdam and Gisbertus. Voetius of Heusden, both delegates.

The outcome was that synod gave the churches freedom of choice. They could use the booklets prepared by the special committee or employ the *Kort begrip der Christelijke Religie voor die sich willen begeven tot des Heeren Heilig Avondmaal* (Compendium of the Christian Religion for Those Who Seek Admission to the Lord's Supper). The explicit reference to the booklet of Herman Faukelius constituted an obvious recommendation. In 1620, the Synod of South Holland decided at Gouda to introduce it everywhere. The example of South Holland, the heartland of the Republic of the Seven United Netherlands, was followed nationally. Beginning in 1637, the Compendium was incorporated in service books that were published in a single volume with the Psalter, a practice that confirmed the great value attached to this summary of the Catechism. The booklet was widely used for the teaching of catechism classes.

Pedagogical principles

The instruction program of the Synod of Dort was based on a number of pedagogical principles that were centuries old. There was a clear delineation of material into three age categories. We further recognize the principle of perception and continuity. In the teaching process, they consciously appealed to existing knowledge and built on this foundation. In the ABC Booklet, the youngest children learned the three catechetical summaries: the Apostles' Creed, the Ten Commandments, and the Lord's Prayer. In addition, some familiarity was established with respect to the three divisions of the Heidelberg Catechism. This groundwork facilitated the use of the Compendium by the intermediate group, who focused on faith, commandments, and prayer in greater detail. With this background, the older students were poised for the deeper and broader material of the Heidelberg Catechism itself, in which confession, commandments, and prayer were discussed and memorized for the third time.

People in those days practiced a culture of memorization, in which the development of memory was assigned a much greater role than is the case today. Knowing something from memory provided people with a degree of pleasure that we no longer experience. Young people in those days had considerably less trouble with memorizing material than do today's youth, who grow up in a culture of images in which everything calls for visualization. Nevertheless, even in those days memorization knew its bounds. The popularity of the Compendium as an ecclesiastical book of instruction leading to admission to the Lord's Supper can be explained to some extent by the difficulty of memorizing the far more comprehensive Heidelberg Catechism.

Catechetical teaching material of the seventeenth century
After the Synod of Dort, it took approximately fifty years before catechism teaching by ordained ministers became general practice. As far as we know, the first catechism class of this type was given in Heusden in 1620. However, enthusiasm on the part of most ministers was not particularly pronounced. Consequently, in a July 29, 1654, directive to all ministers, the Provincial Council of Holland ordered them to offer catechetical instruction on Sunday afternoons after the worship service to all those regularly exposed to the Word of God "and to equip them in this regard more so than ever before with all zeal and diligence, not doubting that in doing so they would be blessed by the Lord."

The Synod of Dort had not envisaged the teaching of catechism classes to children. However, in teaching the Catechism to their congregations at the conclusion of the Sunday afternoon services, ministers discovered that the simultaneous instruction of young and old contributed little to the religious formation of young people. In a number of locations, catechism classes were split into separate assemblies of younger and older persons. The younger group probably consisted of children who were ten to fourteen years old.

Beginning in the fourth decade of the seventeenth century, catechism classes for children increasingly attracted the attention of a number of provincial synods. Only towards the end of the seventeenth century could one speak of a fairly widespread adoption of catechism teaching of children, although encouragement on the part of ecclesiastical assemblies was required on an ongoing basis.

Two categories
By the time catechism teaching had become a generally accepted practice, a series of suitable booklets with questions and answers appeared on the

market. As early as 1641, the church of Middelburg raised objections to this development at the Classis of Walcheren. It was considered to be detrimental to the church of Christ that so many different catechism instruction booklets were being introduced, contrary to classis and synod decrees. The number of published booklets in question-and-answer format in the seventeenth and eighteenth centuries is estimated to have been in the hundreds.

Ministers among the authors of catechetical material often decided on publication in the last church that they served. Sometimes booklets with questions and answers appeared a few months prior to the author's departure. Such publications combined personal views and years of experience. Upon ecclesiastical approbation, whenever such a booklet rolled off the press, it automatically acquired more than local popularity.

The abundance of publications, however, does not necessarily mean that the degree of catechism teaching advanced. Countless encouragements and admonishments from ecclesiastical assemblies imply that family catechism teaching was frequently neglected by parents. In 1678, Christophilus Eubulus, a pseudonym for Jacobus Koelman, painted a rather somber picture of all forms of catechism teaching in *De Pointen van Nodige Reformatie* (Aspects of a Necessary Reformation). The overwhelming majority of parents offered no home catechism instruction whatsoever. Numerous ministers did not visit schools, failed to encourage children, and were ill-suited to conduct catechism classes. Many teachers were quite ignorant of religion and needed further schooling themselves. Numerous school teachers displayed no zeal to teach children the Heidelberg Catechism. The interplay of church and school on catechism teaching was simultaneously the strength and weakness of religious education in the Netherlands.

The importance of catechism teaching

I cannot see how a minister in all conscience can live and die, without making any effort to conduct catechism teaching; for people are usually ignorant, and flowing sermons are not suited to teach them the first principles of truth and godliness: catechism teaching is the ideal means to achieve this, being the same thing as preaching, but reflecting a different approach.

Wilhelmus à Brakel, "Concerning the Office of Pastors and Teachers, of Elders and Deacons,"[2] *De Redelijke Godsdienst* (*The Christian's Reasonable Service*).

---

2. "Van het ambt der herders en leraars, der ouderlingen en diakenen"

Gellius Petri de Bouma

Roughly speaking, two categories of material can be distinguished. In the first place were a number of voluminous publications that were focused on the introduction of catechism teaching after Sunday afternoon worship services or were intended to improve the quality of this teaching. The second category comprised instruction booklets that were targeted at children and young people and envisaged the preparation of those who wished to partake of the Lord's Supper. We give here several short descriptions of books and booklets in both categories, in chronological order. Our choice was guided by their popularity, measured by the number of reprints they achieved.

Gellius de Bouma: Catechism teacher from the start
As early as 1621, De Bouma (1579–1658), minister at Zutphen, published a collection of questions and answers to accompany the Catechism: *Christelicke Catechismus der Nederlandsche Ghereformeerde Kercken* (Christian Catechism of the Netherlands Reformed Churches). He must have been motivated by decisions of the Synod of Dort, because he indicated that "those who had been assigned such a task by the venerable national synod in the year 1619"[3] were aware of the preparation of his publication. He probably had in mind the group of theologians who had been given the task to put together a summary of the Catechism aimed at more advanced children.

---

3. "van de ghene die Anno 1619 van dien Ed. Synodo Nationali daer toe gecommitteert waren"

The author considered his book to be suitable for those who "desired to grow and advance in the knowledge of God and our Savior Jesus Christ."[4] De Bouma did not write his book for catechism teaching by office bearers after catechism preaching, although widespread use was subsequently made of it to this end. He published it specifically "for the benefit of all Christian parents, schoolmasters and schoolmistresses, as well as keen young people."[5]

De Bouma provided an "Onderwijsinge" (Clarification) for each question and answer of the Catechism. In the process, he divided each answer into a series of short questions and answers. He took care to confirm the answers with Scripture references. Practically all authors of catechetical teaching material in the seventeenth and eighteenth centuries followed him in this approach. Frequently, however, he lost track of his own guidelines, and his answers turned into brief expositions.

De Bouma selected this approach to make life easy for the potential users, among whom he also included school children. He adopted this idea from a booklet that appeared in the Palatinate in 1609, which provided additional questions in the margin of the Catechism text.

De Bouma's booklet, which comprised many hundreds of questions and answers, "was received with such eagerness, and gratefully adopted for catechism teaching in a large part of the United Provinces, and continues to be used today, so that it has had to be printed several times in many places."[6] The great popularity of De Bouma's work must have been due to its wide circle of users. Its main purpose seems to have been to encourage "young people"[7]—emphatically so indicated in his prefaces—to make public profession of faith. Of the six appendices to the book, four pertain to the Lord's Supper. The well-known short work by Godefridus Udemans, *Voorbereydinghe tot den H. Avondmaal* (Preparation for the Lord's Supper), belongs in the same category, as does *Kort Onderwys in den geloove* (Brief Instruction in the Faith), which was probably written by De Bouma himself. The latter booklet contained fifty questions and answers that undoubtedly assisted consistories in examinations that preceded public profession of faith and admission to the Lord's Supper.

---

4. "in de kennisse Godts ende onzes Salichmakers Jesu Christi begeeren te wassen ende toe to nemen"

5. "tot dienst van alle Christelijcke Ouders, School-meesters en Schoolvrouwen, als oock de leer-gierige jonge Lieden"

6. "'t Welck met sulcke begeerlickheydt is ontfangen, en in een goed deel der Vereenighde Provincien, om daaruyt te Catechiseren, danckelick aen-genomen, ende oock noch gebruyckt wordt, alsoo dat het tot verscheyde male in veele plaetsen heeft moeten gedruckt worden"

7. "Jonghe Jeucht"

Petrus de Witte

Petrus de Witte: Author of the most popular textbook
Petrus de Witte (1622–1669), minister at Leiden, attained prominence through the publication of his book *Catechizatie over den heidelbergschen Catechismus* (The Teaching of the Heidelberg Catechism). A laudatory poem included in the volume implies that the first edition of this book was published at Hoorn in 1650. In 1697, the thirty-third edition appeared, which probably made De Witte's book the most frequently used textbook among the Reformed community in the seventeenth century.

This book was intended entirely for the introduction of catechism teaching after the Sunday afternoon worship service. Its preface extensively reproduces the decree of the Synod of Dort (1618–1619), as well as the July 29, 1654 directive to ministers issued by the Provincial Council of Holland. Both prefaces to the work itself constitute a major plea for catechism teaching. The entire argument is supported by detailed citations from Willem Teellinck, "that great champion in God's house";[8] and from *Coopmans Roer* (Merchant's Rudder) by Godefridus Udemans, "a bright star among the people of Zeeland."[9]

---

8. "dien grooten Yveraer in Gods huis"
9. "een floncker-ster der Zeeuwen"

Frontispiece of *Catechizatie over den heidelbergschen Catechismus* (The Teaching of the Heidelberg Catechism)

Petrus de Witte on the Catechism

Blessed be this godly work, blessed be the hearts that first conceived it, the mouths that articulated it, the hands and pens that recorded it and brought it to such a desirable conclusion. Through God's blessing, the churches have reaped the desired benefits of this. It has meant the deathblow to the souls of those who sought modernism.

From "Toe-eigeningh" (Appropriation), in *Catechizatie over den heidelbergschen Catechismus der Gereformeerde Christelicke Religie* (The Teaching of the Heidelberg Catechism of the Reformed Christian Religion).

De Witte fully supported the reformation program of the Dutch Further Reformation, in which the introduction of catechism teaching within the family, at school, and in church was a key component. Teellinck's appeal resonated in his heart: "Reform thy home after every sermon that thou hearest."[10] Every father was expected to teach the Catechism to his family, particularly on God's day. "It is these and similar reasons that motivated us to advocate this type of catechism teaching."[11]

---

10. "Reformeert u huis na elcke Predikatie die ghy hoort."
11. "Deze ende diergelijcke redenen hadden ons bewogen deze *Catechizatie* in 't licht te brengen."

There is no shortage of practical suggestions. The reader is to follow the lead provided by the explanation of the Heidelberg Catechism in church. At the start of the week, one should delve into the upcoming material and continue with this until Sunday. "In this manner you will be built up in the knowledge of the truth that leads to godliness; you will be better able to follow the sermon; and you will be in a position to respond to anyone who demands an account of the hope that is within you."[12] Each question and response of the Catechism calls for catechization, a detailed treatment of the material by means of questions and answers, with heavy emphasis on Scripture proof. Although a recurrent theme is the rejection of errors, the explanation of doctrine itself predominates in the more than four thousand questions and answers contained in the book. The answers are usually brief and to the point, but at times they use up as much as a third of a page.

The author repeatedly employs the personal language of the Catechism, but he also presents passages of a more objective nature. Towards the end of his short lesson on question 22 of the Heidelberg Catechism, he focuses on the appropriation of the promises of the gospel through faith. This process includes the so-called mystical syllogism, which permits a believer to draw a conclusion about the faith that he observes at work in his own heart. This line of reasoning was employed in the seventeenth century as an aid to assurance of faith.

Q. To whom were the promises of grace in the gospel meant to bring comfort?
A. To all those who repent of their evil ways.

Q. Is it then sufficient to be aware of these aforementioned promises to qualify as a true believer?
A. Indeed not; but it is necessary to accept personally these promises with a confident heart.

Q. Who can accept these promises and appropriate them within their soul?
A. Penitent sinners, who seek their salvation beyond themselves in Christ.

Q. How is seizing hold of Christ and the appropriation of the promises of grace confessed by the human soul?

---

12. "Zoo zult ghy opgebouwt worden in de kennisse der waerheyd die na de Godzaligheyd is, met meerdere vrucht de Predicatien verstaen, ende bereyd zijn tot verantwoordinge, aen een yegelick die u rekenschap af-eischt van de hoope die in u is."

A. This occurs through the following syllogism that rests on God's promises: The Lord Christ has been promised as Savior to all those who truly repent of their sins; He is indeed their Savior. But through God's grace I have repented from my sins, to serve my God. Therefore, the Lord Christ has also been promised to me as a Savior; He is indeed my Savior.

A catechism student

My dear Father, I desire that thou wilt promise me that thou wilt go to Rev. De Witte and Rev. Ardinois and thank them that they have taught me catechism classes (for they teach the Catechism every Tuesday in the Mare Church, as their colleagues do in due course in other churches) and tell them that those beautiful Scripture references that they have taught me in their catechism classes have brought me so much comfort on my deathbed, indeed have brought me salvation. Oh! Oh! those wonderful and lovely catechism classes that I always attended with so much joy and never once missed in all the time that I attended them ready to respond to questions.

Susanna Bickes (1650–1664)
From: *Laatste Uren van Susanna Bickes* (Last Hours of Susanna Bickes), Rotterdam, 1735.

Cornelius Poudroyen: Interpreter of Voetius's legacy

Poudroyen (d. 1662) was a minister at Fort Crevecoeur. In 1653, he published his *Catechisatie. Dat is, een grondige ende eenvoudige Onderwijsinge over de leere des Christelicken Catechismi: Bestaende in Vragen en Antwoorden* (Catechetical Instruction, That Is, Thorough and Simple Teaching concerning the Doctrine of the Christian Catechism: Comprising Questions and Answers). The author had been a student of the well-known Utrecht professor Gisbertus Voetius (1589–1676). He drew the questions and answers for his book from lecture notes of Voetius, which had been published earlier as a separate booklet. Poudroyen expanded this list of questions on the basis of catechism classes, sermons, and lectures given by Voetius. The latter proofread the text with the utmost care. This book can therefore be thought of as catechetical instruction by Voetius.

Poudroyen's purpose was the same as Petrus de Witte's. In the two prefaces that preceded the text, Poudroyen repeatedly emphasized that the book was intended for "young people, as well as hesitant and ordinary folk."[13] He hoped that they would thoroughly prepare themselves beforehand on the portion of the Heidelberg Catechism that was to be discussed. When the minister or his substitute asked questions on the basis of this book, Poudroyen wanted the students to provide good answers, "thus coming well prepared and ready, not only to answer any questions that might be asked, but also to grow and advance in true knowledge of God from day to day."[14]

The great importance that the author attached to the memorization of questions could leave the impression that he approached the doctrine of salvation intellectually. In his second preface, Poudroyen responded in detail to such criticism. He distinguished between purely human knowledge of Scripture, which can be observed in those who have not been born again, and divine knowledge,[15] which the Holy Spirit works in the heart. To receive the latter knowledge, one must pray to God fervently and earnestly, highly esteem the things of God and His Son Jesus Christ, study the Word of the Lord, and attend catechism classes.

The detailed and concrete treatment of the Ten Commandments in about 350 pages is typical of the book. The Dutch Further Reformation's pursuit of the sanctification of everyday life was transformed here into catechetical exercises that delved into the finest details. For example, the discussion of the fifth commandment indicated that on the basis of Scripture, women could not hold ecclesiastical office. The question was then asked: Can a woman hold political office? "Yes, to ensure legal succession or to safeguard public order and welfare." In connection with the sixth commandment, some ten questions were devoted to the profession of a tightrope walker, who consciously placed himself in danger. On the seventh commandment, fourteen questions discussed the relationship between drunkenness and immorality. When he came to the eighth commandment, the author explicitly discussed theft committed with false yardsticks or measures.

The author realized that his Catechism, which in most editions ran to 1,200 pages and comprised many thousands of questions, was far too detailed and broadly conceived for young people of average ability. Following in Voetius's footsteps, therefore, he differentiated among questions by labeling them as "a," "b," "c," or "d." Questions "a" and "b" were for beginners. However,

---

13. "de jonge jeucht, als oock de swacke ende eenvoudige lieden"
14. "ten eynde sy alsoo wel geprepareert en bereydet komende, niet alleen wel mogen antwoorden op het gene haer gevraegt sal worden, maer oock dagelicks daer door in de ware kennisse Godes mogen aenwassen en toenemen"
15   "Goddelicke kennisse"

this differentiation did not signify much. It did not mean, for example, that the catechism teacher discussed the material differently for every group. Nor did it mean that the "c" questions in a particular chapter belonged together and thus formed one connected whole. Every catechism student simply had to listen to questions that were answered by others and patiently wait for his own "a," "b," "c," or "d" question to be raised.

Johannes Martinus: Author of a manual for the Groningen project
During the second half of the seventeenth century, there was regular preaching from the Catechism in Groningen. After the service, the young people recited the corresponding questions and answers in church. Next, the minister explained that Lord's Day of the Catechism to the children, "also for the benefit of any adults who might be present."[16] However, there was no specific "catechism teaching of older people."[17]

Encouraged by the provincial synod, the consistory conceived of a catechetical project to be implemented by the ministers. In addition to catechetical instruction of children "in the traditional manner,"[18] this project included a new form of catechism teaching for young people. The children not only recited the text of the Heidelberg Catechism, but they were given additional practice by answering short questions concerning its content, "maintaining the precise wording of the Catechism."[19] For older people, catechetical exercises were devised that corresponded with the presentation of the relevant Lord's Day of the Catechism in church.

Johannes Martinus (1603–1665) was the oldest serving minister at Groningen, having already served this church for twenty-eight years. At the request of the consistory, he wrote *Grootere Catechisatie over den Catechismus der waren Christelicken Religie* (Broader Instruction in the Catechism of the True Christian Religion). The goal of Martinus differed little from that of Petrus de Witte and Cornelius Poudroyen. Church members were encouraged to prepare themselves for the preaching of the relevant Lord's Day with the help of questions and answers. Any Scripture references that were not cited in the answers were to be looked up in the Bible at home.

Those who were so inclined could use this book to prepare themselves to answer questions asked by the minister who led the catechetical exercise. The two front pews of the choir in the Martini Church were reserved for

---

16. "tot best ook van de omstaende ouden"
17. "catechetiseeren van de bejaerde"
18. "op den ouden voet"
19. "blijvende precijs bij des Catechismi woorden"

this purpose. Interested people who did not directly participate in answering questions would position themselves around these pews in order to receive the required instruction all the same. Usually the same people supplied the answers. Those who had been thus schooled in public catechism classes frequently became unordained ministers[20] who practiced in the north of the country in the eighteenth century.

The answers for Broader Instruction were generally short and to the point. Their aim was to clarify the text of the relevant Lord's Day of the Catechism and support it with Scripture references. The author indicated that they brought the reader closer to the truth of Scripture "and pointed him to the assurance of faith, ease of conscience, [and] sanctity of life."[21] To this end, Martinus opened and closed each Lord's Day section with "short sighings,"[22] prayers that corresponded to passages of the Old and New Testaments.

Abraham Trommius: Man of good dialogue
Following the completion of Broader Instruction, Johannes Martinus began

20. "oefenaars"
21. "ende deselve tot sekerheyt van 't geloove, troost van de consciëntie, godsaligheyt van 't leven richten"
22. "korte suchtingen"

The Martini Church at Groningen in the eighteenth century

writing a booklet "for the use of young and ordinary folk."[23] After he finished the text for the first two Lord's Days of the Catechism, he passed away. His son-in-law, Abraham Trommius (1633–1719), took up the task of completing the book. Trommius, minister at Haren (Groningen) and author of a well-known concordance, gave to this work the title that his father-in-law had envisaged: *Shorter Catechetical Instruction*. The subtitle is *Tot dienst van kinderen, ende andere eenvoudige personen, die haar eerst in den Catechismo beginnen te oeffenen* (For the Benefit of Children, and Other Ordinary Folk, as a First Exposure to the Catechism).

The author sought to keep the explanatory questions and answers that accompanied the text of the Catechism as brief as possible "to assist those having trouble with memorization."[24] At the same time, he tried to formulate them plainly and clearly, so that everyone would easily grasp their meaning. This approach led to the following formulation for question 29 of the Catechism:

28. Q. But how does Jesus deliver us from all our sins?
    A. In such a way that He sets us free from the guilt, dominion, and punishment of sin.

29. Q. How does He set us free from the guilt of sin?
    A. He has completely paid for all of our sins.

30. Q. How can you prove this?
    A. 1 John 1:7: "The blood of Jesus Christ his Son cleanseth us from all sin."

31. Q. How does He set us free from the dominion of sin?
    A. He no longer lets sin reign in us.

32. Q. Can you prove this also?
    A. Romans 6:14: "For sin shall not have dominion over you."

33. Q. How does He set us free from the punishment of sin?
    A. He has suffered it completely on our behalf.

34. Q. Prove this as well.
    A. Galatians 3:13: "Christ hath redeemed us from the curse of the law, being made a curse for us."

---

23. "tot dienst der Jonge ende Eenvoudige"
24. "om also de memorie der swakken te helpen"

Title page of Shorter
Catechetical Instruction

In this way, the 129 questions of the Catechism were explained and clarified by Trommius with no fewer than 2,173 questions and answers. The author expected the teaching of the Catechism to both young and old to sharpen their minds so that they could listen to and retain sermons incomparably better than before. In 1667, when Trommius had completed "this brief work,"[25] the provincial synod ensured its recommendation to every classis in the Province of Groningen.

Around 1670, Antonius van Oostrum, minister in Den Briel, published his *Korte ende beknopte Catechizatie* (Short and Concise Catechetical Instruction). His approach and scope are reminiscent of the catechism books by Johannes Martinus and Abraham Trommius.

David Knibbe: Focus on the Compendium

David Knibbe (1639–1701), minister at Leiden, agreed with the Synod of Dort that the Heidelberg Catechism was too difficult and too comprehensive "for young people."[26] He therefore wrote catechism lessons to accompany the questions of its Compendium, which had been recommended by the synod for

---

25. "dit kleine werksken"
26. "voor de jonge Jeugd"

intermediate students at schools. His *Katechisatie over het Kort Begrip der Christe-lijke Gereformeerde Religie* (Catechetical Instruction on the Compendium of the Christian Reformed Religion) was intended for home catechism instruction, for the instruction of young people, and for all who desired to partake in the Lord's Supper. The material was explained by means of 974 questions and answers. Special attention was given to the "doctrine of the papacy wherever it might be applicable."[27] Young people and prospective members had to be armed against the teaching of the Roman Catholic Church.

In his preface, Knibbe emphasized that his book was intended first for parents to provide catechetical instruction within the family. They would be wise to mark the most important questions so that children who could not yet read could also memorize some of them. The author did not ignore "stam-mering children."[28] For them, he had printed in the back of his book the "short and sweet"[29] booklet of questions by Jacobus Borstius, minister at Rotterdam: *Korte Vraagen voor de kleine Kinderen* (Short Questions for Small Children). Seventy-one questions on doctrine were followed by 158 questions on biblical history. Knibbe considered Borstius's questions on doctrine, with Bible references, to be the minimum requirement for "folk who were unable to read or were slow in understanding prior to partaking of the Lord's Supper."[30]

Knibbe restructured the book when it was reprinted in 1701. He divided the text of Compendium and his 974 questions and answers into the fifty-two Lord's Days of the Heidelberg Catechism because many children also "took catechetical instruction in church."[31] This way, they could tell what they had to learn for the discussion of each Lord's Day section. The particularly good reception of this booklet undoubtedly reflected his choice of the Compendium, the division of the material according to the Lord's Day sections of the Catechism, and the conciseness of his questions and answers, which were supported by one or two Scripture references. This approach and the incorporation of Borstius's booklet in his own work implied that the author was aware of the development of the intellectual abilities of children and young people. He required only minimal knowledge for those who sought access to the Lord's Supper, which must have contributed to the general appreciation for his work. In the eighteenth century, Knibbe's book would be overshad-

---

27. "Leer van het Pausdom alwaar het maar te pas quam"
28. "de stamelende kinderen"
29. "soete en korte"
30. "lieden, die niet lesen konnen, of swaar van begrip syn eer dat sy ten Heiligen Avondmaal gaan"
31. "katechiseeren in de kercken"

David Knibbe

owed only by the well-known booklet of questions and answers written by one of his own students, Abraham Hellenbroek, minister at Rotterdam.

Catechetical teaching material of the eighteenth century
Near the end of the seventeenth century and the beginning of the eighteenth century, there was a change in the practice of the Lord's Supper in the Netherlands. This development reflected the impact of Reformed pietism, which began as a distinct movement around the end of the sixteenth century. In the seventeenth century, the quest for godliness prompted by this movement was manifested in the ecclesiastical, political, and social renewal program of the Dutch Further Reformation. In the eighteenth century, this program had to be abandoned from a practical point of view. However, an emphasis continued on the experience of Reformed doctrine in the heart through the working of the Holy Spirit and on its culmination in a godly lifestyle.

Under existing practice, all professing members were expected—indeed, emphatically admonished—to partake of the Lord's Supper. In the light of the pietism of the time, a number of ministers came to view this practice as untenable. To these proponents of an experiential orthodoxy, it became increasingly clear that among those partaking of the Lord's Supper were large numbers of people who had not yet been converted and who in their daily walk came through as false, nominal Christians. In preaching, a clear distinction began to be made between professing members who had received a divine right of access from the Lord and professing members who lacked this right. Great emphasis was placed on the self-examination that must precede use of this sacrament. Thus, theological candidate Sicco Tjaden noted in his 1718 travel diary the striking phenomenon that in the Utrecht village of Tienhoven, only forty people participated in the Lord's Supper. Previously, hundreds of people would partake of the Lord's Supper in this church served by the well-known Gerard van Schuylenborch (1681–1770). Presently, however, the great majority of the congregation remained in their pews during the administration of this sacrament.

This development was due in part to gradual shifts in theological thinking. In the relationship between the covenant and predestination, the latter came to be more strongly emphasized. The distinction between the covenant in an external sense (which included all professing and baptized church members) and an internal sense (which included only those who were truly regenerated) became more widely held. Regeneration and the marks of grace received greater attention.

Two illustrations of a new development

This change in the practice of the Lord's Supper led to a shift in how profession of faith was made. It became possible for young people to make profession of faith without being regenerated or possessing personal faith. They professed faith largely to keep up appearances, merely on the strength of historical ties. Many ministers came to assume that although one could not judge people's claims and motives, in most cases profession was a superficial statement coming from the mouth. Consequently, truths needed to be comprehended mentally and appropriated personally. As a result, many books of instruction changed in nature and tone, with the new instruction material presenting biblical doctrine in a more objective, informative manner.

An example of this new development was a frequently reprinted short work by a lesser-known but evidently much-appreciated lay minister and catechism teacher, Cornelis van Vollenhoven. It was published for the first time in 1728 and was still being reprinted in 1790. It was called *De zuivere en beproefde Waarheden Begrepen in den Heidelbergschen Catechismus Zakelyk uitgebreid, en met het H. Woord bevestigd, tot bevordering in die kennesse, die aanzet tot het oeffenen van ware Godzaligheid, en welke hun, die dezelve geloven, belyden en beleven eenen waaren troost geeft in leven en sterven* (Pure and Tried Truths, Contained in the Heidelberg Catechism, Concisely Expanded and Confirmed on the Basis of Holy Scripture, for the Advancement of Knowledge, Encouraging the Practice of True Godliness and Offering True Comfort in Both Life and Death to Those Who Believe, Profess, and Experience the Same). The title of this work and its preface make clear that its author identified with Reformed pietism. It is not sufficient to comprehend truths with the mind and to accept them superficially; their power must also be experienced within one's heart. "Oh! What benefit is there in knowing a great deal, if meanwhile we deny it in practice?"[32]

In Van Vollenhoven's book, the terms "I," "me," and "mine" of the Catechism were replaced by "he," "one," "a person," "they," or some other objective description. Several questions and answers from his discussion of the first Lord's Day section are quoted here:

4.   Q. What presupposes this comfort?
     A. Misery: Revelation 3:17. For if one requires this comfort, one must be aware of it, and feel it. Compare Psalm 38: 5.

5.   Q. Why is it called your comfort?
     A. Because it is not for everyone: but only for the Lord's people. Isaiah 40:1. And a person must be desirous to obtain this comfort for himself.

6.   Q. Why is it referred to as the only comfort?
     A. Because it is sufficient: those who have it, possess everything; this comfort is able to satisfy the soul; it is the only comfort required. Luke 10: 42.

7.   Q. Why is it called a comfort in both life and death?
     A. Because one needs it in both life and death; the comfort that does not forsake us in death is indeed true comfort. Compare Psalm 73: 25, 26.

This development in the direction of a more objective, informative transfer of knowledge was also recognizable in works that supported the presentation of catechetical exercises by ministers. Thus Egbertus Schrader (1711–1785), minister at Landsmeer, became renowned through a work that first appeared in 1733: *Eene gemakkelijke Handleiding om over de Catechismus-Predicatien te Catechizeeren, volgende de woorden van de Heidelbergsche Catechismus in de Verklaringe en Toepassinge, tot gemak en nut der Catechizante* (An Easy Manual for Teaching Catechism Sermons, Employing the Text of the Heidelberg Catechism in Explanations and Applications, for the Convenience and Benefit of Catechism Students). The phrase "for the convenience and benefit of

---

32. "Ach! Wat zal het ons baten veel te weten, zo wy 't ondertusschen loochenen met onze practyk"

catechism students" probably referred to the possibility of using this book to familiarize oneself with the material that the minister was to discuss. This book did not differ much in content from the seventeenth century works of Petrus de Witte and David Knibbe, but the treatment of the material had an entirely objective emphasis. In addition, Schrader provided each Lord's Day section of the Catechism with an application in which he addressed the unconverted with very personal and discriminatory questions. He addressed God's children separately, among whom he further distinguished between those with a weak faith and those with greater assurance.

The books by Van Vollenhoven and Schrader form part of a stream of catechetical publications that continued throughout the eighteenth century. We limit ourselves to a discussion of four popular publications in their order of appearance.

Abraham Hellenbroek: Author of the Voetian question book par excellence
In 1707, Abraham Hellenbroek (1658–1731), minister at Rotterdam, published *Voorbeeld der Godlyke waarheden, voor eenvoudigen die zig bereiden tot de Belydenisse des geloofs: Meest tot particulier gebruik opgesteld* (*A Specimen of Divine Truths, for Those Who Are Preparing for Confession of Faith: Mostly Designed for Personal Use*). The title immediately makes clear that this booklet was not intended for family catechism teaching nor for responding to catechism exercises conducted in church. Whereas the Compendium was intended for those who desired access to the Lord's Supper, Hellenbroek addressed himself to those who prepared themselves to make profession of faith. The difference was not substantive, because profession of faith gave access to the Lord's Supper. Nevertheless, it reflected the shift in practice regarding profession of faith that occurred during the author's lifetime.

As might be expected of a question book aimed at those who desired to make profession of faith, the 612 questions and answers of Hellenbroek's publication are remarkably concise and clear, thus facilitating memorization. Scripture proofs are merely indicated as references. A number of copies survive in which the text is interspersed with blank pages. Catechism students were expected to look up these Scripture passages at home and write them out. The focus on profession of faith is also seen in Hellenbroek's omission of discussions on the Apostles' Creed, the Ten Commandments, and the Lord's Prayer. Instead, he made do with a very concise discussion of faith, the law, and prayer in light of the teachings of the church.

Abraham Hellenbroek

Concerning faith

Here are two questions from Hellenbroek's question book on the justification of faith:

10. Q. What is the primary justifying act of faith?

    A. It is an act whereby the soul not only sincerely wills and desires that the promises of the gospel be true, but also that the soul, with heartfelt surrender and denial of self and all things or persons, desires and actually takes hold of the Lord Jesus as the only cause of its salvation.

11. Q. What is the fruit of the justifying act of faith?

    A. The special and certain application of the promises of the gospel and the Lord Jesus to each believer personally. This application is not always present in all believers because of the temptations of Satan, the accusations of the law, and the allurements of the flesh. All who have truly appropriated Jesus, however, should strive for this.

Why did Hellenbroek leave these topics out? He probably assumed that these three catechetical summary statements received adequate attention in catechetical instruction at school and in public exercises focused on the

Heidelberg Catechism, and therefore they could be omitted in catechetical instruction for profession of faith.

A Specimen of Divine Truths is sometimes interpreted as an elaboration of the Compendium. At most, this description applies to the three chapters dealing with the Mediator of the Covenant and the stages of His humiliation and exaltation—sections that merely resemble the Compendium in its coverage of topics in connection with the Apostles' Creed. For the rest, there is no evidence whatsoever that the author patterned the structure of his work after the Heidelberg Catechism or its Compendium. Hellenbroek certainly interpreted the guidelines set by the Synod of Dort fairly broadly. *A Specimen of Divine Truths*, in fact, provided candidates for profession of faith with a short summary of Reformed dogmatics in twenty chapters. It is noteworthy that its structure closely resembles that of *The Christian's Reasonable Service* by his Rotterdam colleague and friend, W. à Brakel. The latter standard work appeared for the first time in 1700, five years prior to publication of *A Specimen of Divine Truths*.

Around 1759, an anonymous author added to Hellenbroek's question book a chapter on the counsel of peace that employed strikingly long answers; in the editions of that time, it was given a place after the section dealing with predestination. Some questions and answers and a number of Scripture references were added to the text, and the size of the booklet was increased by thirty pages. The original author never laid eyes on the larger version. Only the shorter version from before 1759 can be considered to be original. The "compendium of principal errors found outside the Reformed Church" does not appear in early editions either.

Hellenbroek's question book met with an unprecedented response. In numerous locations, it displaced the Compendium for catechetical instruction of candidates for profession of faith. Before long, it was also used for other catechism teaching, although this was not the author's intention. According to a preface in one of the editions from the second half of the eighteenth century, it was used by ministers "in nearly all important cities and villages." The twenty-fourth edition appeared in 1797, prepared by the Dort bookseller Abr. Blussé and Son. This publisher estimated the number of copies that had been sold since the first edition to be in excess of forty thousand! At any rate, this booklet was reprinted so often that the various publishers lost track of the overall number of copies produced.

In 1798, D. van Wijngaarden, onetime teacher, sexton, and cantor at Willemstad, even published a rhymed version of *A Specimen of Divine Truths*. Each chapter could be sung to the tune of a rhymed Psalm. Van Wijngaarden could not have derived much pleasure from his efforts, for his poetry led to accusations of unorthodoxy. In 1801, Ph. J. Resler published a simplified version of the booklet with the title: *Het leerboekje van Hellenbroek, verkort, door Ph. J. R. tot gebruik zijner leerlingen, bijzonder voor minvermogenden* (The Hellenbroek Question Book, Abridged, by Ph. J. R. for Use by His Students, Especially Those of Limited Ability).

The popularity of the booklet by Hellenbroek was underscored by the publication of two manuals. In 1764, Ary Goedhart, the well-known Rotterdam visitor to the sick and catechism teacher, published *Pit en Merg der H. Godgeleerdheid. Ingericht om dezulken, die het Voorbeeld der Goddlijken waarheden van wijlen de heer A. Hellenbroek, Reeds geleerd hebben, op te leiden tot eene uigebreidere kennis der verhevene Goddelike zaken* (The Core and Marrow of Holy Divinity. Presenting Deeper Knowledge of Sublimely Divine Matters to Those Who Have Already Mastered "A Specimen of Divine Truths" by the Late Mr. A. Hellenbroek). Its ninth edition rolled off the press at Amsterdam in 1782.

The second manual was produced by the Schoonhoven catechism teacher and unordained minister Jan Nupoort, who subsequently became pastor at Batavia. His book appeared in 1777 in two volumes: *Korte en Eenvoudige Catechizatie over het Voorbeeld der Godlyke Waarheden van den Zaligen heer Abraham Hellenbroek. Waar in de Leer van de Hervormde kerk, naar aanleiding van ieder Vraag en antwoord, zaaklyk word opgegeven* (Short and Simple Catechetical Instruction in "A Specimen of Divine Truths" by the Late Mr. Abraham Hellenbroek, in which the Doctrine of the Reformed Church is Concisely Presented with Reference to Each Question and Answer). Its sixth edition appeared in Utrecht in 1799. Following the Secession of 1834 it would be reprinted three more times.

In the course of the eighteenth century, Hellenbroek's *A Specimen of Divine Truths* displaced not only the Compendium but also nearly every other catechetical booklet of instruction within Voetian circles. What factors explain the unprecedented response to Hellenbroek's question book? In the prefaces of various editions and elaborations of this question book, contemporaries invariably mentioned the same reasons: "The natural flow of the material, the clarity and conciseness of the questions and answers, and the encouragement given to more thorough study and further elaboration, make it very useful for both beginners and more advanced students." Another preface praised "its good organization, and concise, clear and pertinent content." Ary Goedhart and Jan Nupoort defended their choice of Hellenbroek's booklet on the basis of its broad appeal.

Hellenbroek's Question Book on the Covenant of Grace

9. Q. How does a sinner enter into this covenant of grace?
   A. God first comes to the sinner, inviting and beseeching him into this covenant with much earnestness and uprightness, thereby resolving all his difficulties (2 Cor. 5:20; Ezek. 33:11; Isa. 55:2)

10. Q. What then does God do as a result of His invitation?
    A. "I drew them with cords of a man, with bands of love" (Hosea 11:4).

11. Q. What in turn does the sinner do who is thus called?
    A. He accepts the Lord as his God and surrenders himself to God (S.S. 2:16).

12. Q. What are the characteristics of such acquiescence?
    A. The sinner consents calmly, willingly, humbly, faithfully, uprightly, fully agreeing with the demands as well as the promises of the covenant (Ps. 51:8).

13. Q. What are the consequences of this consenting?
    A. God remembers His covenant forever (Psalm 105:8), and the partakers of the covenant have the right to request all things necessary unto life and eternal salvation (Ps. 74:19–21).

Compared with books containing thousands of questions, the brief work of Hellenbroek was much to be preferred. The questions were simpler than those of many catechetical works of the seventeenth century, and the author did not fall into the trap of constructing extraordinarily lengthy answers. In an era when unimaginable quantities of material were produced and the average catechism student was inundated with questions, people must have experienced a sense of relief. Hellenbroek's *A Specimen of Divine Truths* excelled in clarity of structure, lucidity, and brevity. He echoed the views of Reformed pietism, which clearly distinguished between the knowledge of faith and intellectual knowledge, and he consequently ushered in a new appreciation for a dogmatic interpretation of Reformed doctrine.

Friedrich Adolph Lampe: Voice of serious Coccceians

F. A. Lampe (1683–1729) initially served as minister in Bremen in northern Germany. He was a confirmed disciple of Johannes Cocceius, "the great Apollo," who placed the key to the treasury of the Word in our hands. At the

same time, his spiritual background was formed by the heritage of the Dutch
Further Reformation. Lampe must be counted among the first representatives of Reformed Pietism in the eighteenth century.

In 1720, he left for Utrecht to take up a professorship. For his catechism
students in Bremen, he left behind an introduction to the Catechism that
they could use to prepare themselves for their catechism classes. This intention explains the title of the book: *Melk der Waarheit volgens aanleydinge van den
Heidelbergschen Catechismus ten nutte van de leer-begeerige Jeugt opgesteld, en zijnen
beminden Catechisanten te Bremen ter gedachtenisse nagelaten* (Milk of the Truth
Gleaned from the Heidelberg Catechism for the Benefit of Young People
Who Are Eager to Learn, and Presented as a Memento to My Beloved Catechism Students). This book was almost immediately translated into German
and was published by an Amsterdam publisher as early as 1721.

In Milk of the Truth, Lampe emphasized that, apart from parents, schools
had the responsibility to impress upon young people "how one can live to
please God, and one day die happily." Since such instruction was largely lacking in most places, it was the responsibility of ministers to fill this gap. The
instruction of young people was one of their most important activities. "If
there is one aspect of their office where they can expect to be blessed, it is indeed this one. In all humility I dare testify on the basis of personal experience
that more people are won over through catechism teaching than through
preaching."[33] Lampe himself devoted more time to catechism teaching than
to preaching. He saw catechism teaching as the ideal way to counteract decay
in the church. The truths of the Word that, under God's blessing, are most
likely to bring about regeneration must be especially stressed and put into
the heart. In catechism teaching, dogmatic material must be blended with
personal questions that encourage young people to focus on their own hearts.
"Have they ever felt troubled about such a wretched state, as the state of nature indeed is? When the Person of the Lord JESUS is discussed, one should
never fail to ask: Dost thou truly love the Lord JESUS?... What is the condition of thy prayer life? Dost thou put any effort into this?"[34]

Lampe always required his pupils to prepare themselves at home by going through the material for their particular level. Beginners were to write

---

33. "Is 'er een stuk van hun Ampt, daarvan zy zeegen te verwachten hebbe, soo is het
waarlyk dit. Ik durf mogelyk in needrigheit door ondervinding daar van getuygenis geven, dat
er door Catechisatien veel meer dan door Predikatien gewonnen werdt."
34. "Of zy haar wel ooyt over sulk een jammerlyken staat, gelyk de staat der natuur is,
verleegen gevonden hebben? Werdt 'er van de Persoon des Heeren JESUS gehandelt, men
vergeete niet te vraagen: Hebt gy den Heere JESUS wel lief?... Hoe staat het met uw Gebedt?
Maakt gy ook werk daarvan?"

out at home a number of key Scripture verses that dealt with the topic to be discussed. Advanced students were to compare a number of good commentaries and books relating to the topic. The catechism teacher also had to assign questions, which catechism students could contemplate at home in order to respond at the next class to the best of their ability.

The author provided commentary on the Heidelberg Catechism by elucidating all questions of each Lord's Day section with the help of a number of questions and answers. This book gained great popularity in both Germany and the Netherlands. The 1758 General Synod of Duisburg went so far as to warn churches not to let Lampe's book displace the Heidelberg Catechism itself. Appreciation for Lampe's book in the Netherlands probably reflected the theological position that Lampe took in the church of the Netherlands in the eighteenth century. He instituted the movement that became known as Lampeanism. Lampeans were strict Cocceians, who manifested a strongly experiential inclination. Within this movement Johannes d'Outrein became the most important author of short catechetical works.

Johan van den Honert: Interpreter of the vision of orthodoxy
Johan van den Honert (1693–1758), son of T. H. Honert, became a professor at Leiden in 1734. He was highly regarded and one of the most famous theologians of his time. Van den Honert maintained numerous contacts with the ruling aristocracy and was a close friend of Stadtholder William IV. A Cocceian himself, he nevertheless sought to mitigate divergences between Voetians and Cocceians. However, he did cross swords with Wilhelmus Schortinghuis for Schortinguis's brand of Reformed pietism, and G. Kuypers in connection with the Nijkerk disturbances. He himself emphasized reason and rationality. Alexander Comrie considered Van den Honert to be a liberal and suspected he was being influenced by the emerging Enlightenment.

In 1748, the Leiden professor published *Eerste Beginselen van de Leer der Waarheid naar de Godsaligheid, in de Hoop des Eeuwigen Levens, By wyze van Vragen en Antwoorden, Ten dienste der Nederlandsche Jeugd* (First Principles of the Doctrine of Truth after Godliness, in Hope of Eternal Life, by Means of Questions and Answers, for the Benefit of the Youth of the Netherlands). This "short work of catechetical instruction"[35] originally comprised two parts. In the second part, the author gave a "broader elaboration and confirmation"[36] of the outline of doctrine in the first part. Van den Honert dedicated his book to Carolina, the young princess of Orange-Nassau. She could use the first part

---

35. "Werkjen van Catechetisch Onderwys"
36. "breder uytbreiding en bevestiging"

immediately, but the second part was intended for a later stage. In the preface to this work, the author provided a useful critical evaluation of catechism books of his time.

In 1755, Van den Honert agreed to the request of a number of ministers and catechism teachers to have the first part reprinted separately as First Principles. In the preface, he presented his criticism of those who argued that "one cannot put the expressions, 'I believe; our Father;' etc. into the mouths of young people; but that they must be shown a different way, considered to be better."[37] At any rate, he had challenged this "new fashion" as early as 1736, in the preface to a new edition of Ursinus's Treasure Book. "If this were not to be the case," he asked, "when could one then read the Word of God, in which such inclusive language so frequently occurs?"[38] In addition, he identified three shortcomings of many existing catechism books that were highly praised.[39] Five fundamental components of religion were not properly

---

37. "men die bewoordingen, ik geloov; onze Vader; enz. in de mond der Jeugd niet legge: maar dat men haar langs eenen andere weg leide, dien men beter keurt."

38. "Mag dit niet syn, wanneer sal dan de Mensch het Woord Gods mogen lesen, in het welke sulke vertrouwende redeneringen soo dikwijls voorkomen?"

39. "ten toppe"

Joan van den Honert,
son of T. H. Honert

treated: the law, the confession of faith, the sacraments, Christian discipline, and the Lord's Prayer. The structure, content, and language employed by the authors inadequately reflected the Catechism itself. This failure was important because this was the way young people were to be prepared for profitable attendance at catechism sermons. The third objection was an inadequate formulation of answers to questions, which frequently did not form complete sentences and apart from the answers made no sense. Catechism teachers had such answers—without questions—memorized, but ultimately young people did not understand anything of what was being learned in this manner, "as anyone who, in receiving such parroted lessons occasionally misses a question but carries on all the same, will experience on a daily basis."[40]

In First Principles, even Van den Honert failed to follow the Heidelberg Catechism step-by-step. He also wrote a miniature Dogmatics in twenty-two short chapters. The five components of religion were discussed with due attention. In the text of his question book, about fifty questions and answers of the Catechism were incorporated in whole or in part, and additional questions and answers were taken from the Compendium. The volume was interleaved with blank pages to facilitate the copying of Scripture passages by students.

Part of Van den Honert's criticism of existing catechism books appeared to apply directly to Hellenbroek's *A Specimen of Divine Truths*: discussion of the law and prayer only in summary form, the total exclusion of questions and answers contained in the Heidelberg Catechism, and the presentation of instruction material in an objective, informative style. Van den Honert maintained the personal approach of the Catechism in his own catechism book.

The great popularity of First Principles, which achieved a seventh printing, must reflect Van den Honert's standing as the leading exponent of Reformed orthodoxy of his time. From a didactic point of view, his work surpassed that of many of his contemporaries, in part through its concentric form of repetition and the elaboration of the instruction material in the second volume.

The Shorter Delft Hellenbroek: Hellenbroek combined with the Compendium
On March 17, 1749, the Classis of Delft and Delfland approved a peculiar instruction booklet: *Kort Begrip der christelyke religie, Voor Eenvoudige, die zich bereiden tot de Belydenisse des geloofs; Geschikt na de Leidinge, door wylen Ds. Abraham Hellenbroek Gehouden in zijn Eerw. alom bekend Boekje, genaamt Voorbeeld der Goddelyke Waarheden* (Compendium of the Christian Religion, For Ordinary

---

40. "Gelyk elk, die, in het horen van sulke Papegaayslesjens, eens ééne Vraag overslaan, en vervolgens voortvragen wil, 't elken dage bevinden sal."

Folk Preparing Themselves to Make Profession of Faith; Structured according to the Leadership Provided by the Late Reverend Abraham Hellenbroek Contained in His Revered and Widely Known Booklet Entitled "A Specimen of Divine Truths"). This new book offered a synthesis of the Compendium by Faukelius and *A Specimen of Divine Truths* by Hellenbroek. It also became known as the *Delfse Hellenbroekje* (Shorter Delft Hellenbroek).

The first two brief chapters of this booklet clearly remind us of the opening chapters of Hellenbroek's *A Specimen of Divine Truths*. The short third chapter contains a reference to Lord's Day 1 of the Catechism and offers a transition to the discussion of the Compendium. The original structure of this document was perfectly maintained by the author and, by means of a larger font, remains typographically recognizable. The additional questions by Hellenbroek were placed within this structure. The author apparently had difficulty with Hellenbroek's very concise treatment of the law and prayer. For the benefit of young people and ordinary folk, he added a "brief elaboration"[41] concerning the law as a whole and each commandment individually (pp. 163–172) as well as the Lord's Prayer as a whole and each petition individually (pp. 179–200). In the preface, the author indicated his objective: "Finally, it is the author's sincere wish for readers and users of this booklet that the Father of lights may grant them from the very beginning and always the necessary grace to rightly know, heartily believe, boldly confess, and devoutly experience the pure doctrine of truth, and thus to receive true comfort for their souls, both in life and death."[42] On the last page we find the three questions for profession of faith that are listed at the end of the Compendium.

The differences of the instruction material in this booklet are very well thought out. It was simply assumed that catechism students would master the questions from the Compendium on their own. The same was true for a large proportion of Hellenbroek's questions. The rest of the material—approximately forty-five percent of the questions of the combined text—was marked with a small half-moon and was intended as additional material for more advanced students.

The author of this booklet remains obscure. It is logical to think of a min-

---

41. "korte uitbreiding"

42. "Voor het overige word den Leezers en Gebruikers van dit Boekje hartelyk toegewenscht, van den Vader der Lichten nodige Genade in haar begin en voortgang, om de zuivere leere der Waarheid recht te kennen, hartelyk te gelooven, vrymoedig te belyden, Godvrugtig te beleeven, en daaruit een weezentlyken troost voor hunne Ziele te ontfangen, in Leeven en Sterven."

Delfse Hellenbroekje

ister of the Classis of Delft and Delfland. However, the rights to this booklet, published in 1749, were held by the publisher, De Erven van Reinier Boitet at Delft. In 1765, a fifteenth edition of this booklet appeared. In 1775, this publisher sold its rights to the well-known publisher Abraham Blussé & Son of Dort, who brought to market the twenty-third edition in 1785. This instruction booklet was still reprinted a number of times in the twentieth century.

On the one hand, this booklet testifies to a great, overall appreciation for the work of Hellenbroek. The anonymous author could not and did not wish to overlook Hellenbroek's leadership. On the other hand, the integrated publication of Hellenbroek's work and the Compendium reflected implicit criticism of Hellenbroek. Making profession of faith had to remain tied to the Compendium, which was recommended by the Synod of Dort as an instruction booklet. Hellenbroek's treatment of prayer and the law was too brief and required further elaboration. The subdivision of the instruction material in this new booklet was a clear step forward from a pedagogical point of view.

The influence of the Enlightenment

In the second half of the eighteenth century, the influence of the Enlightenment on the Reformed church became steadily stronger. Human reasoning determined whether something was lucid and clear, and only those things that could pass this test could be accepted as truth. In this way, the light of reason was increasingly placed above the authority of Scripture. It was reasonable to tolerate each others' views in love. It was equally reasonable to assume that human conscience and the official teachings of various churches were tied to no other bonds than those of the Word. It was believed that there ought to be freedom of thought and feeling without ties to confessional statements. Tolerance, or forbearance, was therefore the manifestation of the Enlightenment in both church and theology. As old-fashioned superstition was being displaced, a natural and reasonable religion would encourage people to love God as the merciful Father of all and to practice virtue according to the example set by the Savior. Over the last few decades of the eighteenth century, Enlightenment thinking also affected catechetical instruction material.

In defense
In 1785, S. van Emdre (1746–1816), minister at Wageningen, published *Het voorbeeld der Godlyke Waarheden van Abraham Hellenbroek, tegen het gevoelen van partyen verdedigd* ("A Specimen of Divine Truths" by Abraham Hellenbroek, Defended against the Feelings of Various Parties). In this apologetical work, he defended the divine truths presented in Hellenbroek's question book "against parties," meaning opponents of Reformed doctrine. In contrast to them, he sought to demonstrate that the teachings of the Reformed church, as contained in its confessional statements, were entirely founded on the Bible. In Van Emdre's view, Hellenbroek had written his booklet specifically to identify and refute prevalent errors. Van Emdre specifically named, explained, and refuted these errors, emphasizing "important doctrines that are currently being attacked."[43] In 1794, a second, considerably expanded edition was published; it contained 868 questions and extremely detailed answers!

With this work, Van Emdre took a clear stand against the influx of various Enlightenment ideas. Nevertheless, the author himself did not entirely escape a moderate spirit of the Enlightenment, which colors his use of language to a certain extent. Natural theology had a prominent place in his thinking, as it did for many of his contemporaries. "Reason provides us with adequate and the clearest proof of the existence of a higher Supreme Being.... If there is anything at all in nature, then there must be a Supreme Being, which we refer to as God." When he discussed Hellenbroek's last three ques-

43. "gewichtige leerstukken die hedendaags bestreden worden"

tions, which dealt with eternal life, he wondered what could be said in this regard. The answer went as follows: "This doctrine not only agrees with God's Word, but is also supported by reason. By denying these truths one questions the existence of a Supreme Being which possesses all perfections and virtues, and one robs the lives of God-fearing people of all comfort as far as their expectation of eternal salvation is concerned."

The breakthrough of the Enlightenment
When Van Emdre applied himself to "defending divinity," the reorientation of a large portion of catechetical instruction material had already been launched. The real breakthrough came in 1782 with the publication at Amsterdam of a work by an anonymous author: *Proeve eener bevatbaarder onderwijzing dan de Heidelbergse catechismus* (Example of a Simpler Teaching Method than the Heidelberg Catechism). Under the influence of this booklet, the Heidelberg Catechism and the instruction booklets based on it began to disappear from schools and catechism classes. In line with this work, some ten authors wrote new catechism instruction booklets that reflected the spirit of the Enlightenment. In 1784, A. Ledeboer, minister at Haastrecht, and W. de Roo, minister at Tiel, wrote *Eenvoudig onderwijs in de voornaamste waarheden, welke de hervormde kerk belijd* (Basic Instruction in Principal Truths Confessed by the Reformed Church). The 1788 booklet by J. W. Tilanus, minister at Harderwijk, was also influential: *Aanleiding tot onderwijs in de leer en pligten van den godsdienst* (Introduction to the Teachings and Obligations of Religion).

These booklets reflected a rejection of a dogmatic treatment of the instruction material. Only "the pure teaching of religion as contained in the Old and New Testaments" was to be presented in terms of concepts. The entire emphasis was placed on life, on the responsibilities of the rationally thinking Christian. They believed that as long as dogmatic diversity could be eliminated, the fire of Christian love could be reignited. The aversion to dogmas was characteristic of these Enlightenment catechism instructors. In 1795, this aversion to dogma was evident in a pamphlet in which Voetians, loyal to the House of Orange, and their preference for Hellenbroek were ridiculed: *Voorbeeld der prinselyke waarheden, voor eenvoudigen, die zig bereiden tot de belydenisse des orange geloofs, meest voor het gemeente opgesteld* (A Specimen of Princely Truths, for Ordinary Folk Who Wish to Prepare Themselves for the Profession of Orange Beliefs: Mostly Designed for Community Use).

The reversal in 1795 brought a separation of church and state, which was not without consequence. Schools were declared neutral ground and every responsibility for catechism teaching was removed from them. In 1807, it was decided that in the future the church itself would provide catechetical instruction on Wednesday and Saturday afternoons. Catechism teaching became the exclusive domain of ministers and elders, as is the case today.

The Reformed undercurrent and the revival of the Compendium

The influence of the Enlightenment on the church was considerable, but a significant Reformed undercurrent remained. In a number of places, the "enlightened" instruction booklets were not adopted. The Catechism was retained, as were the booklets of Hellenbroek and Borstius, both of which were regularly reprinted.

It was not until 1833 that the Compendium was completely revived. In 1833, after his conversion, Hendrik de Cock (1801–1842) of Ulrum republished the Canons of Dort. This confessional statement had become totally ignored. Apparently this was also the case with the Compendium, which was republished in Veendam a month later. In one preface, De Cock sharply protested against various "enlightened" instruction booklets, which presented the truth of Scripture in an entirely erroneous manner, "much more suited to a Remonstrant or Socinian synagogue, leading to eternal perdition." At the same time, De Cock showed his aversion to the plethora of instruction booklets produced by Reformed authors of the seventeenth and eighteenth centuries. None of these booklets was required, since the Synod of Dort had prescribed the Compendium for general use: These authors had "practically inundated the world with instruction booklets"[44] that had not benefited the church but rather harmed it. "May this old, tried, and generally approved instruction booklet once again become widely known and used, and displace the multitude of alternative instruction booklets, however well done in some regards, none of which match this Compendium in every respect, since as a golden gem it combines brevity and comprehensiveness, pertinence and orthodoxy, and can easily be acquired by all in view of its nominal price, and easily absorbed in view of its conciseness."[45]

Incidentally, De Cock himself arranged another republication of Hellenbroek's *Voorbeeld der Goddelijke waarheden* (A Specimen of Divine Truths), which was republished in 1859 by O. L. Schildkamp of Groningen.

---

44. "de wereld schier overstroomd door vragenboekjes"
45. "Mogt dan dit oude, beproefde en algemeen goedgekeurde vragenboekje ook nog eens wederom algemeen gekend en gebruikt worden, en die menigte van andere vraagboekjes

Instruction booklets

One of the nuisances of our church is the multiplicity and diversity of instruction booklets, an affliction which I appear to be exacerbating with the publication of the present booklet, although I desire the opposite effect.

It has at times been pointed out to me, and I believe it to be true, that even the heroes of our faith in our country such as Hellenbroek, Lampe, Alberthoma, Franken, and others, by publishing their instruction booklets, did not benefit but harmed the church. It is not the case that I disapprove of their instruction booklets, which indeed reflect the truth in every sense, but the church had no need of them, because after the illustrious Synod of Dort (for prior to that time it appears that most of the time the Catechism itself was used for general instruction), this brief Compendium was put together by four or six learned and God-fearing ministers for general use and was widely approved, and which may indeed be thought of as a golden gem.

Reverend Hendrik de Cock, "Aan mijn hervormde geloofsgenooten!" ("To my Reformed fellow believers!"), preface to *Kort Begrip der christelijke religie, voor hen, die zich willen begeven tot des Heeren Heilig Avondmaal* (Compendium of the Christian Religion for Those Who Seek Admission to the Lord's Supper) Veendam, 1833.

Assessment

The strong recommendation of the Synod of Dort that its instruction material be presented by way of questions and answers was not honored by all the authors mentioned above. In the seventeenth century, the dialogue approach to instruction was impaired by Gellius de Bouma, Cornelius Poudroyen, and Petrus de Witte because they expanded a number of answers into broader explanations. The method was more effectively employed by Abraham Trommius, Antonius van Oostrum, and David Knibbe. In the eighteenth century, only Abraham Hellenbroek presented the instruction material in dialogue form that best met the demands for brevity, conciseness, and pertinence. Although Johan van den Honert followed in his footsteps, he rendered unduly long answers by quoting relevant Scripture passages in their entirety.

---

verdringen, waarvan schoon ongelijk goed, geen echter in allen opzichte tegen dit mag gerekend worden, daar het als een gouden kleinood, kortheid en uitgebreidheid, zaakrijkheid en regtzinnigheid in zich vereenigd, en door allen gemakkelijk wegens de onkostbaarheid kan bekomen, en wegens de beknoptheid geleerd kan worden."

With the exception of Trommius and Knibbe, the authors discussed here did not show much pedagogical and didactic insight. The Synod of Dort's plea to encourage and reward young catechism students was not honored by anyone. Growing children were frequently viewed as mini-adults. Gellius Bouma considered his catechism instruction book to be appropriate for all ages, including schoolchildren. Although Cornelius Poudroyen realized that not all catechism students possessed the same abilities, his attempt to differentiate between different levels was entirely inadequate.

The eighteenth century witnessed a number of small improvements in the area of education. The interleaving of instruction booklets with blank paper for copying out Scripture passages was a frequent phenomenon. This form of personal initiative enhanced the exposure of catechism students to Scripture. In the Shorter Delft Hellenbroek, we encounter an intelligent differentiation that made it feasible to work at two different levels as far as the quantity of instruction material was concerned. This feature probably largely accounted for the broad appeal of this instruction booklet. Nevertheless, Van den Honert's criticism of the way catechism teachers encouraged their students to memorize answers without paying attention to the corresponding

Hendrik de Cock

questions implies that catechism teaching in the eighteenth century often left much to be desired.

Two authors — Gellius de Bouma and Antonius van Oostrum — included in their instruction booklets a summary of the material in question-and-answer format for purposes of examination by consistory members for admission to the Lord's Supper. Apparently these summaries were preferred to the Compendium. At any rate, there was some awareness that catechism students who had only a few weeks to prepare themselves for such an examination ought not to be inundated with information. David Knibbe must have understood this because he prescribed the minimum amount of knowledge required by illiterate or slow learners.

Seventeenth-century authors gave prominence to the idea that the purpose of teaching the Heidelberg Catechism was knowledge of the faith. This knowledge of the faith was brought about by Word and Spirit in the process of upbringing and instruction within the family, at school, and in church. The personal element—references to "I," "you," "me," and "us"—was emphasized by all. Yet there was also a shift of emphasis from personal to intellectual knowledge of the faith. Petrus de Witte included a number of vigorous passages about spiritual life in an objective style. So did Cornelius Poudroyen and Gisbertus Voetius. In the course of the seventeenth century, a rational approach to doctrine became increasingly popular. Even supposedly concise instruction booklets assumed that catechism students could master many hundreds of questions and answers; the standard set by the many questions of the Catechism and its Compendium was well exceeded. This situation continued into the eighteenth century. With the exception of Johan van den Honert, all of the authors of the period we review here adopted an objective approach to doctrine, whereby the personal perspective of the catechism student was no longer captured in the questions and answers. One might conclude that the eighteenth century witnessed a complete dogmatization of catechism teaching. This probably did occur from time to time, but it did not always occur everywhere. Catechism teaching involves more than an instruction booklet. In his preface to *Melk der Waarheit* (Milk of the Truth), F. A. Lampe emphasized that a catechism teacher was to present the Word to the hearts of his students in a very personal manner. He was clearly aware of the sphere of influence in which the catechism student was placed by God's insistence on repentance and faith.

The most striking phenomenon in catechism teaching in the eighteenth century was the widespread appreciation for the question book published by Hellenbroek, which exhibited remarkable features for that time. However, the thread that connected Hellenbroek with the relevant decisions of the Synod of Dort about instruction booklets was quite thin. His *A Specimen of Divine Truths* can hardly be interpreted as an elaboration of the Catechism or the Compendium. At the same time, the remarkable success of the Shorter Delft Hellenbroek implies a criticism of the abandonment of ecclesiastical decisions of the past. The instruction material presented by Hellenbroek was considered to be enriching, but it was believed that making profession of faith should be linked with the Compendium, as prescribed by the Synod of Dort.

The deluge of instruction booklets that persisted for two centuries reflected a strong desire for individualism within Reformed ecclesiastical life at that time. After all, every movement in the church of those days had its own catechism booklets — a situation that did not contribute to the unity of ecclesiastical life. Criticism of this phenomenon on the part of men like Hendrik de Cock was not unreasonable. Nor was it improper for Van den Honert to observe that an instruction booklet must always display a clear connection with the Catechism and the Compendium. Instruction in the Heidelberg Catechism, a confessional statement of the church of the Reformation, was and is of great significance for the understanding of sermons and the grounding of young people in Reformational doctrine.

CHAPTER 7

The Continued Relevance of the
Heidelberg Catechism

by Willem van 't Spijker

Place and significance

There are few catechisms of the same era as the Heidelberg Catechism that do not reveal evidence of kinship. It is worthwhile to place these documents side by side for a clearer understanding of the character of the Heidelberg Catechism.

Ursinus had connections with Wittenberg, especially with Melanchthon. He had studied with the latter, and in his own teaching in Heidelberg he used the *Loci communes* written by this "teacher from Germany." The textbook that Melanchthon wrote for the training and appointment of ministers was employed by Ursinus as the basis of his lectures. This is obvious from the edition of these lectures published by Ursinus's student, Quirinus Reuter. Melanchthon's influence can be recognized in the definitions that Ursinus presents in his Larger Catechism. We also trace Melanchthon's thinking in Ursinus's description of the relationship between the law and the gospel. The same is true of Ursinus's development of the doctrine of the covenant. According to his thinking, the covenant of nature is connected with the image of God. It became the prototype for the covenant of works and would play an important role in the subsequent development of the overall doctrine of the covenant within Reformed theology. Ursinus's view of the covenant was shared to some extent by all theologians who encountered Anabaptists in their immediate vicinity. This is how the Reformed doctrine of the covenant was born.

In Basel, Oecolampadius employed the concept of the covenant early on to emphasize the unity of the old and new covenants. The same was true in Strasbourg, where Bucer similarly utilized the theology of the covenant in the conflict with Anabaptists. In Zurich, it was Bullinger especially who had to defend Zwingli's heritage and who augmented Zwingli's view on the covenant of grace. Ursinus maintained close contacts with prominent Reformed theologians in Zurich. In the formulation of the Heidelberg Catechism he must certainly have used the catechetical material that had been produced there.

The works of Bullinger himself should also be mentioned here: his *Summa Christlicher Religion* (1556) and his *Catechesis pro adultioribus scripta* (Catechism for Young Adults, 1559). Bullinger knew how to write for ordinary people. However, when compared with the Heidelberg Catechism, his works have a closer affinity with theological works. This probably explains Bullinger's enthusiasm expressed in a letter to Olevianus, in which he praised the qualities of the work of Ursinus and Olevianus: "I have read with great eagerness the Catechism that was produced with the encouragement of the eminent Elector Frederick III of the Palatinate, and while reading it I sincerely thanked God, who initiated and prospered this work. The structure of this book is clear, its content pure truth; everything is very easy to follow, devout and effective. In succinct conciseness it contains the fullness of the most important doctrines. I consider it to be the best catechism that has ever been published. Thanks be to God! May He crown it with His blessing." In terms of form and content, this book of instruction was indeed more accessible, less theologically oriented, and more focused on the immediate benefit of doctrine than Bullinger's work.

Bullinger's colleague, Leo Jud, produced a Short Catechism (1541) that is frequently identified as one of the sources of Ursinus's work. Here, too, the concept of the covenant stands out, without dominating the work. Jud's catechism is an example of the influence of the early Reformation centered in Strasbourg and Basel. The Strasbourg catechisms by Matthias Zell, Martin Bucer, and Wolfgang Capito resurface in some respects in Jud's work. Their practical orientation stands out. The question of the benefit of faith supersedes that of rational insight. Doctrines are presented not so much from a theoretical point of view as from the perspective of their significance for living out one's faith and their importance for ethics. The Heidelberg Catechism has a similar focus. The books of instruction that were used in Strasbourg stand out in terms of their attention to the significance of the church with its ministry, mandate, and discipline. A similar approach was taken in Heidelberg, possibly reinforced by the example of Geneva.

Besides Zurich, Geneva deserves attention. With their catechisms, Calvin and Beza provided material that was liberally used by Ursinus. Calvin produced a catechism in 1537 that could be seen as a summary of his *Institutes,* published in Basel in 1536, and viewed by many as a catechism. Subsequently, in 1543, Calvin published an instruction book written in French, translated by himself into Latin in 1545; it was dedicated to the church of Emden. This work may be thought of as a direct source for the Heidelberg Catechism. Calvin's influence is clearly apparent in the Heidelberg Catechism, not only in direct citations but also through the spirit that it breathes: clarity, godliness, and usefulness for living in God's presence. The two catechisms produced by Calvin's successor, Theodore Beza (1559), undoubtedly also influenced the compilation of the Heidelberg Catechism. Their focus on the instruction of young people stands out, as does a witnessing, confessing, and evangelizing emphasis. Geneva's influence on the Heidelberg Catechism is apparent in its view of the Lord's Supper, in beliefs concerning Christ, and no less in its preferred ecclesiastical system—thus clearing a path for the church order of the Palatinate. Olevianus was especially involved in the establishment of this church order. One must look hard to find his influence in these aspects of the Heidelberg Catechism. Ecclesiastical discipline, which in Lord's Day 31 is discussed in connection with the Lord's Supper, was patterned after the Genevan model, not that of Zurich. A comparison with the work *Der Gnadenbund Gottes* (God's Covenant of Grace), which largely accounts for Olevianus's renown, does not yield anything of substance. The latter work does treat the concept of the covenant in great depth.

In this respect, the Catechism is considerably more sober, which constitutes one of its real strengths. Out of the wealth of Reformational material, the Heidelberg Catechism brings together elements of great value, thus linking a number of traditions. Given its experiential orientation, it focuses on the way people might seek and find the source of all comfort. Through the application of the threefold principle of misery, deliverance, and gratitude, it succeeds in establishing a link between theological content and practical godliness, focusing on the experience of faith. This godliness does not emanate from a theology based on the experience of the human heart. It is derived directly from God's revelation of salvation in Christ as found in Scripture. Scripture is allowed to speak for itself, as the references clearly demonstrate. This is ultimately where the power of the Catechism must be sought, as a confession of faith, in the midst of other confessional statements.

The Catechism and the Belgic Confession of Faith

A comparison of the Catechism with the two other confessional statements of churches in the Netherlands is eminently appropriate. It is noteworthy that these churches adopted the Heidelberg Catechism and the Belgic Confession of Faith practically from the very beginning, together with the Geneva Catechism and the French Confession of Faith. Apparently, it was recognized that the Heidelberg Catechism did not differ in essence from that of Geneva. This early choice also demonstrated that, as far as its theological content was concerned, there was no major conflict between the Belgic Confession of

BELYDENISSE

DES GHELOOFS

DER GHEREFORMEER-
DE KERCKEN

in

NEDERLANT.

Obergheſien in de Synode Nationael **laetſt** gehouden tot DORDRECHT,

Ende uyt laſt des ſelven uytgheven / om voort- aen inde Nederlantſche Gereformeerde Kercken alleen voor autentijck ghehouden te worden.

ToT DORDRECHT,

By Franſoys Bozſaler/ Medeſtander van Iſaac Janſ. Canin.

Met Privilegie voor ſeven Iaren.
1619.

Edition of the Belgic Confession of Faith, adopted as a confessional statement by the Synod of Dort

Faith and the Catechism. The Geneva Catechism eventually made way for the Heidelberg Catechism, in part because the Walloon churches followed the French churches in adopting their Confession of Faith along with Calvin's catechism. The Catechism of the Palatinate and the Belgic Confession of Faith remained the chief confessional statements of the churches of the Netherlands. Despite the essential similarity of these two confessional statements, there are also striking differences. There is, first of all, the role played by the immediate context. Even though the Heidelberg Catechism soon encountered resistance from Lutheran theologians, it was born in a situation of relative peace. In contrast, the Belgic Confession of Faith (1561) emerged in a painful struggle for freedom and independence from an enemy that sought to suppress the church by fire and sword. The fallout from this experience can be recognized in the language of this confessional statement. Guido de Brès, who composed this document, was a martyr. Its final article shows traces of oppression and persecution. Similarly, the articles on the true and false church betray a position of tremendous pressure.

We notice a second difference in the primary purpose of these documents. The Catechism was not primarily meant for the world beyond the church. Its pedagogical aim was principally the upbringing and instruction of the rising generation in the church. Its purpose, therefore, was largely found within the church itself. Presentation to the outside world was an incidental factor, to make a case for the Reformation within the empire. On the other hand, the Belgic Confession of Faith had an apologetic, defensive purpose. It was concerned with presenting information to the outside world, with the goal of removing prejudice. False religion had to be eradicated, which was the responsibility of the government. But the government first had to be adequately informed about the differences between true and false religion—that is, between the false church and the true church of Christ. Like the French and Scottish confessions, the Belgic Confession emerged at a time of persecution and great distress when people testified to the hope that was within them.

A third difference lies in the method. Aside from a catechism's question-and-answer format, we recognize a difference in style in comparison with the Belgic Confession. Although the Catechism focuses on simplicity, edification, usefulness, and comfort, it cannot be denied that its questions reflect a very clear theology that is elaborated in lucid and understandable answers. Its structure is different from that of the Belgic Confession, which reveals a purely theological approach that is apparent from the sequence of its articles, from the doctrine of God to the perspective of eschatology. In the doctrine of God, it is noteworthy that knowledge of God is twofold. Although creation and Scripture are definitely not equivalent in revealing God, each takes its own approach. The former removes all innocence on the part of mankind, whereas the latter reveals to us the Triune God in accordance with Holy Scripture, coupled with stirrings that we sense within our hearts. Scripture and the doctrine of inspiration are explicitly discussed in the Belgic Confession of Faith, but the Catechism does not contain a specific exposition of Scripture per se. Whereas the Catechism is quite succinct in dealing with predestination, the Belgic Confession of Faith devotes an entire article to it. Concerning Christology, the Belgic Confession definitely does not ignore the element of confidence but reminds us that no one loves us more than Jesus Christ. It is precisely here that we find a striking connection between our justification, including the role of faith, and sanctification. Everything follows from the atonement achieved by Christ. When it comes to the church, the Catechism is pertinent but concise, whereas the Belgic Confession discusses the church in considerable detail.

In short, there is a close correspondence between the two statements in terms of content, despite the differences in method. The Catechism is primarily a pedagogical tool, whereas the Belgic Confession has a more theological focus. Perhaps this explains why the Catechism tends to overshadow the Confession in terms of usage and appreciation. With the Belgic Confession of Faith, churches consciously share the Reformed tradition. Despite its clarity, the Catechism manifests a greater openness, which was clearly intended on the part of its compilers. The Catechism's geographic range of dissemination was considerably greater than that of the Belgic Confession, and the Catechism achieved a far greater radius of influence.

The Catechism and the Canons of Dort
A comparison of the Heidelberg Catechism with the Canons of Dort (1619) calls for a different perspective and leads to a different conclusion. In a sense, one could say that the Canons of Dort constitute a long, drawn-out response to criticism voiced by Remonstrants at that time, in part concerning certain points made by the Catechism. Their objections primarily concerned the total depravity of man in terms of sin and guilt. They also objected to the view that even the holiest of people, as long as they remained in this life, only exhibited a mere beginning of the new obedience. In short, they ascribed greater capabilities to man than the Catechism did.

In terms of content, there is no difference between the two confessional documents. Even when it comes to predestination by grace, one cannot speak of profound differences. The conciseness with which the Catechism discusses predestination is no reason to deduce a difference of view. An instruction book for people of all ages cannot contain the same material and follow the

IVDICIVM
SYNODI
NATIONALIS,
REFORMATARVM
ECCLESIARVM BELGICARVM,
habitæ
DORDRECHTI,
Anno 1618. & 1619.

Cui etiam interfuerunt plurimi insignes Theologi
Reformatarum Ecclesiarum Magnæ Britanniæ,
Palatinatus Electoralis, Hassiæ, Helvetiæ, Correspondentiæ VVedderavicæ, Genevensis, Bremensis, & Emdanæ,
DE
QUINQUE DOCTRINAE
Capitibus *in Ecclesiis Belgicis Controversis.*

Promulgatum VI. May, cIↃ. IↃc. xix.

Cum Privilegio.

The convictions of the Synod of Dort with respect to the Canons of Dort

David Pareus was an irenical theologian. In 1598 he became professor of theology in Heidelberg. A student of Ursinus's, he produced in accordance with the lectures of Ursinus the latter's commentary on the Heidelberg Catechism.

same structure as a theological tract such as the Canons of Dort. One might say that the article of the Belgic Confession of Faith that deals with eternal election by God (article 16) was significantly expanded in the Canons. It can now be studied from many different perspectives. At the same time, one can benefit from the many practical and experiential references contained in the Canons. It is very evident that the Canons of Dort emerged at a specific point in the history of Reformed theology. In some sense, one can discern a direct link between Geneva and Dort as far as predestination is concerned. Among the delegates at the Synod of Dort of 1618–1619, one can recognize supporters of both the Canons and the Catechism. In content, their views were largely identical. The rejection of Remonstrantism was lucid and clear because the essence of the Reformation was at stake. When the Catechism was produced, this was definitely not yet the case. Within the Reformed tradition of those earlier days, there were indeed some variations of views that could make a subsequent parting of ways understandable. But given this situation, the Catechism took a clearly recognizable stand, reflecting positions taken by Luther, Bucer, and Calvin. Lutherans subsequently abandoned, to some extent, the views of their great leader. The belief on the part of the Remonstrants that they could appeal to Melanchthon was fiercely disputed by the Contra-Remonstrants. At any rate, the influence of that great friend of Luther on the Catechism on this precise point is difficult to demonstrate.

Despite the Reformed community's evident diversity, which was even greater than that among Lutherans, there was a deep-seated unity in the Reformed conflict with the Remonstrants. The church of France also accepted the doctrinal decisions of Dort and ascribed synodical authority to them. At the Synod of Dort, the delegates from the Palatinate were not the only defenders of their Catechism. The elderly David Pareus (1548–1622), a former student of Ursinus's, submitted a tract to the assembly that was read aloud in its entirety. In Heidelberg, he subsequently presented a detailed lecture to his students on the significance of what was at stake in Dort. In his view, there was no difference between the Catechism and the pronouncements of the Synod of Dort. Despite differences in approach, in part reflecting developments within the Reformed tradition, there were no essential differences in view. The importance of advances in theology becomes abundantly apparent when we compare the Heidelberg Catechism with the outcome of the great assembly that was held in Westminster Abbey thirty years after the Synod of Dort: a confession and two catechisms. The latter documents have been just as significant for the history of the church as has the Heidelberg Catechism.

Comparison with subsequent catechisms

Important confessional developments in England after the Reformation can only be sketched briefly here. As could have been expected, the English Reformation under King Henry VIII (1509–1547) was not very clearly defined. Its breach with Rome rested on grounds that had little to do with the teachings of the gospel that were rediscovered by Luther and others. As a matter of fact, initially Henry personally opposed Luther and, in the process, acquired the title *defensor fidei* (defender of the faith) from the pope. Nevertheless, under Henry's government, a gradual reorientation took place along the lines of the Reformation on the Continent. A delegation from England that visited Wittenberg produced the Wittenberg Articles (1536). Somewhat earlier, the king had endeavored to establish contact with Melanchthon. The latter's influence was recognizable in the articles. The nexus of penance, faith, justification, and good works showed Luther's discovery to full advantage. Faith must be part of penance. Faith brings us to place our confidence in forgiveness. The terrified conscience is lifted up and comforted, not in recognition of the worthiness of our repentance or other works, but for Christ's sake. Good works are part of the new obedience. In the same year, Henry VIII formulated the Ten Articles, which spoke of justification by faith, combined

Thomas Cranmer

with repentance and conversion. Two years later, these fundamental concepts were reiterated in the Thirteen Articles, although they continued to be embedded in previous liturgical practices.

The Reformation did not fully break through until the reign of Edward VI (1547–1553), although his rule was too short to affect the hearts of his people. Nevertheless, a new catechism was produced (1548) that achieved three printings in a relatively short time. For this purpose, Archbishop Thomas Cranmer made use of the work of Osiander, who in turn borrowed a good deal from Luther's Small Catechism. Furthermore, a new edition of the Book of Common Prayer (1549) was published in 1552, which incorporated a new form for the administration of the Lord's Supper. A confession of faith was also added, which offered instruction about free will, original sin, justification, and good works along Reformational lines. Justification was described as the perfectly certain and most wholesome doctrine of Christianity. Noteworthy in this confession is the emphasis on the doctrine of election or predestination to life: "God's eternal resolve, whereby He decided from before the foundation of the world, according to His hidden purpose, to free from the curse and perdition those whom He predestined from among the human race, bringing them as vessels of honour to eternal salvation through Christ.

Therefore, those who are granted such a glorious benefit of God through His Spirit, who works at the appropriate time, are called according to His plan. They obey His call through grace, are freely justified and adopted as children of God, are made to conform to the image of His only begotten Son Jesus Christ, walk holily in good works and through God's mercy ultimately attain eternal life." The contemplation of our election in Christ leads to a sweet and inexplicable comfort to those who experience themselves to be within the power of the Holy Spirit, who destroys the works of the flesh and its earthly members and lifts up their consciences to heavenly and exalted things. With this confession, Cranmer succeeded in bringing the Reformation in England under the sphere of Bucer and Calvin's influence. The doctrine of predestination would take on lasting significance in the teachings of the church.

When, after the reign of Bloody Mary (1553–1558), the pursuit of reformation could be resumed, a Declaration of the Chief Articles of Religion, called the Eleven Articles (1559), was adopted. These entrusted spiritual power to bishops under the head of the church, Queen Elizabeth. Under her government (1558–1603) there emerged the beginnings of the movement that would

Robert Rollock

be known as Puritanism. Under Queen Mary, numerous spiritual leaders had fled to the Continent, where, in the centers of the Reformation, they absorbed ideas about the confession as well as the structure of the church. After her death they returned to England, where they sought to implement their new vision of a further reformation through manifestos and programs. To them, the doctrine of predestination was and continued to be crucial. In 1595, nine articles were adopted that came to be known as the Lambeth Articles, which adopted the doctrine of double predestination as the official teaching of the church. That this view was more than a temporary fad is confirmed by the great influence achieved by the Irish Articles of Religion (1615).

The Irish Articles referred to a covenant of the law engraved in man's heart at the time of creation. God promised him eternal life, on condition of perfect obedience to His commands, while disobedience was threatened with the penalty of death. Man fell into sin, but Christ became the Mediator of the Second Covenant. All those predestined by God were inseparably united with His body. United with Christ, they were reborn and made partakers of Him and all of His benefits. In these Irish Articles, we are struck by the emphasis on predestination, covenant, and justification. These three aspects of doctrine were to be combined into a single whole, especially at the Westminster Assembly. Unity among these components of doctrine was feasible because of several factors. We first mention the development of covenantal theology. In this regard there was a noticeable difference from the Heidelberg Catechism. In the Catechism, we do encounter the doctrine of the covenant, but in a subdued fashion. At Westminster the covenant played a special role in sacramental doctrine. In the confession and catechisms of Westminster, the covenant served to present the entire doctrine of faith in a transparent manner. This approach reflected the prominent place of the covenant in Puritan thinking.

There was an early connection between the confessional statements of Westminster and the Heidelberg Catechism. The head of the University of Edinburgh, Robert Rollock (1555–1599), presented lectures there on the Heidelberg Catechism and theological aspects of Beza's publications (*Quaestiones et responsiones*). Rollock was among the first to employ covenantal theology in a systematic manner, on the basis of the thesis that the entire Word of God reflects a covenant because God did not address man apart from a covenant. Therefore, every rational creature necessarily fell under one of two covenants: that of works or that of grace. Rollock addressed this idea in his *Questions and answers concerning God's covenant and the sacrament which represents a seal of God's covenant, compiled for the benefit of ordinary people* (Edinburgh, 1596). The covenant that God established with man consisted in the fact that He promised

Assertion of Liberty of Conscience by the Independents in the Westminster Assembly of Divines (painting by J. R. Herbert, ca. 1844)

man a certain benefit, which was based on a certain condition. Man accepted this condition. Like Ursinus, Rollock referred to the initial covenant as a covenant of nature or works and the subsequent covenant as a covenant of grace. The context of the first covenant was the good, holy, and unimpaired nature received by man in creation. The condition of the covenant of works consisted of good works proceeding from the good, holy, and unimpaired nature of man. This condition had nothing to do with faith in Christ, nor with the works of grace and regeneration. After the fall into sin, the covenant of grace persuaded people to seek refuge in the covenant of grace. This covenant was based on satisfaction obtained through Christ; atonement was achieved through the establishment of a new covenant with man. In the covenant of grace, God promised justification and eternal life on condition of faith in Christ the Mediator. Man accepted this requirement to believe. In this context, reference was made to a condition of the covenant of grace; at this point, it was obvious that this condition was entirely based on the grace of God. Thus, justification was incorporated into the doctrine of the covenant. The Westminster Assembly further elaborated this initial formulation.

In the Westminster Shorter Catechism, God's decrees preceded creation, providence, and particularly, the covenant. In the first covenant, once God had created man, He established a covenant of life with him, on the condition of perfect obedience. Following the fall into sin, all of humanity found themselves in a state of sin and misery. But God established a covenant of grace with the elect, in order to deliver them from this state of sin and misery. The Lord Jesus Christ, who is the Redeemer of the elect, and the Son of God, became incarnate. On the authority of His threefold office, He saved them from sin and misery. The Spirit makes us share in His benefits by binding us to Christ through effectual calling.

The Shorter Catechism places most of the emphasis on the inner workings of the Holy Spirit. He convicts man of sin and enlightens the mind to know Christ. He renews our will and thus leads us to embrace Christ, who is graciously offered to us in the gospel. This office of grace might have been given more emphasis. As a rule, there is no effectual calling apart from the sincere offer extended through the proclamation of the gospel — a fact fully emphasized in the Canons of Dort. It is obvious that the Westminster Confession, as well as both catechisms, were produced at a later stage than were the Canons of Dort. The resistance against Dort in France and the emerging rational manner of conducting theology led to a strongly defensive attitude at Westminster. It is clear that the progress of Reformed theology reflected further doctrinal refinements.

In England and Scotland of those days, the concept of the covenant had significance that was not only broadly political and purely ecclesiastical, but also deeply personal. It was a common custom for people of faith to draft a document in which they entered into a personal covenant with God. Examples of this are well known. This variegated background definitely affected covenantal thinking at the Westminster Assembly. It implied a connotation of "covenant" that was foreign to both the Canons of Dort and the Heidelberg Catechism.

The view of the Canons of Dort on the covenant is clearly described in the preface to the Authorized Translation of the New Testament. God has established a covenant with mankind "to grant them eternal life under certain conditions; which covenant is twofold, the old and the new." The old covenant was established prior to the fall into sin, and is referred to as the covenant of the law. Since its conditions can no longer be met, "salvation must be sought in a different covenant, which is referred to as *the new one* and signifies that God has ordained His Son to be a Mediator and promises eternal life on condition that we believe in Him; and is called the covenant of grace." It cannot be put more simply than this. This view is also found in the Canons of Dort: no elaborate doctrine of the covenant, but a biblical representation of the difference between the old and new covenants as presented in the Reformation by Bucer, Calvin, and others. In essence, there is a single covenant, which is differentiated only in terms of its administration.

The Heidelberg Catechism speaks of God's covenant especially in connection with the doctrine of the sacraments. Its explanation is also considerably simpler than those of the Westminster catechisms. This difference in language reflects the way in which theology and biblical research were practiced in the seventeenth century. As far as the main issues are concerned, there are essentially no differences; yet there is a shift in emphasis. Like the statements of the Westminster Assembly, the Heidelberg Catechism contains good Reformational theology, but its formulation reflects a simpler methodology. It is based more directly on Scripture, while avoiding theological refinements. The experiential nature of the Heidelberg Catechism with its scheme of misery, deliverance, and gratitude, succeeds in speaking directly to the heart of its readers. The confessional statements of Westminster reflect a more refined theology and give more explicit recognition to the involvement of the Holy Spirit. Each approach has its own appeal and has had lasting implications within their own spheres of influence. In this connection, we cannot ignore the fact that in the Netherlands, the Heidelberg Catechism has played a significant role in the practice of godliness. This book of instruction also served as a confessional basis for a rapprochement of churches in the Netherlands. Although the Catechism was not incorporated into a church order, as was the case in the Palatinate, it was at least as significant for church governance.

Criticism of the Catechism
Criticism directed at the Heidelberg Catechism to some extent reflects issues related not only to tensions within Protestantism but also to its conflict with Rome. The Catechism addresses a number of issues in far more detail than we would find necessary today. There are a number of other elements of criticism that deserve closer investigation.

If this book of instruction were to be written today, wouldn't it have to mention some doctrines to which we feel deeply attached but that were hardly referred to in the Heidelberg Catechism, if at all? We are thinking of our current views with respect to the church, or a description of the work of the Holy Spirit. Doesn't it speak too little about the great future of Christ, so that all of eschatology receives too little attention?

It is indeed true that the Catechism reveals remnants of a conflict that at the time of the Reformation caused a rift between Luther and Zwingli, between subsequent Lutherans and adherents of the Reformed persuasion. However, in view of the history of the emergence of the Catechism, it would have been surprising not to find any traces of these frictions within its questions and answers. We are thinking particularly of views with respect to the Lord's Supper.

The Lord's Supper

We owe to the conflict between Lutherans and the adherents of the Reformed persuasion not only the exhaustive explanation of the essence of the Lord's Supper, but also the description of the mystery of this sacrament as contained in questions 75 through 79. Frederick III decided to align himself with the Reformation because he had personally delved into the significance of the Lord's Supper. It is therefore not surprising that the difference with Lutheranism came to the forefront. This issue threatened to estrange him from his own family and his immediate colleagues within the empire. It is clear that the compilers of the Catechism consulted Calvin in connection with the interpretation of the Lord's Supper. This Genevan Reformer was not primarily concerned with the question concerning the presence of Christ. To him the critical issue was our partaking of the true body and blood of Christ. A shift in focus was implied, so that the issue was not so much the *how* of His presence, but whether we partake "of that one sacrifice of Christ, accomplished on the cross, and of all His benefits" (Q. 75). In Luther's judgment, a subjective element had taken the place of the real, objective presence of Christ. He thus felt justified in regarding Zwingli and Oecolampadius as fanatics. Subsequent Lutherans also applied this judgment to the Reformed persuasion, particularly Calvinists. In the process, we acquired in the Heidelberg Catechism a particularly thorough description of the great mystery that takes place in the celebration of the Lord's Supper by believers. We truly participate in communion with Christ through faith. We acquire a sincere and inward bond with Him who makes us eat and drink unto eternal life.

In the meantime, the question of the implication of Christ's ascension became particularly pertinent. How should we imagine Christ's presence at the table of the covenant in the light of His presence in heaven? The Catechism teaches that Christ is truly present at His Supper. "With respect to His Godhead, majesty, grace, and Spirit, He is at no time absent from us," although as "true man"—that is, "with respect to His human nature"—"He is no more earth," but in heaven (Q. 47). The question that now arises is whether this response implies that the two natures of Christ are so intertwined as to affect His person. We owe question 48 to this conundrum. Here the Catechism asks whether "these two natures in Christ [are] separated from one another." This question gives rise to the well-known "extra" dimension implied by the Catechism: Christ's Godhead is omnipresent. It is

The second edition of the Heidelberg Catechism (February 1563), in which question 80 was incorporated

not limited to His assumed, human nature. Although it remains completely united with His human nature, it is not limited to it. It is also present beyond this humanity. This "additional" presence of Christ or presence beyond His humanity has been interpreted as a typically Calvinistic idiosyncrasy. It could open the door to speculations concerning God's revelation or the operation of the Divine Logos outside Christ. As a rule, we do not encounter such speculation on the part of Calvin or the Reformed community. This digression of the Catechism reflects the far-reaching set of issues associated with the conflict surrounding the Lord's Supper. Whether Christ's church can still benefit from these ideas today remains an open question.

Whereas the above conflict over the Lord's Supper involved regrettable differences of interpretation among various movements within the Reformation, the issues surrounding the mass constituted an enormous conflict. To some Reformers the "popish mass," referred to in question 80, represented a supremely refined form of justification by works. It was in conflict with the threefold *sola* of the Reformation, particularly the *sola* of grace and the *sola* of faith. Doctrinal developments pertaining to the mass led in the world of

Roman Catholic scholastic thought to a theologically pervasive and influential system of views concerning the church, the doctrine of grace, and atonement and forgiveness by means of indulgences. It was not so much the theological concept of the mass that was advocated at universities and schools that was at issue. The initial Reformational criticism targeted particularly the practice of this doctrine among ordinary people as manifested in a sort of trade in grace. The violent reaction of the Catechism must be understood against this background. The Lord's Supper is conducted in remembrance of the sacrifice of Christ; it is not a repeated act.

At the personal initiative of Elector Frederick III, Olevianus added question 80 at the very last minute. The rather provocative inclusion of this question must be ascribed to the Council of Trent's having pronounced its anathema against the Reformed view of the Lord's Supper. It is quite certain that the text of the canons and decrees of the Council of Trent was not available at Heidelberg at this time; the solid anathema, however, was well known. We may well conclude that the Catechism particularly opposed the perverted malpractices of the fifteenth and early sixteenth centuries. Actually, the theology of Trent turned against medieval practices in no uncertain terms. But in the process, it also condemned the Reformational and evangelical views. The Catechism definitely does not advocate an empty celebration of the Lord's Supper as a ceremonial event that ignores Christ's *presentia realis* (true presence). On the other hand, nothing should ever detract from the one-time sacrifice of atonement accomplished on the cross of Golgotha. The real question is how we are made partakers of the person of the living Christ and His benefits.

Spirit, church, and prophecy

Apart from these points, there are several other issues that must be raised in the context of "shortcomings" of the Catechism. In part, these questions concern the authority of the Catechism as a confessional statement, which will be left aside in the present discussion. Ever since the sixteenth century, there have been differences of opinion regarding the authority of confessional statements — including the Catechism — especially regarding their relevance to our own time. Here we limit ourselves to three topics: the Holy Spirit, the church, and the significance of prophecy.

Many who allow themselves to be led by the modern charismatic movement, or who subscribe to evangelical thought, experience in the confessional statements a painful lack of focus on the Holy Spirit. According to them, the answer to the question: "What do you believe concerning the Holy Spirit?"

(Q. 53) contains too few biblical elements. The declaration that the Holy Spirit "is true and co-eternal God with the Father and the Son" is thought to have too little content. "That He is also given me, to make me by a true faith partaker of Christ and all His benefits, to comfort me, and to abide with me forever" apparently has too little content for someone who wants to see a description of the gifts and the fruits of the Spirit in their fullness. In the meantime, however, they miss the real significance of what is confessed here. The Spirit is the *Creator Spiritus*, the creating Spirit. He is just as much the Spirit of Christ. The unity of the work of the Triune God is found in creation, redemption, and consummation. In comparison with this perspective, the modern charismatic understanding of the Holy Spirit implies a diminution of reality, a shallow interpretation of certain charismatic gifts. What the Catechism further testifies concerning the Spirit and His work is inexpressibly rich. He makes us partake of communion with Christ. He comforts and guides those who are His own in a very individual manner. He forever abides with believers. Those who allow these ideas to sink in can only be amazed by the richness of the work of the Holy Spirit as it is described in the Catechism. The essence of the Person and the work of the Holy Spirit are clearly pointed out.

When we consider what the Heidelberg Catechism further teaches us about the Holy Spirit, we recognize aspects that can only enrich our understanding. The Spirit of Christ "assures [us] of eternal life, and makes [us] heartily willing and ready, henceforth, to live unto [the Lord]" (Q. 1). The Catechism places special emphasis on the connection between "the blood and Spirit of Christ" (Q. 69–71, 73), which indicates that the atonement through the cross and the Spirit are interconnected. Good Friday and Pentecost cannot be separated from each other. The Spirit of Pentecost is none other than the Spirit through whom Christ sacrificed Himself, and who also raised Him from the dead. It is also the Spirit who makes us appropriate what we have in Christ. According to the Catechism, the relationship between Christ and the Spirit is experienced in that the Spirit binds us to Christ. We are governed by one Spirit—the Spirit who dwells in Christ as the Head and in all of us as His members (Q. 76). This unbreakable relationship between Christ and the Spirit is of vital importance for a proper understanding of the reality of Christ's work and guards us from interpreting the work of the Spirit in His relationship to Christ as spiritualism. The latter signifies a form of godliness that functions in isolation. It is our view that the Catechism clearly and satisfactorily presents the elements for a sound doctrine of the Holy Spirit.

Is the same thing true for the church? It is understandable that people consider Lord's Day 21, which discusses the church, to be all too brief. Nevertheless, it does present the essential elements for a biblical ecclesiology. Nowhere is a tiresome and exhausting view of the church rejected more effectively than in this concise description: it is the work of the living Christ. He "gathers, defends, and preserves" His church. This expresses the richness of God's gracious election. Behind the church stands the miracle of God's grace. It is this vision of the church that is presented to us so clearly in the first edition of Calvin's *Institutes* (1536). The church and predestination go hand in hand. The church of Christ reveals the power of God's eternal good pleasure. This is where the Lord dwells and where His salvation is obtained. What is here confessed in our book of instruction directly contradicts the disunity of the church that can only be ascribed to self-serving religion.

The Heidelberg Catechism does not ignore the structure of the church, as is clear from the model that it presents: a church where Word and discipline function as means of grace, administered by the office bearers of the church. Indeed, an image of the church emerges here in which Christians serve each other with the gifts that they have received as partakers of Christ's person and gifts. In times of persecution and suppression, this structure of the church could help to keep the foundation of God's house intact. In this regard, nothing of relevance has been lost over the centuries that have elapsed since the birth of the Catechism.

Our final point concerns prophecy that reaches out to the future, the culmination of God's promises in the last days, particularly concerning Israel. Does the Catechism fall short in this regard? One might think so when, towards the end, in the discussion of the Lord's Prayer, the church is equated with the kingdom of God (Lord's Day 48). We tend to be more hesitant in this regard, in agreement with what the Lord teaches us about the kingdom in His parables. His kingdom is broader—infinitely broader—than the church. And the future is richer than what is pictured here for God's kingdom. But we do not ignore the fact that the prophecies whose fulfillment is still anticipated are not equally clear and transparent in every respect. The fulfillment of prophecy is its best explanation. Restraint is advised. However, those who desire to hold back will nevertheless find in the Catechism sufficient material to prove that God's future is certain. It will be more excellent than what we have ever been able to imagine.

According to the explanation of the Catechism, this—and no less than this—is the content of the Lord's Prayer: "Thy kingdom come." All "the works of the devil, every power that exalts itself against [God], and all wicked counsels conceived against [God's] holy Word" will not be able to prevent the fullness of the kingdom from arriving when one day the voice of all prophecy will be fulfilled. This kingdom will have come. And God will "be all in all."

Continued relevance

Among the Reformed confessional statements, the Heidelberg Catechism has justifiably taken an enduring and important place. This was originally the primary purpose of this document. Frederick III took a convincing position within the Reformed tradition of his time. Many of his contemporaries also considered the adoption of this book as an important event. What was a decisive choice on the part of the elector 450 years ago continues to be a meaningful confessional statement to us. It definitely does not fall short in terms of theology. Nevertheless, our first impression is not of a theological dissertation but of a pastoral reaching out—even to modern man. To churches in the Netherlands and elsewhere, the Heidelberg Catechism remains an essential confessional statement. Its place beside the Belgic Confession of Faith is indisputable, especially since it addresses the church, which must be built up in the faith that was once delivered to it. The material that is presented in the Canons of Dort plays the same role but takes a different approach than that selected by the book of the "only comfort."

In the wider Reformed context, in which numerous confessional docu-

---

Kohlbrugge on the Heidelberg Catechism

Through God's faithfulness the Catechism became the Catechism of the Palatinate and particularly the Netherlands. In the Netherlands this booklet has always been retained, so that it also became the Catechism for the Reformed church here in Elberfeld. All those who were ever converted to God agree with this Catechism. In contrast, those who remained unconverted continued to tinker with it.

The great truth has not been expressed in any book of instruction adopted by the Reformed church as clearly as in this document, namely this truth: that man is saved without himself contributing anything in the process, out of pure, free grace through Christ, and that for the entire life of faith, the life of sanctification and of good works, Christ is the Omega and the Alpha, the last and the first. In this way man is entirely bypassed in this doctrine of salvation; it is solely and exclusively the work of almighty grace.

Dr. H. F. Kohlbrugge, *De eenvoudige Heidelberger* (The Simple Heidelberg Catechism), Lord's Day 1.

ments have found a home, the Heidelberg Catechism continues to be the best-known statement. Its status is undisputed. It appears to be an essential characteristic of the Reformed tradition that it manifests itself in a multitude of confessions. Those who consult the collections of confessional statements contained in scholarly works are impressed with what tradition has produced in terms of such classical documents, which definitely do not have merely a historical significance. Among all of these, the Heidelberg Catechism occupies a recognized place of honor. Its significance has been far more enduring than a great number of onetime efforts that constituted pronouncements in concrete situations and established particular points of view. Many such declarations have had no lasting significance. The Catechism is in an entirely different category. It continues to figure among the church documents in which the compilers sought to focus on the testimony of Scripture.

It is fair to ask whether in a changing ecclesiastical context, with broadening horizons, the Heidelberg Catechism will retain its place. The recent publication entitled "Belijdenisgeschriften voor de Protestantse Kerk in Nederland" (Confessional Statements for the Protestant Church of the Netherlands) includes, beside the three confessional statements of the early church — the Apostles' Creed, the Nicene Creed, and the Athanasian Creed — the unaltered Augsburg Confession, Luther's Catechism, the Heidelberg Catechism, the Geneva Catechism, the Belgic Confession of Faith, and the Canons of Dort. In addition to these, a place was assigned to the Theological Declaration of Barmen and the Concord of Leuenberg. The position of the Protestant Church on the authority of the latter two documents differed to some degree from its stance on the other confessional statements. This difference was carefully worded; the significance of Barmen was recognized, and the Leuenberg Concord was believed to demonstrate that the Lutheran and Reformed traditions had found common ground in their joint understanding of the gospel.

The Barmen Theses and the Leuenberg Concord have found a place in virtually all modern editions of the Reformed confessional statements in Germany, France, Switzerland, and America, albeit not without dispute. The question of how the Heidelberg Catechism is related to these statements is important. The ecclesiastical position described in the Theological Declaration of Barmen must be interpreted in the light of its 1933–1934 context. The declaration reflects an attempt by the church to keep a place open for the gospel in society. This declaration made a very clear statement against the background of forces in the Third Reich that conspired to thwart the church and the gospel.

The situation is somewhat different for the "Concord of European Reformational Churches" (March 16, 1973). Lutheran and Reformed churches sought rapprochement in an ecumenical context. This document presented a dubious historical interpretation of the situation between Lutherans and the Reformed community in the sixteenth century. If this concord were correct, the compilation of the Catechism would have resulted from an erroneous interpretation of the reality of those days. In that case, the Catechism would contain a number of passages that would have to be discredited today. Not every Reformed believer would go this far without a fight.

The Heidelberg Catechism cannot be dismissed as merely a historical document. The comfort referred to in Lord's Day 1 applies to a large number of situations that trouble modern man. It addresses the foundations of the *consolatio animae*, the comforting of man's deepest essence and longings.

The Heidelberg Catechism also has lasting significance as a book of instruction, although present-day pedagogy would employ different methods and means. It is primarily written for the church. The theology on which it is based is rooted in the church, although it is not a theology of the church. Such a theology would fail to do justice to the richness and freedom of Holy Scripture and ignore the real work of the Holy Spirit. The Catechism recognizes a living relationship with the church, but its source is Scripture: "Word and Spirit" (Q. 31 and 123) or "Spirit and Word" (Q. 54). It seeks to be a book of instruction for the church, but always from the perspective of faith. That this is not just an external matter is obvious from its entire structure and its description of faith. It is the fervent language of experience that reveals salvation as an existential reality. We do not hesitate to identify this as the real power of this book. The Catechism has many great qualities. It serves simplicity without ignoring the broader dimensions of God's truth. Virtually everywhere and always it recognizes the central fact of God's love in Christ, which through atonement wins over the sinner to faith and strengthens him in this faith. What ultimately was the secret of the Reformation according to Luther, Bucer, Zwingli, and Calvin—namely, communion with Christ—is also the secret of this presentation of doctrine. At the center are the cross, Christ's blood and Spirit in atonement, forgiveness, renewal, and assurance. None of this can ever be separated from the *unio mystica*, the mystical union and hidden communion with Christ. Originating in Christ, the Catechism draws lines from doctrine to life, ethics, and the anticipation of the kingdom to come.

It is this true unity of doctrine and life, of knowledge and confidence, that gives the Catechism its own character. With God's blessing, its impact, which proved to be so powerful in the past, may also be anticipated for the future.

BIBLIOGRAPHY

Primary Sources

Acta der Provinciale en Particuliere Synoden, gehouden gedurende de jaren 1572–1620 (Acts of the Provincial and Regional Synods, held in the Northern Netherlands during the years 1572–1620). Collected by J. Reitsma and S. D. van Veen. 5 vols. Groningen: J. Reitsma and S. D. van Veen, 1892–1896.

Acta van de Classis Neder-Veluwe, Harderwijk van 1592–1620 (Acts of the Classis of the Lower Veluwe, Harderwijk 1592–1620). Goes: G. van der Zee, n.d.

Acta van de Nederlandsche Synoden der zestiende eeuw (Acts of Dutch Synods of the sixteenth century). Edited by F. L. Rutgers. Reprinted ed., Dort, 1980.

Acten van Classikale en Synodale Vergaderingen der verstrooide gemeenten in het land van Cleef, Sticht van Keulen en Aken, 1571–1589 (Acts of Classis and Synod Meetings of the dispersed churches in the District of Cleve, Bishopric of Cologne and Aachen, 1571–1589). Utrecht: H. Q. Janssen and J. J. van Toorenenbergen, 1882.

Allgemeine deutsche Biographie. Auf Veranlassung und mit Unterstützung Seiner Majestaet des Königs von Bayern, Maximilian II, hrsg. durch die historische Commission bei der Königl. Akadmie der Wissenschaften (Comprehensive German Biography). Leipzig: The Historical Committee of the Royal Academy of, 1875–1912.

Bakhuizen van den Brink, J. N. *De Nederlandse belijdenisgeschriften. In authentieke teksten met inleiding en tekstvergelijkingen* (The Dutch confession statements. Authentic texts with introduction and text comparisons). Reprinted ed., Amsterdam, 1976.

Bullinger, Heinrich. *Catechesis pro adultioribus scripta…* (Catechism for young adults…). Zürich, 1559.

_____. *Summa Christlicher Religion* (Summary of the Christian Religion). Zürich, 1556.

Calvin, John. *De Catechismus van Calvijn (Calvin's Catechism)*. Translated out of French by the Reverend J. J. Buskes. Baarn, n.d.

Catechismus oder christlicher Unterricht, wie der in Kirchen und Schulen der Churfürstlichen Pfalz getrieben wirdt in dt. U. lat. Sprache. Reprint-Ausg. Heidelberg 1563–Zürich 1983 (Catechism or Christian Instruction, as taught in the churches and schools of the Paltz Electorate in German and Latin. Reprinted edition of Heidelberg 1563Zürich 1983).

de Bouma, Gellius. *Christelicke Catechismus der Nederlansche Ghereformeerde Kercken: mitsgaders: sekere maniere van Catechizatie, ofte onderwijsinghe der jonghe jeugdt in deselve: met klare getuygenisse der H. Schrift, volghens de Nieuwe Oversettinge des Bybles bevesticht…* (Christian Catechism of the Reformed Churches in the

Netherlands: certain approaches to catechism teaching, or instruction of young people in the same, with clear testimony of Holy Scripture, confirmed with references to the New Translation of the Bible...). Utrecht, 1654.

Decades duae continentes vitas theologorum exterorem principum qui ecclesiam Christi superiori seculo propagarunt, et propugnarunt coactae a Melchiore Adamo Silesio. Frankfurt, 1653.

de Cock, Hendrik. *Verzamelde geschriften* (Collected works). Houten, 1984.

de Witte, Petrus. *Catechizatie over den Heidelbergschen Catechismus der Gereformeerde Christelicke Religie* (The Teaching of the Heidelberg Catechism of the Reformed Christian Religion). Hoorn, 1662.

Hellenbroek, A. *A Specimine of Divine Truth for Those who are Preparing for Confession of Faith.* Translated by Joel R. Beeke. Grand Rapids: Reformation Heritage Books, 1998.

Kerkelyk Handboekje, zijnde een kort uittreksel, van de Voornaamste Actens (Short Church Manual, i.e. a brief summary of the Most Important Acts). Rotterdam, 1764.

Knibbe, David. *Katechisatie over het Kort Begrip der Christelijke Gereformeerde Religie* (Catechetical Instruction regarding the Compendium of the Christian Reformed Religion). Leiden, 1771.

Lampe, Frederik Adolf. *Melk der Waarheit volgens aanleydinge van den Heidelbergschen Catechismus ten nutte van de leer-begeerige Jeugd...* (True Milk gleaned from the Heidelberg Catechism for the benefit of young people who are eager to learn...). The Hague, 1739.

Martinus, Johannes. *Grootere Catechisatie over den Catechismus der waren Christelicken Religie, de welcke in de Nederlandse Kercken geleert worden...* (Broader Instruction concerning the Catechism of the true Christian Religion, taught in the churches of the Netherlands). Amsterdam, 1700.

Martinus, Johannes and Abraham Trommius. *Kleyndere Catechisatie over de Catechismus der Gereformeerde Nederlandsche Gemeenten...* (Shorter Instruction concerning the Catechism of the Reformed Churches in the Netherlands). Amsterdam, 1728.

Melanchthon, Philippus. *Bekenntnisschrifte und kleine Lehrschriften* (Confession statements and shorter textbooks). Edited by Robert Stupperich, Melanchthons Werke in Auswahl (Selected works by Melanchthon), Volume VI. Gütesloh, 1955.

Micron, M. *De Christlicke Ordinancien der Nederlandscher Gemeinten te Londen* (Christian Ordinances of the Dutch Church in London), 1554, ed. W. F. Dankbaar. Reprint ed., The Hague, 1956.

Montanus, Arnoldus. *Religionis Christianae Catechesis, in Ecclesiis et Scholis Germaninae Superioris et Inferiores usitata, cum Analysi ad marginem subjectisque Scripturae locis adornata, et nunc ultima manu sedulo recognita.* Ex Illustrium

Ordinum Hollandiae et West-Frisae decretoin usum Scholarum ejusdem Provinciae... ex Festi Hommii Tabulis. Amsterdam, 1717.

Rollock, R. *Quaestinones et responsiones aliquot de foedere Dei, deque Sacramento quod Foederis Sigillium est.* In gratiam rudiorum collectae (Questions and answers concerning God's covenant and the sacrament which represents a seal of God's covenant. Compiled for the benefit of ordinary folk). Edinburgh, 1596.

Schrader, Egbertus. *Eene gemakkelyke handleidinge om over de Catechismus-Predicatien te catechizeeren...* (An easy Manual for Teaching Catechism Sermons…). Amsterdam, 1753.

Ursinus, Zacharias. *The Commentary of Dr. Zacharius Ursinus on the Heidelberg Catechism.* Translated by G. W. Willard. Phillipsburg, N. J.: P&R, n. d.

vanden Honert, Jo(h)an. "Voorreede" (Preface). In Z. Ursinus et al., *Schat-boek der Verklaringen over den Nederlandschen Catechismus* (Treasure book of Commentaries on the Catechism of the Netherlands). Gorinchem, 1736.

_____. *De Leer der Waarheid naar de Godsaligheid, in de Hoop des Eeuwigen Levens...*(The Doctrine of Truth after Godliness, in Hope of Eternal Life…). Leiden, 1764.

_____. *De eerste Beginselen van de Leer der Waarheid naar de Godsaligheid, in de Hoop des Eeuwigen Levens...* (First Principles of the Doctrine of Truth after Godliness, in Hope of Eternal Life…). Leiden, 1776.

van Emdre, Samuel. *Het Voorbeeld der Godlyke Waarheden van Abraham Hellenbroek tegen het gevoelen van partyen verdedigd* (*Specimen of Divine Truths* by Abraham Hellenbroek, defended against the feelings of various parties…). Utrecht/Leiden, 1794.

van Oostrum, Antoninus. *Korte en Beknopte Catechezatie over den Heidelbergschen Catechismus...* (Brief and Concise Instruction concerning the Heidelberg Catechism). Deventer, 1741.

van Vollenhoven, Cornelis. *De zuivere en beproefde Waarheden, begrepen in den Heidelbergsche Catechismus...* (Pure and tried Truths, contained in the Heidelberg Catechism…). Amsterdam, no date [1790], without indication of edition.

Vitae germanorum theologorum, qui superiori seculo ecclesiam Christi voce scriptisque propagarunt, congestae ad annum usque 1618, deductae a Melchiore Adamo. Frankfurt, 1653.

Secondary Sources

Alblas, J. B. H. *Johannes Boekholt (1656–1693). The first Dutch publisher of John Bunyan and other English authors.* Nieuwkoop, 1987.

Arrenberg, R. *Naamregister van de bekendste en meest in gebruik zynde Nederduitse boeken* (Register of names of the best-known and most popular Lower German books). Rotterdam, 1788; reprint ed., Rotterdam, 1999.

Barth, K. *Learning Jesus Christ through the Heidelberg Catechism.* Translated by Shirley C. Guthrie, Jr. Grand Rapids: Eerdmans, 1981.

———. *Die Theologie der reformierten Bekenntnisschriften.* Vorlesung Göttinger Sommersemester 1923, Herausgegeben von der Karl Barth-Forschungsstelle an der Universität Göttingen, Leitung Eberhard Busch, Karl Barth—Gesammtausgabe, Im Auftrag der Karl Barth-Stiftung herausgegeben von Hinrich Stoevesandt, II. Akademische Werke 1923 (The theology of the Reformed confession statements. Lecture given at the University of Göttingen during the summer semester of 1923, published by the Karl Barth Research Institute in Collected Works, at the request of the Karl Barth Foundation. Reprinted ed., Zürich, 1998.

———. *Einführung in den Heidelberger Katechismus* (Introduction to the Heidelberg Catechism). Zürich, 1960.

Beck, D. *Spiegel van mijn leven. Een Haags dagboek uit 1624* (Mirror of my life. A journal from The Hague in 1624). Edited by S. E. Veldhuizen. Hilversum, 1993.

Berkelbach van der Sprenkel, S. H. F. J. *Catechetiek* (Catechetical instruction). Nijkerk, 1956.

Beyer, U. *Abendmahl und Messe. Sinn und Recht der 80. Frage des Heidelberger Katechismus* (The Lord's Supper and the Mass. Significance and correctness of Question 80 of the Heidelberg Catechism). Neukirchen, 1963.

Bierma, Lyle D., Charles D. Gunnoe, Jr., Karin Maag, and Paul Fields. *An Introduction to the Heidelberg Catechism: Sources, History, and Theology.* Grand Rapids, 2005.

Biographisch-bibliographisches Kirchenlexikon. Bearb. und hrsg. von (Biographical-bibliographical dictionary of churches). Edited by Friedrich Wilhelm Bautz. Hamm, 1970ff.

Blaak, J. *Geletterde levens. Dagelijks lezen en schrijven in de vroegmoderne tijd in Nederland 1624–1770* (Lettered lives. Daily reading and writing in early modern times in the Netherlands 1624–1770). Hilversum, 2004.

Bouwmeester, G. *Zacharias Ursinus en de Heidelbergse Catechismus* (Zacharias Ursinus and the Heidelberg Catechism). The Hague, 1954.

———. *Caspar Olevianus en zijn reformatorische arbeid* (Caspar Olevianus and his Reformational work). The Hague, 1954.

Brienen, T., et al. *De Nadere Reformatie en het Gereformeerd Pietisme* (The Dutch Further Reformation and Reformed Pietism). The Hague, 1989, pp. 186–187, 197–200.

Coenen, L., ed. *Handbuch zum Heidelberger Katechismus* (Manual for the Heidelberg Catechism). Neukirchen. 1963.

Cuperus, S. *Kerkelijk leven der Hervormden in Friesland tijdens de republiek* (Ecclesiastical life of the Reformed in Friesland during the time of the Republic). Leeuwarden, 1916.

de Boer, D. E. L. *Het oude Duitsland. Een geschiedenis van de Duitse landen van*

1450 tot 1800 (Early Germany. A history of German countries from 1450 to 1800). Amsterdam, 2002.

Decavele, J. *De eerste protestanten in de Lage Landen. Geloof en heldenmoed* (The first Protestants in the Low Countries. Faith and heroic courage). Zwolle, 2004.

Den Hartogh, G. *Voorzienigheid in donker licht. Herkomst en gebruik van het begrip 'Providentia Dei' in de reformatorische theologie, in het bijzonder bij Zacharias Ursinus* (Predestination seen in a dark light. Origin and use of the concept "Providentia Dei" in Reformational theology, especially according to Zacharias Ursinus). Heerenveen, 1999.

de Reuver, A. *De drie stukken in de theologie van Luther, Calvijn en Kohlbrugge* (Three aspects of the theology of Luther, Calvin, and Kohlbrugge). Heerenveen, 2004.

Doedes, J. I. *De Heidelbergsche Catechismus in zijn eerste levensjaren* (The Heidelberg Catechism in its first few years of existence). Utrecht, 1867.

_____. *De Nederlandsche Geloofsbelijdenis en de Heidelbergsche Catechismus als de belijdenisgeschriften der Nederlandsche Hervormde Kerk in de negentiende eeuw getoetst en beoordeeld.* Tweede deel: de Heidelbergsche Catechismus (The Belgic Confession and the Heidelberg Catechism as confession statements of the Reformed Church in the Netherlands in the nineteenth century gauged and evaluated). Utrecht, 1881.

Evenhuis, R. B. *Ook dat was Amsterdam* (Amsterdam was also like this). Amsterdam, 1967.

Fabricius, D. C. *Die Kirche von England, ihr Gebetbuch, Bekenntnis und kanonisches Recht*, Conf. 17. Abt. Anglikanismus, I. Band (The Church of England, its Prayer Book, Confession and Canon Law, Conf. 17, Section on Anglicanism, Volume I). Berlin/Leipzig, 1937.

Forde, Gerhard O. *On being a Theologian of the Cross. Reflections on Luther's Heidelberg Disputation, 1518.* Grand Rapids, 1997.

Fühner, Jochen A. *Die Kirchen-und die antireformatorische Religionspolitik Kaiser Karls V. in den siebzehn Provinzen der Niederlande 1515–1555* (Churches and the anti-Reformation policy of Emperor Charles V in the seventeen provinces of the Netherlands 1515–1555). Leiden/Boston, 2004.

Glasius, B. *Godgeleerd Nederland. Biographisch Woordenboek der Nederlandsche Godgeleerden* (Theological Netherlands. Biographical Dictionary of Dutch Theologians). 's-Hertogenbosch, 1853.

Goeters, J. F. G. "Caspar Olevianus als Theologe" (Caspar Olevianus as Theologian). In *Monatshefte für Evangelische Kirchengeschichte des Rheinlandes*, 37. und 38. Jahrgang 1988/1989. Im Auftrag des Vereins für Rheinische Kirchengeschichte, hrg. von H. Faulenbach, u.a. (Periodical for Evangelical Church History, volumes 37 and 38, 1988–1989. At the request of the Society for Rhineland Church History, edited by H. Faulenbach et al). Köln/Bonn.

Golverdingen, M. *Avonden met Teellinck. Actuele thema's uit zijn werk* (Evenings with Teellinck. Relevant topics gleaned from his works). Houten, 1993.

Gooszen, M. A. *De Heidelbergsche Catechismus. Textus receptus met toelichtende teksten. Bijdrage tot de kennis van zijne wordingsgeschiedenis en van het gereformeerde protestantisme* (The Heidelberg Catechism. Textus receptus with explanatory texts. Contribution to the knowledge of the history of its compilation and of Reformed Protestantism). Leiden, 1890.

_____. *De Heidelbergsche Catechismus en het boekje van de breking des broods, in het jaar 1563–1564 bestreden en verdedigd. Oorkonden en dogmen-historisch onderzoek. Nieuwe bijdrage tot de kennis van het gereformeerde protestantisme* (The Heidelberg Catechism and booklet of the breaking of the bread, fought and defended in the year 1563–1564. Historical study of documents and dogmas. New contribution to the knowledge of Reformed Protestantism). Leiden, 1893.

Green, Ian. *The Christian's ABC: Catechisms and Catechizing in England c. 1530–1740*. Oxford, 1996.

Haitsma, J. *De leer aangaande de kerk in de reformatorische Catechismi uit het Duiste en Nederlandse taalgebied van 1530–1600* (The doctrine concerning the church in the Reformational catechisms of the German and Dutch language areas of 1530–1600). Woerden, 1968.

Häusser, L. *Geschichte der Rheinischen Pfalz nach ihren politischen, kirchlichen und literarischen Verhältnissen*, 2 vols. (History of the Rhineland Paltz from political, ecclesiastical and literary perspectives). Heidelberg, 1845.

Henss, W. *Der Heidelberger Katechismus im konfessionspolitischen Kräftespiel seiner Frühzeit. Historisch-bibliographische Einführung* (The Heidelberg Catechism in the power play of confessional politics in its early days). Zürich, 1983.

Herrenbrück, W. and U. Schmidt. *Warum wirsrt du ein Christ genannt? Vorträge und Aufsätze zum Heidelberger Katechismus im Jubiläumsjahr 1963* (Why are you called a Christian? Presentations and essays on the Heidelberg Catechism in its anniversary year 1963). Neukirchen, 1965.

Hofman, T. M. *Eenich Achterdencken, Spanning tussen Kerk en Staat in het gewest Holland tussen 1570 and 1620* (Suspicion and tension between Church and State in the Netherlands, 1570–1620). Heerenveen, 1997.

Hollweg, W. *Neue Untersuchungen zur Geschichte und Lehre des Heidelberger Katechismus* (New research on the history and teaching of the Heidelberg Catechism). Neukirchen, 1961.

_____. *Der Augsburger Reichstag von 1566 und seine Bedeutung für die Entstehung der Reformierten Kirche und ihres Bekenntnisses* (The Augsburg Legislative Assembly of 1566 and its significance for the emergence of the Reformed Church and its confession statements). Neukirchen, 1964.

Jaanus, H. J. *Hervormd Delft ten tijde van Arent Cornelisz 1573–1605* (Reformed Delft at the time of Arent Cornelisz, 1573–1605). Amsterdam, 1950.

Jacobs, P. *Theologie reformierter Bekenntnisschriften in Grundzügen* (Key principles of the theology of the Reformed confession statements). Neukirchen, 1959.

Kaajan, H. *De Pro-acta der Dordtsche Synode in 1618* (The Pre-Acts of the Synod of Dort of 1618). Rotterdam, 1914.

Keizer, G. "De Catechismusprediking voor onze tijd" (Catechism preaching for our time), *Gereformeerd Theologisch Tijdschrift* (Reformed Journal of Theology), XXII (1921): 225–250, 287–296.

Kluckhohn, A. *Friedrich der Fromme. Kurfürst von der Pfalz; der Schüzer der reformirten Kirche 1559–1576* (Frederick the Pious: Elector of the Paltz; Protector of the Reformed Church, 1559–1576). Nördlingen, 1879.

Koecher, J. C. *Catechetische historie der gereformeerde kerke* (Catechetical history of the Reformed Church). Amsterdam, 1763.

Lang, A. *Der Heidelberger Katechismus und vier verwandte Katechismen: Leo Juds und Microns kleine Katechismen sowie die zwei Vorarbeiten Ursinus, mit einer historisch-theologischen Einleitung herausgegeben* (The Heidelberg Catechism and four related catechisms: Leo Jud's and Micron's shorter catechisms as well as the two preliminary works by Ursinus, published with a historical-theological introduction). Reprint ed., Darmstadt, 1967.

Läpple, A. *Kleine Geschichte der Katechese* (Short history of catechetical instruction). München, 1981.

Latzel, Th. *Theologische Grundzüge des Heidelberger Katechismus. Eine fundamentaltheologische Untersuching seines Ansatzes zur Glaubenskummunikation* (Key theological principles of the Heidelberg Catechism. A basic theological analysis of its approach to the communication of the faith). Marburg, 2004.

Leurdijk, G. H. *Jan Nupoort. Zijn leven en arbeid en betekenis voor de catechese* (Jan Nupoort: His life, work, and significance for catechetical instruction). Veenendaal, 1981.

Mau, R., ed. *Evangelische Bekenntnisse. Bekenntnisschriften der Reformation und neuere Theologische Erklärungen*, Teilband I. II. (Evangelical Confessions. Confession statements and more recent theological declarations. Bielefeld, 1997.

Metz, W., *Necessitas satisfactionis? Eine systematische Studie zu den Fragen 12–18 des Heidelberger Katechismus und zur Theologie des Zacharias Ursinus* (*Necessitas satisfactionis?* A systematic study of Questions 12–18 of the Heidelberg Catechism and the theology of Zacharias Ursinus). Zürich, 1970.

Moersch, K. *Geschichte der Pfalz. Von den Anfängen bis ins 19. Jahrhundert* (History of the Paltz: From its beginnings to the 19th century). Landau, 1987.

Molhuysen et al, P. C., ed., *Nieuw Nederlandsch Biografish Woordenboek* (New Biographical Dictionary of the Netherlands). 11 volumes. Amsterdam 1974 articles on P. Dathenus, 2:367–382, and H. Faukelius, 6:507–509.

Morsink, G. *Joannes Anastasius Veluanus: Jan Gerritz. Versteghe, levensloop en ontwikkleing* (Course of life and development). Kampen,1986.

Mullan, David George. *Scottish Puritanism, 1590–1638*. Oxford, 2000.

Nauta, D., et al (ed.). *Biografisch Lexicon voor de geschiedenis van het Nederlandse Prot-*
estantisme (Biographical dictionary for the history of Protestantism in the
Netherlands). 5 volumes. Kampen, 1978–2001.

Niesel, W. *Das Evangelium und die Kirchen, Ein Lehrbuch der Symbolik, Zweite, über-*
arbeitete Auflage (The Gospel and the Church: A textbook on Symbolism,
revised edition). Neukirchen, 1960.

op 't Hof, E. J. "De verschillen tussen voetianen en coccejanen in het licht van
hun verklaringen van de Heidelbergse Catechismus" (The differences between Voetians and Cocceians in the light of their interpretations of the
Heidelberg Catechism). In F. G. M. Broeyer en E. G. E. van der Wall, *Een*
richtingenstrijd in de Gereformeerde Kerk. Voetianen en coccejanen 1650–1750 (A
conflict between movements in the Reformed Church: Voetians and Cocceians, 1650–1750). Zoetermeer, 1994, 54–73.

Peters, A. *Kommentar zu Luthers Katechismen*, Band 1: Die Zehn Gebote, Luthers
Vorreden. (Commentary on Luther's catechisms, Volume 1: The Ten
Commandments, Luther's Preface) Edited by Gottfried Seebass. Göttin-
gen, 1990.

Plasger, G./M. Freudenberg (ed.). *Reformierte Bekenntnisschriften. Eine Auswahl von*
den Anfängen bis zur Gegenwart (Reformed confession statements: A selection from the beginning to the present time). Göttingen, 2005.

Polman, A. D. R. *Onze Nederlandsche geloofsbelijdenis verklaard uit het verleden,*
geconfronteerd met het heden (Our Belgic Confession explained from the perspective of the past, contrasted with the present). Franeker, n.d., vol. 1.

Post, R. R., *Scholen en onderwijs in Nederland gedurende de Middeleeuwen* (Schools
and education in the Netherlands during the Middle Ages). Antwerp,
1964.

Realencyklopädie für protestantische Theologie und Kirche (Encyclopedia of Protestant
theology and church). Begründet von J.J. Herzog. Leipzig, 1896–1913.

Reu, J. M. *Quellen zur Geschichte des kirchlichen Unterrichts in der evanglischen Kirche*
Deutschlands zwischen 1530 und 1600 (Sources for the history of ecclesiasti-
cal instruction in the German Evangelical Church between 1530 and 1600.
Reprinted ed., Hildesheim-New York, 1976.

Rohls, J. *Reformed Confessions: Theology from Zürich to Barmen*. Translated by John
Hoffmeyer. Louisville, 1988.

Schotel, G. D. J. *Geschiedenis van den oorsprong, de invoering en de lotgevallen van den*
Heidelbergschen Catechismus (History of the origin, introduction and adven-
tures of the Heidelberg Catechism). Amsterdam, 1863.

Schotel, G.D. J. and H. C. Rogge. *De openbare eerdienst der Nederl. Hervormde Kerk*
in de zestiende, zeventiende en achttiende eeuw (Public worship services of the
Reformed Church in the Netherlands during the sixteenth, seventeenth,
and eighteenth centuries). Leiden, n.d.

Seeling, W. *Johannes Willing (1525–1572). Ein Schicksal zwischen Luthertum und*

Calvinismus: Versuch einer Biographie (A destiny between Lutheranism and Calvinism: Attempt at a biography). Otterbach, 1972.

Soly, Hugo (ed.). *Karl V. 1500–1558 und seine Zeit* (Charles V [1500–1558] and his times). Cologne, 2003.

Staedtke, J., "Entstehung und Bedeutung des Heidelberger Katechismus" (Birth and significance of the Heidelberg Catechism). In *Reformation und Zeugnis der Kirche, Gesammelte Studien*, edited by Dietrich Blaufuss (Reformation and Testimony of the Church, Collected Studies). Zürich, 1978.

Steubung, Hans, ed. *Bekenntnisse der Kirche. Bekenntnistexte aus zwanzig Jahrhunderten* (Confessions of the church. Confession texts from twenty centuries). Wuppertal, 1970.

Tazelaar, J. P. *De Heidlebergsche Catechismus, beschouwd als het leerboek onzer vaderen* (The Heidelberg Catechism, viewed as the instruction book of our fathers). Leiden, 1899.

Troelstra, A. *De toestand der catechese in Nederland gedurende de vóór-reformatorische eeuw* (Catechetical instruction in the Netherlands during the century preceding the Reformation). Groningen, 1901.

Troelstra, A. *Stof en methode der catechese in Nederland vóór de Reformatie* (Material and method of catechetical instruction in the Netherlands prior to the Reformation). Groningen, 1903.

Tukker, C. A. *De Classis Dordrecht van 1573 tot 1609. Bijdrage tot de kennis van in- en extern leven van de Gereformeerde Kerk in de periode van haar organisering* (The Classis of Dort from 1573 to 1609: Contribution to the knowledge of life inside and outside the Reformed Church during the period of its formation). Leiden, 1965.

van de Bank, J. H., et al. *Kennen en vertrouwen. Handreiking bij de prediking van de Heidelbergse Catechismus* (Knowledge and trust: Manual for preaching on the Heidelberg Catechism). Zoetermeer, 1993.

van der Haar, J. *Schatkamer van de gereformeerde theologie in Nederland c. 1600–c. 1800. Bibliografisch onderzoek* (Treasury of Reformed theology in the Netherlands, circa 1600–circa 1800: Bibliographical study). Veenendaal, 1987.

_____. *Internationale ökomenische Beziehungen im 17. und 18. Jahrhundert. Bibliographie von aus dem englischen, niederländischen und französichen ins deutsche übersetzten theologischen Büchern von 1600–1800* (International ecumenical connections: Bibliography of English, Dutch, and French theological books translated into German from 1600–1800). Ederveen, 1996.

_____. *Drielandenverkeer. Bibliografische studie betreffende 1: Uit het Duits in het Nederlands vertaalde theologische boeken, 2: Uit het Frans in het Nederlands vertaalde theologische boeken* (Exchange among three countries: Bibliographical study regarding Theological works translated from German to Dutch, and from French to Dutch). Ederveen, 1997.

van der Hoeven, A. "Ursinus en Olevianus. Heidelberger Catechismus" (Ursinus and Olevianus. Heidelberg Catechism). In *Kerkelijke klassieken. Inleidende beschouwingen over geschriften van oude en nieuwe kerkvaders*. Compiled by J. Haantjes and A. van der Hoeven, with collaboration from H. Berkhof *et al.* (Ecclesiastical classics. Introductory reflections concerning works of old and new church fathers). Wageningen, 1949.

Van Deursen, A. Th. *Bavianen en Slijkgeuzen. Kerk en kerkvolk ten tijde van Maurits en Oldenbarnevelt* (Baboons and Mud Beggars: Church and church people in the days of Prince Maurice and Oldenbarnevelt). Assen, 1974.

———. *Rust niet voordat gy ze van buiten kunt. De Tien Geboden in de 17e eeuw* (Do not rest before you know them by heart: The Ten Commandments in the 17th century). Kampen, 2004.

———. *De last van veel geluk. De geschiedenis van Nederland 1555–1702* (Burden of great fortune: History of the Netherlands, 1555–1702). Amsterdam, 2004.

van Lieburg, F. A. *Repertorium van Nederlandse hervormde predikanten tot 1816*. Deel 1: predikanten, deel 2: gemeenten (Repertory of Reformed ministers of the Netherlands up to 1816. Volume 1: Ministers; volume 2: Churches). Dort, 1996.

van Rongen, G. *De Westminster Confessie met de Grote en de Kleine Catechismus*, translated and introduced by G. van Rongen with collaboration from M. J. Arntzen (The Westminster Confession together with the Larger and Shorter Catechisms). Barneveld, 1986.

van Sliedregt, C. *Calvijns opvolger Theodorus Beza. Zijn verkiezingsleer en zijn belijdenis van de drieënige God* (Calvin's successor, Theodore Beza: His doctrine of predestination and his confession of the Triune God). Leiden, 1996.

van Sterkenburg, P. G. *Een glossarium van zeventiende-eeuws Nederlands* (A glossary of seventeenth century Dutch). Groningen, 1981.

van 't Hooft, A. J. *De theologie van Heinrich Bullinger in betrekking tot de Nederlandsche Reformatie* (The impact of Heinrich Bullinger's theology on the Reformation in the Netherlands). Amsterdam, 1898.

van 't Spijker, W. "Ursinus praedicator" (Ursinus as preacher). In J. van Genderen, W. van 't Spijker, J. de Vuyst (ed.), *Ten dienste van het Woord* (In the service of the Word). Essays offered to Dr. W. H. Velema, Professor at the Theological University of the Christian Reformed Churches in the Netherlands to commemorate his twenty-five years in office. Kampen, 1991, 158–179.

van 't Spijker, W., R. Bisschop, and W. J. op 't Hof. *Het puritanisme. Geschiedenis, theologie en invloed* (Puritanism. History, theology and influence). Zoetermeer, 2001.

van 't Spijker, W., et al. *De Synode van Dordrecht in 1618 en 1619* (The Synod of Dort of 1618 and 1619). Houten, 1987.

van 't Spijker, W., et al. *De Synode van Westminster 1643–1649* (The Westminster Assembly, 1643–1649). Houten, 2002.

van Veen, S. D. *Het godsdienstonderwijs en de aanneming van lidmaten in de Gerefor-*

meerde Kerk (Religious instruction and the acceptance of members into the Reformed Church). Revised edition arranged by L. F. Groenendijk. Dort, 1979.

Verboom, W. *De catechese van de Reformatie en de Nadere Reformatie* (Catechetical instruction of the Reformation and the Second Dutch Reformation). Amsterdam, 1986.

_____. *De theologie van de Heidelbergse Catechismus. Twaalf thema's: de context en de latere uitwerking* (The theology of the Heidelberg Catechism. Twelve themes: the context and the subsequent consequences). Zoetermeer, 1996.

_____. *Hulde aan de Heidelberger. Over de waarde van de leerdienst en de catechismuspreek* (Praise for the Heidelberg Catechism: The value of the catechetical worship service and the Catechism sermon). Heerenveen, 2005.

Vierhonderd jaar Heidelbergse Catechismus (The four hundredth anniversary of the Heidelberg Catechism). The Heidelberg Catechism commemorated in a national gathering on 19 January 1963 at Amersfoort. Amersfoort, 1963.

Visser, D. *Zacharias Ursinus: The Reluctant Reformer—His Life and Times.* New York, 1983.

Vos, G. *De verbondsleer in de Gereformeerde Theologie.* Rede gehouden bij het overdragen van het rectoraat aan the Theol. School te Grand Rapids, Mich., den 2n September 1891 (The doctrine of the covenant in Reformed Theology. Lecture given at the transfer of the headmastership of the Theological School at Grand Rapids, Michigan, the 2nd September 1891). Grand Rapids, 1891.

Weber, Otto. "Analytische Theologie. Zum geschichtlichen Standort des Heidelberger Katechismus" (Analytical Theology. On the historical significance of the Heidelberg Catechism). In Otto Weber, *Die Treue Gottes in der Geschichte der Kirche.* Gesammelte Aufsätze 2 (The true God in the history of the church). Neukirchen, 1968, 131–146.

Weir, David A. *The Origin of the Federal Theology in Sixteenth-Century Reformation Thought.* Oxford, 1990.

Wezel-Roth, Ruth. *Thomas Erastus. Ein Beitrag zur Geschichte der reformierten Kirche und zur Lehre von den Staatssouveränität* (A contribution on the history of the Reformed Church and the doctrine of state sovereignty). Lahr/Baden, 1954.

Woelderink, J. G. *De inzet van de Catechismus. Verklaring van de zondagen I–VII van de Heidelberger* (The aim of the Catechism: Explanation of Lord's Days 1–6 of the Heidelberg Catechism). Franeker, no date.

Wolf, E. *Ordnung der Liebe. Gottesgebot und Nächstenrecht im Heidelberger Katechismus* (The place of love: God's command and our neighbour's rights according to the Heidelberg Catechism). Frankfurt on the Main, 1963.

Wumkes, G. A. *De Gereformeerde kerk in de Ommelanden tussen Eems en Lauwers 1595–1796* (The Reformed Church in the Ommelanden region of the

Dutch Province of Groningen between the Ems and the Lauwers Sea 1595–1796). Groningen, 1904.

Wijminga, P. J. *Festus Hommius*. Leiden, 1899.

Ypeij, A. and I. J. Dermout. *Geschiedenis der Nederlandsche Hervormde Kerk* (History of the Reformed Church in the Netherlands). Breda, 1819–1827, vol. 4.

Zwanepol, K. *Belijdenisgeschriften voor de Protestantse Kerk in Nederland* (Confessional statements for the Protestant Church in the Netherlands). Zoetermeer, 2004.

NAME INDEX

PLACE INDEX

CONTRIBUTORS

Willem van 't Spijker is Emeritus Professor of Church History and Canon Law at the Theological University of Apeldoorn.

Christa Boerke is Associate at the Library of the Theological University of Apeldoorn and the Institute for Research on the Reformation.

Martinus Golverdingen is Minister of the *Gereformeerde Gemeente* (Reformed Congregation) at Waarde.

Willem Jan op 't Hof is Minister of the *Hersteld Hervormde Gemeente* (Restored Reformed Congregation) at Nederhemert and Professor of Reformed Pietism at the Free University of Amsterdam on behalf of the *Hersteld Hervormde Kerk* (Restored Reformed Church).

Teunis M. Hofman is Professor of New Testament at the Theological University of Apeldoorn.

Wim Verboom is Professor of the History of Reformed Protestantism on behalf of the *Gereformeerde Bond* (Reformed League) and Lecturer for ecclesiastical formation at the University of Leiden.